The Daily Telegraph

Military Obituaries

BOOK THREE

The Daily Telegraph

MILITARY OBITUARIES

BOOK THREE

Edited by

DAVID TWISTON DAVIES

Foreword by Field Marshal
the Lord Bramall, KG, GCB, OBE, MC

GRUB STREET • LONDON

Published by
Grub Street
4 Rainham Close
London SW11 6SS

Photograph on page 7 of Field Marshal the Lord Bramall courtesy of Michael Pattison

A CIP data record for this title is available from the British Library

ISBN-13: 9781909808317

Printed and bound in Spain by Novoprint

FOREWORD

I am delighted to write a foreword to this third collection of *The Daily Telegraph* military obituaries, which have appeared in print over the last sixteen years. With its well-written pen portraits of some 100 military men and three women who have made their mark over a wide spectrum of conflict, this new volume provides a fascinating insight into contemporary military history at ground roots level and often at the very 'sharp end'.

The obituaries are set out in the chronological order in which death occurred, but describe actions and activities going back, in one case, as far as the Battle of Passchendaele in 1917. They cover virtually all the theatres of operations in World War II; post-war conflicts include Korea, the withdrawal from Empire and revolutionary war as well as more limited wars such as the Falklands Campaign and, more recently, those in the Middle East.

Any reader browsing through them will soon have no illusions about the realities of battle and of the human qualities of courage and resourcefulness which come to the fore under the stresses of war and combat; nor, indeed of the emotions which are avowed and help to motivate an individual. There are plenty of examples of extreme heroism and gallantry. No less than six are of those who won the VC; two of GC holders; and two others (one unarmed) who twice won the DCM – the next highest award for gallantry in the face of the enemy, which is now called the Conspicuous Gallantry Cross.

There are also numerous others which recount the winning of lesser awards, sometimes more than once. No reader will want to overlook the contribution of Bill Millin, Brigadier Lord Lovat's personal piper, who become almost immortalised in the D-Day film, *The Longest Day*. Amidst shot and shell with many killed or wounded, Piper Millin continued to play stirring Scottish airs to encourage and inspire the commandos as they stormed across the beaches and, eventually, under heavy fire, relieved Pegasus Bridge.

There are so many other inspiring stories of daring and enterprise which emphasise the ubiquity, versatility and professionalism of those who serve their country in war, mostly from the British Army, but also from the Commonwealth.

For me personally, reading the obituaries was a particularly moving and sometimes humbling experience. Covering every rank from private soldier to full general, they helped me to recall the quite large number whom I knew personally from my own service, and in some cases – albeit it indirectly – became involved in their actions and activities. In the case of more senior officers, I remember them as close and respected colleagues; in one case when I was a captain and he a major. Moreover my own experience of similar circumstances and situations covered in the obituaries made me fully able to appreciate the emotions and stresses which I must have felt at the time.

I therefore commend this volume to those who are keen followers of military history, as so many

are, and who want to obtain and share in a greater knowledge of the realities of battle and what makes an individual 'tick' under pressure.

Field Marshal the Lord Bramall,
KG, GCB, OBE, MC

DRAMATIS PERSONNAE
(in order of appearance)

INTRODUCTION

A century after the First World War began it is disconcerting to realise how dangerous a place the world has become again. Terrorism poses threats at home; Russia is bent on swallowing Ukraine; Isil is raging in the Middle East and North Africa while the Chinese are flexing their muscles on the South China Sea. One spark could ignite a rolling conflagration of limited but unpredictable proportions.

There are plenty of experts to explain the latest hardware needs of our national defence, and the government is at last showing signs of waking up to the danger caused by the blind cutting of recent decades. But this third collection of *Daily Telegraph* military obituaries is a reminder that when significant hostilities break out our forces, along with those of our Commonwealth kinsmen whom we have so often neglected, will be able to draw on the example and resolution shown by our grandfathers' and fathers' generations.

In today's rule-dominated society these stories offer badly needed lessons in command and tactics. They show the importance of initiative, flexibility and courage; of comradeship and loyalty; and, above all, the need to retain the trust of those serving down the command chain untrammelled by the constraints of health and safety.

It should be appreciated that military technology and economic power may have greatly advanced in the past seventy years, but the essentials for conducting war on the ground remain simple; and, while horror is ever-present, the senseless reality of it all is so often made bearable by the comedy caught up in its coat-tails.

These obituaries, published over the past sixteen years, range from Private Harry Patch – the last survivor of the trenches on the Western Front who died aged 111 in 2009 still enraged by the waste of war – to Staff Sergeant Olaf Schmid, a demolition expert awarded a posthumous George Cross in Afghanistan, aged 30.

All the senior commanders of the Second World War have gone by now, but a slightly younger generation of significant figures is to be found in these pages. Major General Harry Grimshaw saw almost twenty years of continual service in pre-war India, Burma, Iraq, Libya, Alamein, Malaya, Kenya, Suez and finally Cyprus. Lieutenant Colonel Kendal Chavasse distinguished himself in Tunisia, leading a newly formed reconnaissance unit nicknamed 'Chavasse's Light Horse'. General Sir Frank Hassett led 3rd Battalion, Royal Australian Regiment, in a model assault on Maryang San above the Korean front line.

Younger officers include Captain Ewen Frazer who won a DSO attacking enemy machine guns on the first night at Alamein. Brigadier General Denny Whitaker, a Canadian football star, charged into a casino at Dieppe to clean up the enemy but found nobody with whom to link up; racing back to the shore he was the first on his feet in London to tell Lord Louis Mountbatten that the Germans must have been waiting.

None could have succeeded without the courage,

dash and loyalty of the men they led. Havildar Lachhiman Gurung, VC, lost his fingers and was shot in the body and leg while resisting a four-hour Japanese attack alone in his trench in Burma ("I knew I was going to die so I might as well die standing"); Sergeant Eric Batchelor was known as 'the Ferret' in Italy for the deadly, silent skills he had learned as a poacher in New Zealand; Company Sergeant Major Noel Ross proved an invaluable messenger who took on anyone he encountered on the battlefield of Arnhem before finally holding onto the back of a boat to cross the Rhine. Special Constable Terry Peck, the former Falklands police chief, was drafted into 2 Para for the battle of Mount Longdon in 1982.

Major Martin Clemens was a district officer in the Solomon Islands who organised a guerrilla group to keep fighting against the Japanese and helped a large number of American Marines who kept getting lost after they arrived. Colonel Bill Becke, who earned an immediate DSO for a dramatic struggle over a Tuscan church in 1944, showed he still retained the right stuff some twenty years later when, monocled and bristling, he marched beside a piper as a mob tried to sack the British embassy in Jakarta.

No less brave on the battlefield were the unarmed. The stretcher bearer Corporal 'Nutty' Hazle won two Distinguished Conduct Medals for tending the wounded under fire in North Africa and Italy while under constant fire and seriously wounded himself. Brigadier the Reverend David Whiteford of the Scots Guards had to jump into graves when attacked while conducting funerals. Also well favoured above was

Piper Bill Millin who was never hit while playing on the beach at D-Day; he was later told the Germans thought he was mad.

Whoever they were, wherever they were sent, all were subject to the changeable fortunes of war. In 1940 Lieutenant Philip Martel was posted to enemy-occupied Guernsey to liaise with a Commando landing which never arrived; unable to communicate with his superiors on the mainland, he scurried around the island for some weeks before being urged by the islanders to surrender; he spent the remainder of the war as a POW. Four years later Major Tony Hibbert took part in the failed raid on the Arnhem Bridge. He was captured, then escaped to help organise an evacuation over the Rhine in which he broke his leg; still on crutches on the final day of European hostilities he hobbled up to the German commander at Kiel to receive the surrender, 4 hours ahead of the Russians.

The expectation of any captured officer was that he would try to escape or help others to do so. Lieutenant Colonel 'Jumbo' Hoare first bailed out of his burning tank in 1940. Later he dived off a sinking ship and jumped from a moving train taking him to Germany, before being hidden under a nun's bed; Major Hugh Fane-Hervey won an MC as a tank officer in the desert before being captured; he escaped to Rome, where he called himself Count Fattorini as one of some sixty officers on the run in the Eternal City. A significant figure in what he called 'the escaping community' at Colditz Castle was Captain Kenneth Lockwood who looked after the escapers' finances and was the post-war secretary of their association.

Commander Penny Phillips of the Mechanised Transport Corps briefly fell into the hands of bemused Germans during the Fall of France, but resolutely turned round her ambulance and set off unhindered in the opposite direction. In later life her crisp efficiency as a Somerset county councillor led her to be known as the 'Ayatollah'.

Perhaps the most dramatic story is that of Colonel Tony Hewitt in Hong Kong. After stealing a boat he was attacked by robbers, fired on by Chinese Red Guards who then asked him to train their men before he finally left them to fight off pirates on the East river to reach the British military mission at Kukong. The most charming tale is that of Major Michael Ross. After being released from prison camp when Italy sued for peace he was hidden by an Italian family until finally reaching liberated Monte Carlo in time for breakfast; after the war he returned and married his protector's beautiful daughter. A story with an even longer sequel is that of Private Isaac Fadoyebo, a Nigerian medical orderly left for dead in Burma who was hidden and nursed by a Rohingya Muslim. Almost seventy years later a resourceful television reporter, Barnaby Phillips, found him and carried the elderly Fadayebo's message of thanks to his rescuer's children.

The adage that time waits for no man may be true – but groups can lag behind. Although the British Army abandoned horses early in the war, in 1941 General Amedeo Guillet led 250 Italian cavalry in a charge which cut through the armoured cars of Skinner's Horse in East Africa.

Colonel Richard Heaven commanded a mule unit which would march five miles an hour before being halted to stand in a neat circle. But none could match Colonel Garforth-Bles's unprecedented experience pig-sticking in pre-war India, when a friend disappeared and was found in a well with his horse and the pig which was trying to bite it.

Although Europhiles who like to champion political correctness might not approve, success can go to those who push matters to the edge and sometimes beyond. Colonel Clive Fairweather, who, in 1980, masterminded the assault on the terrorists who seized the Libyan embassy in Kensington, was in a succession of scrapes throughout his career. Sergeant Dougie Wright earned a reputation as a hard man in Greece, and retained it afterwards. When he retired to the Royal Hospital Chelsea he kept a dagger on the wall by his bed; none of his comrades doubted his claim to have strangled nine enemy. Obergefreiter Henry Metelmann was a Panzer driver on the Eastern Front who saw no point in apologising for the atrocities in which he had been involved; but the boys at Charterhouse School, where he worked as a groundsman, appreciated the honesty in his talks. Sergeant 'Smoky' Smith, who won a VC with the Canadian Seaforths in Italy, had clear views on prisoners: "I'm paid to kill them. That's the way it is". Yet scattered throughout this book are small hints that, even in action, opponents recognised the humanity of those they were fighting – the exchange of a nod, a reluctance to shoot a man already wounded, the dip of an aircraft's wing over a field hospital.

What is especially striking is the diversity of their post-war occupations. Some returned to their old jobs, such as colliery drivers and postmen. Others ended up aiding their comrades at the Royal Chelsea Hospital. Signalman Arthur Titherington came home, after three years as a Japanese slave labourer in a copper mine, to campaign for the rest of his long life for a proper apology from the Emperor. Nancy Wake, the high-spirited SOE agent in France, tried to become an MP in Australia before spending her later years happily ensconced at the bar of the Stafford Hotel in Knightsbridge, which she had known in the war. Sir John Gorman, who won the Irish Guards' first MC in Normandy, became an RUC policeman, airline executive, and then a member of the Northern Ireland Assembly where his polished military manner astonished Gerry Adams and Martin McGuinness.

Always retaining the long view was Val, the 8th Duke of Wellington. He inherited his titles through a cousin killed leading his men in Italy and earned an MC in Iraq to champion the Army in the House of Lords. But he never forgot the achievement of his great ancestor, the 1st Duke. In 1995, he wrote a letter to the *Telegraph* pointing out that the large number of 'N' flags at the field of Waterloo suggested that Bonaparte had really won. Shortly after the column's deadline had passed, he rang the Letters Editor to add another line under his signature: 'Prince of Waterloo'.

This book continues the great tradition of obituary writing established under the late Hugh Massingberd who, twenty years ago, edited the first in this *Telegraph* series. Its leading writers are Charles Owen, Bill Barlow, Julian Spilsbury and Michael Smith. One cannot be sure what will happen after the last veteran of the Second World War passes. But with the two earlier military books being reprinted it is reasonable to suggest that there is no sign of the formula ageing. The opening obituary, Lieutenant Colonel 'Jumbo' Hoare, was written by our first military writer, the late Philip Warner. The Canadian Lieutenant Colonel Jeffery Williams is no longer with us, but his work is also to be found here.

Hugh Massingberd was the first editor of the expanded column in the mid-1980s. When he stepped down in 1994 he was succeeded in the chair by David Jones, Kate Summerscale, Christopher Howse, Andrew McKie and Harry de Quetteville; now Andrew Brown is proving a worthy successor. They have been aided by writer-editors who include the recently retired Jay Iliff, Katharine Ramsay, Georgia Powell, Robert Gray, Philip Eade, George Ireland, James Owen, Christian House and Kate Moore. Occasional writers have included David Blair, Sebastian O'Kelly, Bill Duff, Henry Porter, Will Heaven and the late Philip Snow.

All have been shepherded by our secretary, the incomparable Dorothy Brown. Always ready to help have been Captain Peter Hore and Air Commodore Graham Pitchfork, who produce our Royal Navy and RAF obituaries. Two other invaluable friends to the column have been Didy Grahame, who recently retired as secretary of the Victoria Cross-George Cross Association, and Lord Bramall who has kindly contributed a foreword.

Lastly thanks are due to the regimental secretaries on whom we depend for so much, and not least, the paper's editor, Chris Evans.

David Twiston Davies
Sutton Courtenay, Oxon

LIEUTENANT COLONEL 'JUMBO' HOARE

Lieutenant Colonel 'Jumbo' Hoare (who died on December 19 1999, aged 83) won an MC during the Battle of France in 1940 when he leaped from a burning tank and pulled his sergeant from another; he dived off a sinking ship; jumped from a train taking him to a German prison camp; then, suffering from malaria, he was sheltered at an Italian convent in the hills near Rome where he swapped his uniform for a nun's habit to proceed into chapel.

When a search party arrived at the convent, the Mother Superior hid him and a comrade under her bed, refusing point blank to let the Germans search her room. "No man," she informed them, "has ever entered my bedchamber." After the coast was clear, Hoare recalled, she told him that she would have "to do a lot of penances for telling the Germans those lies". Although the local mayor warned there would be shootings if the British soldiers were discovered, the nuns sheltered them until they could join up with the advancing Allies.

The son of an engineer rear-admiral, James Gordon Hoare was born on July 22 1916 and educated at Weymouth College. He was commissioned via the Supplementary Reserve into 4th Royal Tank Regiment, which had small Matilda tanks with a top speed of 8 mph. Large and muscular, he had difficulty climbing in; and, once inside, he had to fire a machine gun and operate a radio.

Posted to France on the outbreak of war in 1939, Hoare's troop was involved in the fierce counter attack around Arras which was thought to have temporarily prevented the Germans entering Dunkirk. After extricating himself and his sergeant from their tanks he walked ninety miles to find his brother Henry in a ditch outside Dunkirk with some Wiltshires, and told him to get up as the Germans were coming; they reported home in Weymouth within an hour of each other.

'Jumbo' was next sent to East Africa, where 4RTR took part in the conquest of Keren and Eritrea, before being posted on to the Western Desert. When Tobruk was besieged in 1941, 4RTR was sent into the port by sea and took part in the battles for the break-out when Hoare was wounded in the leg and head. He was evacuated but his ship was torpedoed and sank rapidly, drowning many. But he leaped over the side and grabbed a piece of floating wreckage to be eventually rescued by a destroyer.

After recovering from his wounds he was posted to Palestine where his unit was re-equipped with Valentine tanks and sent to North Africa where, in the final battle for Tobruk, 4RTR fought until its last tank was on fire. Hoare was captured and sent to Italy.

When Italy sued for peace in 1943, the Germans started to move British POWs to Germany. But Hoare and a friend jumped from their train at night to make for the mountains, where a shepherd showed them to a cave and fed them. Soon he was so stricken with malaria that the shepherd took him to the nearby convent so weak at first that the local undertaker measured him up for a coffin. But gradually he recovered, and, heavily disguised, even took part in feast day processions despite the local mayor demanding he be sent on his way immediately.

As the Allies finally drew nearer Hoare was led through minefields to reach the British lines. He then spent a long time in hospital undergoing surgery on his leg. In 1945 he was posted to the Staff College at Haifa and then Quetta. Subsequent postings took him to Holland and Germany.

'Jumbo' Hoare was an extremely sociable, modest and independent man, who had been a fine rugby player and swimmer, and enjoyed fishing and sailing in his 27ft yacht in later life. After the war he returned to Italy several times to thank those who had helped him, including one of the nuns and the shepherd who had led him to the convent. In 1945, he married Ida Rifaat, an Egyptian who had nursed him in hospital. She predeceased him, and he was survived by a son.

LIEUTENANT COLONEL HENRY HOWARD

Lieutenant Colonel Henry Howard (who died on May 6 2000, aged 85) was awarded an MC in Palestine in 1936, a Bar in the Western Desert and a DSO in north-west Europe, earning the description 'absolutely fearless' from one fellow officer.

His first MC came while serving with the Buffs (Royal East Kent Regiment) during the Arab uprising in protest against Britain, the mandatory power, allowing too many Jewish immigrants into the country. They expressed their resentment by ambushing and sniping at patrols, then hiding among the villagers, which made them almost impossible to detect.

When the 2nd Battalion were patrolling the roads and clearing the Arabs from strategic points on a hillside near Tarshiha, a small party commanded by Howard, then a second lieutenant, came under fire from a large group of rebels. He was immediately shot through both thighs but picked himself up and managed to lead the platoon to the top of the hill, which he held for four hours until the surviving Arabs dispersed.

Frederick Henry Howard was born on February 25 1915 and educated at Gresham's School, Holt, and Sandhurst before being commissioned into the Buffs in 1935. Later he was seconded to the King's African Rifles, with whom he earned a mention in despatches, serving against the Italians operating mainly behind the lines in Kenya, Somaliland and Abyssinia.

After the Battle of Sidi Rezegh in 1941, in which the Buffs had sustained heavy casualties, Howard rejoined the regiment and was with the 1st Battalion through all the actions in the Western Desert, including Alamein, until the fall of Tunis. It was during this period of intense fighting that he was awarded a Bar to his MC. On the night of January 21 1943 – his fourth running without sleep – Howard led a moonlight attack down the Tarhuna Pass towards Tripoli and drove the enemy back two miles. Four nights later he seized the strongly defended Kidney

Hill and held it in spite of heavy enemy counter-attacks.

The Buffs were particularly successful in the Mareth battle of March 1943 when, according to the official history 'patrolling was a feature of life with the Buffs and many calls were made on the battalion in the quest for the enemy's intentions'. Howard was particularly prominent, probing right forward into the enemy defences and often being involved in a brisk exchange of fire.

After Staff College at Haifa he was given command of 1st Battalion, Ox and Bucks, with whom he cheerfully strode around the European battlefield, immaculately dressed with his green regimental cap on very straight to hearten many an uneasy soldier. Leading them through heavy floods, he crossed the Ruhr river on the Dutch-German border to secure many prisoners, and earned a DSO. He considered the German resistance the hardest in the Ardennes before going on to the Reichswald forest and the Rhine crossing.

In 1946 Howard commanded 2nd Reconnaissance Regiment in Singapore, where he kept a tame pygmy elephant presented to him by the Sultan of Johore. It was invited to parties in the mess, and would trumpet loudly in appreciation when offered a plate of sandwiches. Howard was then advised by General Sir Miles Dempsey, commanding Second Army in Europe, to join the Royal Armoured Corps as being especially suited to his talents and style. Transferring to 3rd Hussars as second-in-command at Bielefeld he was then appointed commander of the Tactical Wing at Lulworth, Dorset.

Anxious to relieve his boredom in that final posting, he caused surprise by driving to work from his quarters at Lulworth in an old butcher's van and generally failing to treat senior officers with the respect they thought they deserved. But he never did anything which might have impaired the fighting efficiency of the troops under his command. On retiring he moved to the Isle of Ulva to farm cattle and sheep on an estate his wife had inherited.

Henry Howard was a courageous and extremely effective leader whose men knew that he had their interests at heart. He represented the Army with the javelin and was a good golfer who shot, hunted and loved fishing and sailing. In 1952 he married Jean Parnell, second daughter of the 6th Lord Congleton. They had two sons and a daughter.

CAPTAIN EWEN FRAZER

Captain Ewen Frazer (who died on November 11 2000, aged 81) was awarded a DSO for single-handedly clearing enemy machine-gun positions on October 23/24 1942, the first night of the battle of El Alamein.

He was commanding a platoon of A Company, 1st Battalion the Gordon Highlanders, in the first wave of 30 Corps' advance on Rommel's positions. Soon after crossing the start line the leading two units, A and C Companies, were held up by heavy German machine-gun fire. Taking one section to cover him, Frazer moved forward and successfully attacked the position from the flank.

When he returned both the A and C Company commanders had become casualties so he promptly took command and led them forward to dig in on their objectives. When they came under fire from a second position, he went forward on his own to bayonet the occupants of four dug-outs and silence the machine gun with grenades.

At dawn, Frazer's company came under fire from a third position to their front. Armed only with a rifle and bayonet, he crawled his way forward to another position and forced its seven occupants to surrender. For his actions that night he was awarded an immediate DSO.

Ewen Forbes Frazer was born at Perth on February 7 1920. Three years later his family moved to Bournemouth, where he attended prep school before going on to Clifton. In 1939 he started work for a shipping company in London and joined the Territorial Army, obtaining his commission in the London Scottish. Since this had been affiliated to the Gordon Highlanders since 1916, Frazer was posted to that regiment's 1st Battalion when the 51st Highland Division was reformed following its surrender at St-Valery.

Always a proud Gordon Highlander, Frazer nevertheless insisted, throughout his wartime service, on wearing the hodden grey kilt of the London Scottish. After Alamein, he remained with A Company as second-in-command for the remainder of the North African campaign. But in Tunis, just as the battalion was preparing for the invasion of Sicily, he was taken ill.

Treated at first for malaria, he was eventually diagnosed as having polio by doctors who believed he would never walk again. However, as a highly competitive sportsman, he was possessed of enormous willpower, and by 1945, after a period of recuperation at Stoke Mandeville Hospital, was walking unaided.

On demobilisation he was employed by Butlin's, setting up their new holiday camp in Ayr and advising the company on sports and fitness. In 1950 he bought a farm in Ayrshire, converted it for pigs, and later built a factory where he produced his own bacon – a business he ran successfully until his retirement in 1986. Despite gradually increasing infirmity, Frazer maintained his interest in sport, and although in later years he could walk only with the aid of two sticks he continued to play golf.

LIEUTENANT COLONEL KENDAL CHAVASSE

Lieutenant Colonel Kendal Chavasse (who died on March 31 2001, aged 96) was awarded a DSO in Tunisia in 1942 while commanding 56 Reconnaissance Regiment, a new formation which took on the tasks of cavalry which had been converted to tanks. Its flair and panache led to it being nicknamed 'Chavasse's Light Horse'.

The Germans responded to the Allied landings by flying in reinforcements which, operating with air superiority on shorter lines of communication, put up fierce resistance in the mountainous country shielding Tunis to the west.

Between November 25 and December 10, 56 Recce operated from a position east of Oued Medjerda where outnumbered, outgunned and dive-bombed, it dominated the area, thanks largely to Chavasse's "personal example, dash and daring", according to his citation. Throughout this period, German tank and armoured car patrols were prevented from interfering with Allied operations, and much valuable information on enemy movements was obtained.

By the autumn of 1943, 56 Recce was operating west of Termoli, on the east coast of Italy, which had been taken by Commandos the previous day. The same day, Chavasse's B Squadron had captured a German motorcyclist belonging to the 16th Panzer Division, which had until then been believed to be on the other coast.

A few hours later, the Germans launched a strong counter-attack. Leading a mixed force composed of his own squadron, 3 Commando, a troop of the Special Raiding Squadron and an anti-tank battery, Chavasse took up position on high ground to the west of the town.

The Germans attacked with armour and infantry, under cover of heavy shelling and mortar and machine-gun fire. Both flanks of the position were driven in, but he maintained the defence throughout the daylight hours, despite being surrounded on three sides by enemy infantry and tanks.

As night fell, he advised his men that they had 'an all-round shoot' and by the time he was ordered to withdraw they could hear the enemy infantry's voices through the shelling. Despite this, Chavasse extricated his entire command except for a few immobile vehicles. Next morning a counter-attack by the Irish Brigade, supported by Canadian tanks, drove the Germans out of Termoli.

Praising Chavasse's "exceptional leadership, coolness and devotion to duty", the citation for his second DSO stated that his personal example was "the mainspring of a gallant and effective defence which did much to ensure the successful outcome of the operations". Two of Chavasse's brothers, Paul and Evelyn, joined him at Buckingham Palace in July 1945 when King George VI presented them with a total of five DSOs and one DSC.

Kendal George Fleming Chavasse was born on September 28 1904 at Whitfield Court, near Waterford, Ireland, and educated at the Royal Naval College, Osborne, and the Royal Naval College, Dartmouth.

A bout of illness made him too old to join the navy as a cadet. Neverthelesss with a father who had served with 4th Cameronians in the Boer War and his cousin Noel, who had won a Victoria Cross and Bar as a medical officer in the First World War, he obtained a commission into the Royal Irish Fusiliers in 1924, and was soon posted to India.

As a one-time whipper-in of the Britannia Beagles, he devoted much of his spare time in India to shooting, playing polo and pig-sticking. After serving with his battalion in Egypt, Sudan, Malta and Cyprus, he attended staff college in 1939.

In March 1940 Chavasse was appointed brigade major, 150th Infantry Brigade, with whom he took part in the evacuation from Dunkirk. After serving on the staffs of Eastern and South-Eastern Commands he became, in January 1942, second-in-command of the 3 Reconnaissance Regiment before leading and taking over 56th Recce a few months later.

Promoted temporary colonel in 1945, he served briefly as Deputy Chief of Staff at HQ Fifth Army, before returning to England to run the Reconnaissance Training Centre at Catterick. In March 1946 he went to Padua as GSO1 1st Armoured Division, he then took command of 2nd Battalion Royal Irish Fusiliers in December. After commanding the battalion in Egypt and Palestine he retired in 1947.

He proceeded to his new family home in County Waterford – which his wife had bought after having a dream, and which he had not yet seen. There he embarked on a new career as a farmer, becoming one of the first in his district to make silage, use electric fences and obtain a milking machine.

Chavasse was a founder member of the Irish Farmers' Association and secretary of the West Waterford Hunt for nineteen years. He was vice-chairman of the Dungarvan Show. Always a devout man, he became a lay reader and helped with the taking of services, including the annual Armistice Day service, throughout his diocese, which he represented at the World Anglican Conference in Toronto in 1963. He became the longest-serving lay reader in Ireland and a member of the Diocesan Council and the General Synod of the Church of Ireland. In 1930 he married Oonah Perceval-Maxwell, who died in 1994, and was survived by their son and daughter.

STAFF SERGEANT LEONARD PEARSON

Staff Sergeant Leonard Pearson (who died on April 3 2001, aged 80) was awarded a Military Medal as a demolition expert in Burma, where he operated behind enemy lines with the Special Operations Executive's Force 136.

Pearson arrived in January 1945 to train Karens and Burmans in the use of small arms and explosives. His skills were such, however, that he soon became an operative, completing a parachute course in such haste that his final training jump was made operationally.

His group was charged with recruiting while disrupting enemy supply lines and communications as a prelude to General Slim's final assault on the Japanese. They had been operating for nine months when a decision was made at headquarters to take the town of Toungoo before the monsoon, in order to prevent the Japanese reinforcing it to block the way to Rangoon. The intention was to inflict maximum damage on the enemy, destroying their morale by ambushing convoys and blowing up roads and bridges.

Pearson's job was to lay explosives in potholes on a five-mile stretch of road, remaining close by waiting for the leading vehicle to drive directly over the charge before setting it off by hand. The convoy would then be forced to halt and Pearson's Karen soldiers would shoot the Japanese troops as they piled out of their vehicles in search of their ambushers.

Meanwhile he had to remain in position until he was certain that his men had got away, a risky business which resulted in some close shaves. Under mortar attack on one occasion, he escaped to where he thought his comrades were waiting and called out the password, only to discover that he was in the thick of a group of Japanese soldiers who opened fire on him. Thoroughly shaken but uninjured, he managed to escape, resolving never to allow himself to be taken alive.

Pearson accounted for more than 100 Japanese vehicles, demonstrating extreme bravery on numerous occasions and behaving with great coolness and determination. He was seen to be operating well beyond his rank and was offered an immediate commission. But unfailingly modest he declined, judging himself to be from the wrong social background.

Leonard Pearson was born in Yorkshire on August 8 1921. After joining the Army he enlisted as an apprentice at Chepstow, and soon became a boy sergeant-major before being posted for service in Persia. It was feared that the Germans might try to link up with the Afrika Korps from the Caucasus, and Pearson was employed mining possible lines of approach.

In 1944, whilst helping to transport Kenya-bound Polish POWs released by Stalin, he contracted typhus and almost died, being sent to recover at Poona, where he was recruited by Force 136.

Pearson's prolonged experience behind the lines in Burma took its toll, and he was evacuated to England. He was posted to a bomb disposal unit in Cornwall where thousands of mines around the coast had to be disarmed. Again he showed immense courage and presence of mind, but contracted tuberculosis and was medically discharged.

After recovering he pursued a successful career with Imperial Tobacco until a stroke paralysed his left side. Despite his disability, he took a job in health service management, where he was a well-liked and impressive employee for fifteen years before retiring early.

The loss of his home to a fire, and his wife's death shortly after, prompted Pearson to move to the Royal Hospital Chelsea, where he worked in the Surveyor of Works Department. At the time of his death he had contended with the effects of his stroke for more than thirty years but was determined to remain independent, showing great courtesy but gently reprimanding anyone who inconvenienced themselves to help him. He never complained or lost his sense of humour. Leonard Pearson married Eileen Roberts in 1947. They had three children.

BRIGADIER GENERAL DENNY WHITAKER

Brigadier General Denny Whitaker (who died May 30 2001, aged 86) won the DSO on the Dieppe Raid and a Bar in the Rhineland; as a relaxation in between he organised a North American football match between Canadian and American Army teams at White City.

The fixture was the result of his meeting in a pub with an American officer who remarked that equipment for six teams had just arrived in Britain.

Whitaker, a star quarterback with the Hamilton Tigers in southern Ontario, issued a challenge, and then rounded up a team of Canadian players from the troops assembling for the invasion of Europe. After six weeks' training the 'Canadian Mustangs' turned out on February 13 1944 for a 'Tea Bowl' game before a crowd of 30,000.

There was no score in the first half, which was played to slower American rules. But in the last quarter, Whitaker received a dramatic 40-yard pass to romp over the line, helping to bring the Canadians to a 16-0 victory. It had been agreed beforehand that there would be no further match; but during the game a Canadian general present agreed with his American counterpart to a 'Coffee Bowl' return match the following month.

Fifty thousand spectators were in the stands. The Spitfires flying over the ground were said to be there to ward off any sudden German attack. But the Canadians had lost several of their best players to the campaign in Italy, and the American team, which included the crack professional Sergeant Tommy Thompson, late of the Philadelphia Eagles, ran roughshod over them to a convincing 18-0 victory.

The son of an Army officer, William Denis Whitaker was born at Calgary on February 27 1915 and educated at the University of Toronto Schools and the Royal Military College, Kingston. A small, wiry man, he captained their football and hockey teams, then played for the Hamilton Tigers, earning an unofficial $25 a game for three seasons, while employed as a supervisor at a steel works.

After mobilising as a militia officer with the Royal Hamilton Light Infantry in 1939, Whitaker was soon sent to England as a staff officer. When the ill-planned day trip to Dieppe was launched on August 19 1942, he landed on White Beach, only to find himself immediately pinned down by heavy German fire. Crouching as if he were carrying the ball, Whitaker led his men in a desperate dash to a casino where they eliminated a machine-gun emplacement, took out a pillbox and cut through barbed wire before crashing in through a verandah firing Sten guns.

A bullet struck the wall close to Whitaker's head; German snipers were shooting from the upper storeys and rolling grenades down the corridors. After control was established on the lower floors, he led his group out through slit trenches at the back filled with dead Germans to a shed which turned out to be a latrine. When the enemy mortars eased up he was off again, zig-zagging 150 yards across the esplanade to the town where, still under machine-gun fire, he climbed in a window.

But it was clear that there was nobody with whom to link up, as planned, so Whitaker made his way back to the casino where he was part of the all-officer rearguard which made a final rush down the beach. The rescue boat was so overloaded that he ordered bailing with helmets. He tried to pull on board one of his men swimming alongside; but his grip slipped. The helmsman refused to turn back, and the man was never seen again.

At the conference held at the War Office shortly after the raid, Whitaker was the first on his feet to state bluntly that the Germans had been expecting them, only for Lord Louis Mountbatten to cut him off with the assurance that he was satisfied there was no breach of security. Whitaker was awarded the DSO for his part in the raid and returned on leave to Canada where he sustained his first injury of the war by slipping on ice.

He commanded the Rileys, as the Royal Hamilton Light Infantry are nicknamed, when they landed in Normandy. He was wounded in the face by shrapnel and evacuated to England when his command post near Verson received a direct hit.

But he was back at the front by September, commanding the battalion in the fighting around Antwerp and in the Scheldt estuary, which gave the Allies free use of that vital port. His seizing of the village of Woensdrecht, which was the key to clearing South Beveland, was carried out in the teeth of fierce resistance and in appalling weather. The Rileys sustained more than 100 casualties a week, and many of their reinforcements lacked the experience or training for such difficult operations.

In February 1945, they captured and held for four days the strategically important road between Goch and Kalkar against repeated counter-attacks from the Panzer Lehr Division. Whitaker proved inspirational both in his tenacity and tactical skill, especially in the use of artillery support. The Bar to his DSO was awarded for restoring "situation after situation by cool and deliberate planning", according to the citation.

After being demobilised in 1946, he became commercial manager of a radio station in Hamilton, while maintaining his connections both with the Army, as a volunteer officer, and the Hamilton football club. In 1961, he joined the O'Keefe brewery, rising to become chief executive officer. He then became consultant to a firm of stockbrokers. Although he also maintained an active interest in water skiing and squash (becoming the Canadian veterans' champion in his mid-forties) his main sporting interests were equestrian.

A founder-member of the Hamilton Hunt Club, where he was Master for many years, Whitaker hunted both in Ireland and with the Belvoir and Duke of Beaufort's hunts in England. From 1960 to 1976 he was chairman and chef d'equipe of the Canadian equestrian team when it successfully competed in three Olympic Games and won two world championships. He was also a member of the Executive of the Fédération Equestre Internationale, chaired by Prince Philip.

After retiring from business Whitaker wrote (with his wife, the journalist Shelagh Dunwoody) four anecdotal books about the war. *The Battle of the Scheldt* (1984), *Rhineland* (1989), *Dieppe* (1992) and *Victory at Falaise* (2000) copiously quoted survivors and expressed forthright opinions about the political background to the Canadian effort. To conduct their research the Whitakers interviewed veterans in Canada, the United States and Europe, spending five months touring Britain in a second-hand Volkswagen.

If the results were unvarnished, Denny Whitaker had developed what many authors would consider the best way to write a book. He dictated the narrative. His wife took it down. He would then explode – "Jeez, Shelagh, don't you know the difference between a bombardment and a barrage?" – until the text was completed.

Denny Whitaker was appointed an officer of the Order of Canada in 1990 and a member of the French Legion of Honour in 1995. He was survived by his widow, and three children from an earlier marriage.

COLONEL HENRY 'TOD' SWEENEY

Colonel Henry 'Tod' Sweeney (who died on June 4 2001, aged 82) was with the first glider-borne troops to land in France on D-Day; the following day he won an MC for rescuing a member of his platoon while under heavy fire.

On the night of June 5 1944, six Horsa gliders of D Company, 2nd Airlanding Battalion, under the command of Major John Howard, took off from England towed by Halifax bombers. A few minutes after midnight, the lead glider was cast off at 7,000 ft as it crossed the north coast of France. The company's objective was Benouville (now Pegasus) bridge over the Caen canal and another over the river Orne at Ranville. On the Allied left flank these were vital links in the supply line from the beaches.

The first group of three gliders landed close to the canal bridge and achieved complete surprise. A pillbox was knocked out, the enemy cleared from their slit trenches and, after a fierce fight, the bridge was taken. Sweeney's glider, however, hit an air pocket and landed precipitately several hundred yards short of the river.

As he scrambled out of the mangled doorway, he could hear the noise of the battle for the canal bridge. Then a patrol could be heard coming down the towpath from Caen. A challenge was shouted, to which the response sounded like German, and the entire section opened fire, killing all four men.

Later Sweeney was resting beside the road when a young paratroop officer who was to star in the film *The Longest Day*, pushed through the hedge. They had met the week before. "I'm Richard Todd," the captain had announced, "my friends call me Sweeney." "I'm Sweeney," came the reply, "my friends call me Tod."

In the early hours of June 7, Sweeney was ordered to take two soldiers to make contact with the rest of the battalion. After taking a wrong turning in the dark, they saw an indistinct shape and heard the clang of a steel door. Realising they had stumbled across an enemy armoured vehicle, Sweeney hurled a grenade inside and beat a rapid retreat. As he ran down the road, pursued by enemy tracer, he was disconcerted to find himself overtaken by his private, a heavily-built, unathletic farm lad, prompting him to shout, "Here, Private, wait for me."

During the battle, one of his corporals was wounded and left in an exposed position. With no regard for his own safety, Sweeney went forward under mortar and machine-gun fire in full view of the enemy and rescued him. He was awarded an immediate MC.

Henry John Sweeney was born on June 1 1919 at Blyth, Northumberland, the son of a customs officer. He was educated at Douai Abbey School, and entered the monastery as a novice. But when war broke out he left to join first the Pay Corps and later the 2nd Airlanding Battalion, Oxfordshire and Buckinghamshire Light Infantry.

In July 1944, a few weeks after winning his MC, Sweeney was wounded and evacuated to England, but he rejoined his battalion for the fighting on the Maas river in Holland and then the large-scale airborne landing assault across the Rhine and the advance across Germany.

In 1946, he was appointed instructor at the School of Infantry near Haifa. After staff college, he was posted to Berlin as GSO2 and then to the Canal Zone as adjutant of the Ox and Bucks. At the Queen's Coronation in 1953, he commanded the regimental guard of honour.

Three years later, Sweeney was sent to Cyprus during the EOKA troubles, where he earned a mention in despatches. In 1962, he commanded the 1st Battalion Green Jackets (into which the Ox and Bucks had been subsumed) at Penang, moving it to Brunei at short notice to help to put down a serious revolt; again he was mentioned in despatches.

From 1966 to 1969, Sweeney was defence adviser to the UK Mission to the United Nations in New York during the Six Day War and the Russian invasion of Czechoslovakia. He then was appointed deputy commandant of the School of Infantry before retiring three years later to become director general of the Battersea Dogs' Home.

His charm and persistence in reminding people of the borough that the home was their local charity resulted in a substantial increase in donations.

Purpose-built kennels were installed for the first time in 1975, and a country annex near Windsor was acquired in 1979 to provide extra accommodation and to serve as a training school for kennel maids. After retiring to Warwickshire, he lectured on Normandy and the Rhine Crossing. He married, in 1942, Geraldine Follett, with whom he had two sons and three daughters.

MAJOR HUGH FANE-HERVEY

Major Hugh Fane-Hervey (who died on January 11 2003, aged 86) won an MC as a tank commander in North Africa and a Bar for his exploits as an escaped prisoner.

His first taste of action came when leading a troop of 7th Royal Tank Regiment in General Richard O'Connor's lightning attack on the Italians south of Sidi Barrani on December 9 1940. His men engaged anti-tank and field-guns at point blank range, and by 10 am a camp had been captured, together with large quantities of arms and more than 2,000 prisoners. Despite receiving a number of direct hits (one in his third tank), he rallied his troop and led his two remaining tanks into an attack on Tummar where he knocked out more enemy guns. The next day, Fane-Hervey was once more in the leading troop in the attack on the base at Sidi Barrani before it was immobilised, with all radio communications gone.

He ordered his crew to bail out and set the vehicle on fire to prevent its capture. But although he seemed to be a prisoner, he persuaded the Italians that they were surrounded, and an Italian officer surrendered after being assured that he and his men would not be castrated (as was alleged to have occurred in the Abyssinian campaign of 1935–6.) As they were marched away the captives were gradually joined by others until they eventually numbered several hundred on arriving at the British lines. Fane-Hervey was awarded the MC for his part in the two-day action.

On January 3 1941 he was involved in the attack on the encampment at Bardia. After Phase One, he withdrew his battered vehicle, which had received about forty direct hits only to be told by his commanding officer Roy Jerram, "There's my tank, Hugh. You're in Phase Two – off you go." The CO was more than six feet tall, and Fane-Hervey just 5ft 6in; but there was no time to adjust the height of the seat so he returned to battle standing on the ammunition boxes.

In June 1942 he had another tank catch fire outside Tobruk. Pulling his trapped wounded gunner free he earned the open applause of watching German soldiers, according to one witness. Wounded and suffering from burns, he was taken prisoner this time. But with a brother officer he escaped from hospital during the night and passed through the enemy lines with three other escapers. After hiding for eight days, with little food or water and moving only by night, they tried to steal a truck. Three Germans were killed in an exchange of fire, but Fane-Hervey and most of his group were re-captured.

He was subsequently transferred to Italy, where

he was the senior British officer in Fontanellato prison camp when it was abandoned after the Italian armistice. After making arrangements for the accommodation of those who hoped to wait for the arrival of the Allies, he and a Royal Marine headed south where he was recaptured ten miles from the Allied lines, and incarcerated in a civilian prison at Frosinone.

Soon after his arrival, he broke out through the roof just as the guards conducted a snap roll call. But by the time a recount was taken, he had dropped down from the roof and slipped in behind the guards to take his place among the other prisoners.

Following the Italian armistice the Germans decided to send the POWs to Germany. Fane-Hervey and his comrades badgered the guards into allowing them a hot bath. When a Polish conscript was ordered to chop wood to heat the boiler, he secretly stole his hatchet which was then used to hack through the floor of the truck. Twenty-four escaped.

He then made his way to Rome in the company of Flight Lieutenant Garrad-Cole, who subsequently wrote *Single to Rome* about their adventures. Some sixty Allied officers and 300 other ranks were thought to be hiding in the Eternal City. Although speaking imperfect Italian Fane-Hervey took the name 'Count Paolo Fattorini' and was befriended by a marchesa who invited him to her box at the opera, where he once proffered his programme to be signed by the German commander next door.

Contacts with the Venerable English College and

Monsignor O'Flaherty's resistance organisation obtained him rooms in the abandoned British Embassy, where he used a curtain rod with a noose on the end to extract bottles of champagne from a barred wine cellar to celebrate the Christmas of 1943. When Rome was later liberated he captured five Germans whom he handed over to the Allies.

The son of a member of the Indian Civil Service, he was born Hugh Frederick Fane Hervey at Trichinopoly, India, on January 2 1917. He completed his education at Ashburton Grammar School, Devon, and joined the 3rd County of London Yeomanry (Sharpshooters). After being sent to Sandhurst he was commissioned into 7RTR, and amended his surname to Fane-Hervey to avoid confusion with another officer over mess bills, only to be known as 'Fanny'.

After his exploits as an escaper, Fane-Hervey had a period of home leave, before returning to Italy where he was severely wounded at the battle of Senio in April 1945, then sent to recover at Sir Archibald McIndoe's burns unit at East Grinstead. He held various post-war appointments until returning to 7RTR, as second-in-command before retiring in 1959.

Fane-Hervey became a stockbroker in the City, and settled in East Sussex where he farmed for several years. A gregarious man of stocky build, he played for Harlequins RFC before the war and represented the Army at hockey. He boxed at regimental level, and was a leading member of the squash team and the golf society.

Hugh Fane-Hervey married Eileen Kerbey in 1938 (the marriage was dissolved in 1946). They had a twin son and daughter. He then married Patricia Brennan in 1950. They had three sons and a daughter.

MAJOR JIM DAVIES

Major Jim Davies (who died on February 28 2003, aged 89) was a Special Operations Executive officer whose efforts against the Germans in the Peloponnese were complicated by the approaching civil war in Greece.

In October 1943 he was parachuted in to work with ELAS – the Communist-led largest branch of the Greek Resistance – when a series of attacks on enemy airfields was planned as part of the ill-starred Dodecanese campaign. The attacks were designed to prepare for 'Noah's Ark', which was aimed at harassing the eventual German withdrawal from Greece; but by then ELAS's priority was to combat any possible rivals.

A tense stand-off between SOE and ELAS resulted. Davies recalled one meeting with the Greeks, when his mission leader, Lieutenant Colonel John Stevens, became so exasperated that he got up to throw open a window and exclaim loudly in Greek: "It stinks in here." Despite the strain, Davies continued his work of recceing demolition targets.

By June 1944, however, ELAS had made conditions so difficult that Stevens withdrew the main body of the mission, though not before Davies had demolished part of the main road and railway along the north coast. As he and his party withdrew on mules up the mountainside at dawn, they saw a German light aircraft flying low past them to photograph the damage.

James Thomas Mann Davies was born on January 1 1914 at Bushey, Hertfordshire. When he was seven his parents bought a hotel at Villars in Switzerland, where he became a first-class skier. After Aldenham, young Jim went up to Pembroke, Oxford, where he studied Forestry and obtained a half-blue for skiing. He then joined the Bombay Burma Trading Corporation to work in the Gangor teak forest of north-west Burma. It was an isolated life, in which his superior would drink plenty of whisky, then pull out boxing gloves and invite Davies to spar with him.

In 1937 Davies was sent to the Siam border to receive a herd of some thirty elephants which was needed to drag logs to rivers for floating downstream. This involved coaxing them on to a raft, on which they were shackled for the crossing of the Salween River, an operation which took three days.

After a year Davies was sent to Shwebo, where he worked with Lieutenant Colonel J. H. Williams, author of the bestseller *Elephant Bill*. Williams recorded how Davies was sleeping with his two dogs in a jungle hut raised 10ft off the ground on stilts, when he was woken by a yelp: he saw a leopard disappearing with his Labrador in its mouth.

Davies leaped out of bed and fired his revolver, to no avail; but his brindle bull terrier set off in hot pursuit, and attacked the cat so ferociously that it dropped its prey and vanished into the scrub;

unfortunately, the Labrador was so badly mauled that it had to be destroyed.

When war broke out Davies found himself in a reserved occupation, since teak was considered as important as steel. However, after the Japanese entered the war in 1941 he was transferred to government service to help supervise the building of a road into Manipur along which the British could retreat to India. He helped to run a vaccination programme during a cholera outbreak, then returned home after being stricken with malaria and dysentery.

He was treated on board ship by the drug Atebrin, which cured him of malaria for life; but he was not to return to a tropical climate. Commissioned into the Royal Engineers, Davies was serving as a sapper platoon commander with the 52nd (Lowland) Division when he met an officer on a troop train to Scotland who recruited him into SOE. He was then posted to Cairo as an expert demolitions officer.

After his work in Greece, for which he was appointed MBE (Mil), Davies and Charles Holland, who had also been in the Peloponnese, were snapped up by SOE's Italian unit, No 1 Special Force. They were briefed to drop an Italian parachute battalion behind enemy lines in the Central Apennines, ahead of the American Fifth Army which was advancing towards the Gothic Line.

Davies and Holland went in as members of an advance party, but soon found that the enemy, alerted by the supply drops of arms, had launched an element of the Hermann Goering Panzer Division to clear the area; Davies managed to get the main drop cancelled just hours before take-off. Together with a British radio operator, he and Holland headed west to set up a new mission with partisans in Parma. Davies was then recalled to base, after six men were lost in a surprise attack on his mission.

His report, one of the first by a British liaison officer in the field in Italy, received a wide circulation. It included a timely and balanced military and political assessment of the current state of partisan formations. After spending Christmas 1945 with his widowed mother in Switzerland, Davies was dropped by day into the province of Modena to prepare the partisans to aid the Allies' Spring offensive.

On the night of April 20/21 he rode down from the mountains on a parachuted motorcycle, a prototype for the post-war Italian Vespa, and entered the city of Modena, which was already under Resistance control ahead of the entry of the first American column. Forty-two years later, he was to return as an official guest at their Liberation Day celebrations.

When No 1 Special Force was run down, Davies, who was awarded an MC, served as Allied Military Governor of Rho in Piedmont, and ended his military service in Austria. He next embarked on a post-war career with ICI, representing the company in Dublin, South Africa, Belgium and Switzerland. In 1951 Jim Davies married Wendy Gillbanks, who died in 1995, after which he went to live in Switzerland. They were survived by their three children.

LIEUTENANT PETER JOHNSEN

Lieutenant Peter Johnsen (who died on June 4 2003, aged 79) served throughout the latter years of the Second World War with Phantom and the SAS, operating behind the lines in Occupied France.

In his first operation on D-Day + 2, Johnsen was parachuted just south of Rennes with his patrol from Phantom and thirty men from 2SAS. Their mission was to report on German troop movements, mostly reinforcements being rushed up to the Allied bridgehead. They operated unobserved for nearly a fortnight, calling in a squadron of Typhoons to attack and destroy trains and road convoys.

Ordered east towards Le Mans to link up with another squadron of SAS (commanded by the Colditz escaper Major Airey Neave), they were denied a drop of jeeps, so commandeered civilian vehicles. They made their way across northern France, successfully linking up with Neave's force just as the main German force was pulling out.

Johnsen and a small group then made an unauthorised dash for Paris before being called back to rescue some 100 escaped British POWs who were in hiding in the area. He was mentioned in despatches.

In August, 120 men from 2SAS, including Johnsen, were parachuted by night into the Vosges Mountains to arm and organise the French resistance and create as much diversionary activity as possible behind the German lines. For three months they hid in the thick forests, blowing up roads, railways and other strategic installations. By October, they were being chased by two German divisions, including one crack SS armoured division which thought it was dealing with a far superior force.

The force could not have survived without the assistance of the inhabitants of Moussey and the surrounding area who, until the British came, had led a largely unaltered existence despite a strong German presence. Nevertheless, they often hid and fed small parties of SAS along with three servicewomen (one British and two French) working with SOE.

Finally the Gestapo rounded up all the French civilian men from Moussey and the surrounding area in the main square of the town, offering an amnesty if they disclosed the whereabouts of the British. Not a man moved. As a result, 220 Frenchmen were marched off to concentration camps; 140 never returned. The area is still known as 'the Valley of the Widows'.

In October the SAS unit split up into small groups of three or four, and were ordered to head westwards in the direction of the Allied lines some 200 miles distant. Johnsen led one group consisting of himself, Private Bannerman and Private Johnston. Almost within sight of the American lines, they were ambushed by a German patrol. As they split and ran, all three were hit; only Johnsen survived, wounded in an arm and a leg.

Johnsen completed one further operation, with 1SAS in early 1945, which was codenamed Operation Howard and led by Lieutenant Colonel Paddy Mayne. This force of fifty, mounted in jeeps with twin Vickers machine guns in the front and .5

Browning guns in the back, was sent in to an area opposite 4th Canadian Armoured Division, which found itself outgunned by the German Tiger tanks. The job of the SAS was to disrupt enemy supply lines. At his demob in October 1946, Johnsen was awarded the Croix de Guerre with Palm Leaf.

Peter Bowater Johnsen was born on October 12 1923 at Balcombe House, West Sussex, the fifth of eight children of Captain 'Billy' Johnsen, DFC, and May Bowater. Peter's father was a scion of a Norwegian family which had been attracted by business opportunities in Britain in the early 19th century.

As land and forestry owners, the Johnsens established increasingly strong trading links with paper and pulp manufacturers in Scotland and the north of England. In 1885, Johnsen & Jorgensen became established in the City of London to supply much of Fleet Street with its newsprint. Later it gave Peter Johnsen great satisfaction that the company had never accepted any business from Robert Maxwell, from whom he instinctively recoiled after seeing him cheat someone out of ten shillings at cards.

Peter was educated at Eton, where his housemaster was Humphrey Lyttelton's father, George. The bohemian side of Lyttelton family life was never far away; Humphrey was often to be heard practising his jazz trumpet in Warre House, and his mother once brought her sick horse into the drawing room to nurse it.

After leaving school, Johnsen was commissioned into the King's Royal Rifle Corps and posted to the 7th Battalion, training for deployment in North Africa. In 1943 he was recruited into Phantom, which had originally been constituted in 1940, when Army Group headquarters needed faster and more accurate information. Young officers were trained to speed up to the front line, usually on motorcycles, assess the situation and report back – a ploy developed by Napoleon; though Montgomery claimed it as his idea.

Johnsen enjoyed the company of such comrades as the film star David Niven, the future law lord Nigel Bridge, the jump jockey John Hislop and many other colourful characters who, when back in England, never failed to take advantage of their camp's proximity to the West End.

After the war, Johnsen initially joined Bowaters. But he became ill at ease with the autocratic style of his uncle, Sir Eric Bowater, and in 1950 joined his brothers at JJ & W, in their offices at Old Bailey, taking turns as nominal chairman.

They successfully managed the transition of the company from an old-fashioned family firm into part of an international public company. Peter Johnsen became a main board director of Ibstock (from 1971 to 1988), helping oversee its development from a large regional brickmaker into a multi-national building products company.

During this period, when the uncertainties engendered by aggressive takeover battles between London Brick and Hanson often seemed to engulf Ibstock too, he enjoyed touring the plants at times of industrial unrest to explain to workers on the shop floor what was going on.

In 1954 he married Nina Raben-Levetzau, granddaughter of the Lensgreve Raben, sometime Foreign Minister and Chancellor at the Danish Court of Christian IX. In retirement, Peter Johnsen devoted much time to Business in the Community, the charity established by the Prince of Wales. After finally settling in Gloucestershire he and his wife started a spectacular garden within the old walled garden of Oddington House.

It gave him particular pleasure to support the initiative of his former troop sergeant, Joe Owen, to erect a permanent memorial to members of Phantom, the SAS and their many French Resistance allies who lost their lives during Operation Loyton at the National Arboretum in Staffordshire. Peter Johnsen was survived by his wife; they had four children, one of whom died shortly after childbirth.

COLONEL TONY HEWITT

Colonel Tony Hewitt (who died on June 30 2004, aged 89) was awarded an MC for a daring escape from a Japanese POW camp after the fall of Hong Kong on Christmas Day 1941.

In the month before, Japan launched a massive offensive against the Crown Colony with infantry, artillery and supporting air cover. British, Canadian and Indian forces put up a gallant defence but they were overwhelmed and the garrison forced to surrender.

Captain Hewitt, adjutant of 1st Battalion Middlesex

Regiment, was imprisoned in Sham Shui Po POW camp on the Kowloon Peninsula. It was only lightly guarded because the Japanese believed that escape was impossible; but Hewitt had a detailed knowledge of the New Territories beyond the mountains with their terraced valleys, walled villages, bays and inlets and was determined to make a break.

Warning that he had no more than one chance in a hundred of succeeding, General C.M. Maltby, GOC China Command, authorised the paymaster to provide his escape party with $800.

Early on the cold, moonlit night of February 2 1942, Hewitt and two comrades – Eddy Crossley, a pilot officer with the Royal New Zealand Air Force, and Douglas Scriven of the Indian Medical Service – concealed themselves in a dank, smelly slipway waiting for a sampan to deliver food to the camp. As soon as this was unloaded, the three men rushed the boat, thrust $300 into the boatman's hand and paddled into the darkness, pursued by the Japanese sentries' machine-gun and rifle fire.

When it reached the mainland, they crossed the Shing Mun River and began a 200-mile journey to reach the Chinese Regular Forces. While sheltering in a gully, they were attacked by seven robbers armed with axes. Hewitt killed one, but sustained serious head wounds and had tendons in his right hand severed. Crossley and Scriven set about the others with heavy sticks and put them to flight.

From villagers, they learned that the gang had captured some foreigners the previous day and handed them over to the Japanese, who had beheaded them in the market square. Two days later, the three were attacked by a party of sixty armed robbers. They fought back with clasp knives but were badly beaten and robbed of most of their possessions.

Near Shunchun, they learned that the Japanese occupied all the surrounding towns and that patrols were only a few hundred yards away. After spending the night hidden in a tomb, they crossed the Sham Chun River into China. Any euphoria was quickly dispelled when four Chinese brigands armed with knives and bayonets jumped on them and pushed them into a creek.

They were rescued by a large Jamaican-Chinese who ran a radio shop in Kowloon and who recognised Hewitt. He arranged for an escort of friendly bandits to guide them to the Wung Tu Mountains. Passing a wedding ceremony held under an old lychee tree to the sound of gongs beating and crackers exploding, the escapers met the village patriarch who praised them for their escape and predicted they would reach freedom safely.

The Japanese had built a line of block houses interspersed with picquets, and the only way through them was by a steep ravine, where the enemy were reported to be on the crest. But after climbing an almost perpendicular incline and scaling a cliff at the top, they found that the Japanese had moved on a few hours earlier. By negotiating slit trenches and barbed wire entanglements, they passed through the enemy lines.

Next day, the trio were spotted by soldiers of the Communist Red Army who opened fire and arrested them. But after they had agreed to help train the soldiers, the local commander returned from skirmishing with the Japanese and held a banquet in their honour. He provided them with an escort of guerrillas who accompanied them for four days before melting away as they made contact with the Chinese National Army at the badly damaged city of Waichow, where they were received like conquering heroes.

They then travelled up the East River by motor launch, but had to switch to a barge crowded with refugees when this broke down. They reached Long Chun on March 3, and for the next three days travelled with thirty-two Chinese refugees clinging to salt sacks in a three-ton Chevrolet. Finally at Kukong, Hewitt contacted the British Military Mission. With his hand now swollen to the size of a football he was sent to the Methodist Hospital, where he learned he was to be awarded the MC.

Anthony George Hewitt, the son of an Army chaplain, was born on September 13 1914 at Dharwad, southern India, in what he described as an old pre-Mutiny bungalow with a sunken grave in the garden and the ghost of a murdered British officer. His early years were spent in Ahmednagar, north-east of Poona, but when he was 10 he came to England to attend prep school then Epsom College.

In his first term, Hewitt was awarded his house colours for cricket by a school prefect named Stewart, afterwards the film star Stewart Granger. He entered Sandhurst in 1933 and was commissioned into the Middlesex Regiment, Duke of Cambridge's Own. After being posted to 1st Battalion in Egypt his unit moved to Singapore and thence Hong Kong.

On returning to India following his escape, Hewitt joined 1st Battalion Lancashire Fusiliers in Cawnpore. Promoted to major, he commanded a detachment at Ranikhet, in the foothills of the Himalayas, before rejoining his battalion.

Hewitt moved to Belgaum, southern India, as an instructor at the officers' training school. He then returned to England, where he received his MC from King George VI at Buckingham Palace. He subsequently returned to the Middlesex Regiment and, with 2nd Battalion, took part in the Normandy landings and the liberation of Brussels before ending the war on the Baltic coast.

After attending staff college, Camberley, he was anxious to see something of the Empire, and joined 1st Battalion Sierra Leone Regiment, which was part of the Royal West African Frontier Force. He subsequently commanded the Gambia Regiment and was appointed MBE following his second tour in West Africa.

He served in Germany, Austria, Norway and Ghana before moving to Canberra in 1962 as military adviser to the British High Commissioner. After two years as deputy commander of Singapore District, he retired in 1967. Hewitt lived in Sydney for some years, working as secretary of the University Club, before settling at Buderim, Queensland. He wrote *Bridge with Three Men* (1986), *Corridors of Time* (1993) and *Children of the Empire* (1995) about his adventures. Tony Hewitt married, in 1948, Elizabeth Weedon (née Hayley-Bell).

LIEUTENANT RODNEY WILKINSON

Lieutenant Rodney Wilkinson (who died on August 13 2004, aged 80) won an MC in the last days of the Italy campaign, when the Allied armies were racing to prevent the Germans withdrawing behind their Alpine barrier.

The 27th Lancers had crossed the Po and were leading 6th Armoured Division's pursuit of the enemy towards Austria. On May 1 1945, Wilkinson, a lieutenant in B Squadron, was in command of a troop of armoured cars, close to the town of Maniago which was held by 1,000 enemy troops equipped with seven self-propelled guns. Although twelve miles from the rest of his squadron, he delivered an ultimatum to the German commander, exaggerating his own strength and threatening an immediate air attack.

The ruse succeeded, and Wilkinson personally supervised the disarming of the force before escorting it fifteen miles to a holding area. The citation for his MC stated, "his leadership and disregard of personal danger over many months had been a magnificent example to his men."

Rodney Norman Wilkinson was born on March 9 1924 in St John's Wood, London. His father, Norman, was a well-known landscape artist who drew the LMS railway posters and invented 'dazzle' paint to protect merchant ships from U-boats in the Great War.

Young Rodney was educated at Stowe, then Sandhurst, before being commissioned into the 27th

Lancers and sent to Egypt. After a spell in Cyrenaica, Palestine and Syria, 27L landed in Italy in July 1944 and took over from two squadrons of the 12th Royal Lancers, from which it was formed, in the Upper Tiber valley. There was a friendly rivalry between the two regiments; 12RL, which had first been formed, dubbed the new arrivals the 'Desert Mice'.

The terrain consisted of barren ridges divided by deep valleys where it was impossible to make much use of the armoured cars and most of the patrolling was carried out in jeeps or on foot. In September, at Piandimeleto, near Pesaro, Wilkinson dispersed a patrol of ten Germans single-handed, killing two with his revolver and bringing back two prisoners.

As the Germans fell back, 27L followed; but the mountains west of Urbino became almost impassable for wheeled transport. Oxen had to be employed to pull the massive Staghound armoured cars out of the mud, and the regiment largely depended on mules.

On one occasion, Wilkinson had made up a bridge four with members of his troop in a farmhouse near Gubbio when a German patrol of twelve soldiers arrived. Both parties were taken by surprise. Wilkinson and his comrades took cover in a ditch over which the Germans had to jump to get away. He fired off all six chambers of his revolver as they leaped over him but only succeeded in hitting a straggler in the backside which expedited the man's departure. In December, elements of 27L were among the first into Ravenna. Bottles of wine appeared, the women came out of their houses with cakes and the children ran up with gifts of fruit.

At the officers' club, Wilkinson was one of four cavalry officers who let off a smoke discharger from a destroyer which resulted in more than thirty people being removed on stretchers, though none was permanently injured. The perpetrators were fined a year's pay – but the ringleader, to their great relief, settled the bill for all the other participants.

In April 1945, Wilkinson took part in the Battle of Commachio where he commanded a troop of fantails – tracked amphibian vehicles – carrying sappers and explosives. After crossing the Po, 27L were heading for Treviso when Colonel General Graf von Schwerin, commanding 76 Panzer Corps, came down the road in a Mercedes staff car carrying a white flag and surrendered to Wilkinson; the commanding officer of 27L asked to be allowed to use the Mercedes, a much more exciting car than his Humber, but the corps commander kept it for himself. Wilkinson was mentioned in despatches.

B Squadron met stiff resistance at Conegliano, where it fought an eight-hour battle before the 1,500-strong garrison surrendered. On May 2, the squadron found seven German tanks and 400 infantry holding the entrance to a pass near Gemona. Wilkinson, after his successful stratagem at Maniago, decided to try to bluff them into surrendering and dispatched an Italian priest with a white flag to inform the commander that he was surrounded by twenty tanks and a brigade of infantry.

The Germans called his bluff and, next day, they attacked Gemona. Armoured cars and half-tracks were no match for the Panthers and Panzer IV tanks but B Squadron, reinforced by part of C Squadron, held off the assault until further reinforcements arrived.

Shortly after the end of the war, Wilkinson had a lucky escape when the brakes failed on a Churchill tank which rolled down a hill and over the tent in which he was sleeping. It did not seem possible that he could survive and there was a rumour that he had levitated himself and shot horizontally out of the flap. Unsurprisingly, he was somewhat shaken by the experience.

In August 1945, 27L was disbanded. Wilkinson transferred to the 7th (Queen's Own) Hussars, and was demobilised two years later. He became a student at the Byam Shaw Art School until 1952 when he embarked on a career as a portrait painter. His commissions included Princess Mary, the Queen's aunt, the Bishop of Ipswich and the Dean of Westminster. There was also one of his own father, with whom he often found himself exhibiting in the Royal Academy summer shows, as well as his own wife.

In 1956, he returned to the Byam Shaw where he taught drawing and painting for the next twenty years. Maurice de Saumarez, the principal, was influential in his decision to abandon portraiture and focus on abstract landscape and cityscape painting.

Wilkinson was greatly interested in Bristol docks, where he executed a number of major works which demonstrated his fascination with the geometry of the picture plane, much inspired by Cézanne. An accomplished snooker player, he later moved to Dorset, where he concentrated on landscape painting.

He was perhaps a better painter than his father but a less astute businessman. Settled in his motoring habits, he drove a 1937 Lancia Aprilia for the rest of his life. He was a first-class fisherman and a proficient golfer. In 1954 Wilkinson married Angelina Pawle, daughter of the stained glass artist Hugh Pawle; the marriage was dissolved in 1982. Their son and two daughters survive him.

BRIGADIER PAUL CROOK

Brigadier Paul Crook (who died on August 20 2004, aged 89), led 3 Para Group in the assault on El Gamil airfield during the Suez Crisis. In the summer of 1956, President Nasser of Egypt nationalised the canal, which was owned by a joint Anglo-French company, and closed it to Israeli shipping. At the end of October, Israel invaded the Gaza Strip and the Sinai Peninsula and advanced towards the Canal Zone.

Meanwhile, Britain and France bombed Egyptian targets in an attempt to force the reopening of the Canal, and deployed their troops in readiness for an invasion. 3 Para Group, commanded by Crook, was ordered to capture El Gamil airfield, and advance to the east of the town to link up with the seaborne Royal Marines.

The first transport aircraft in Operation Musketeer took off from Nicosia airport at dawn on November

5. El Gamil airfield was long and narrow and largely surrounded by water. Hard intelligence as to the dispositions of the Egyptian forces was limited, and when Crook and 600 men were dropped into action at first light the leading companies came under mortar, machine-gun and tank fire from an Egyptian battalion group.

One enemy company, armed with medium machine guns, was operating from two pillboxes, and another strong company position was located in a cemetery closer to the town. Crook's command team dealt with the enemy positions, firing at them from a distance by calling on the weapons of Support Company and strikes by the Fleet Air Arm.

The airfield was quickly secured, and, following an airstrike by Venoms and Sea Hawks, at 10.30 am an attack went in against the unit deployed in the cemetery. Some Egyptian soldiers fought with considerable courage, but few employed aggressive tactics and no counter-attacks were mounted.

3 Para Group was reinforced by a second drop of men and equipment in the afternoon. By dusk it had overwhelmed an enemy superior in numbers, and secured an area considerably larger than that originally demanded of them. It had also captured large quantities of arms and ammunition while sustaining light casualties.

A French parachute battalion held Port Fuad and, the following day, a seaborne invasion took place. After intense pressure from the United Nations and the Soviet Union, however, the French and British were forced to withdraw and, shortly before midnight on November 6, a ceasefire took effect.

The citation for Crook's DSO stated that, "his gallantry under fire, his inspiring leadership and the skill with which he handled his force made an immeasurable contribution to the success of the action."

Paul Edwin Crook was born at Croydon, Surrey, on April 19 1915 and educated at Uppingham before going up to Emmanuel College, Cambridge, to read Classics and Law. He was commissioned into the Queen's Own Royal West Kent Regiment (QORWK) in 1935 and went with 2nd Battalion to Karachi as a platoon commander.

Crook served in Palestine on internal security operations for two years before the Second World War and then moved to HQ Military Forces West Africa at Accra. After returning to England to attend staff college, he was posted to 147 Infantry Brigade, part of 49 West Riding Division.

He went to Normandy with his brigade, but his troopship was damaged in the Thames Estuary and he arrived on the beaches 12 hours after the landings. He took part in tough fighting in the bocage country and in the capture of Le Havre, before being posted to the United States Command and General Staff School.

In September 1945 Crook was posted to Singapore, and was present at the signing of the Japanese surrender. As commander of HQ 2RAPWI (Repatriation of Allied Prisoners of War and Internees), he and his small staff were immediately faced with the problem of organising the feeding, clothing, documentation, hospitalisation and embarkation of 34,000 prisoners from thirteen widely-scattered Japanese camps.

Working 20 hours a day, by the end of October he had played a leading part in repatriating 50,000 former detainees. He was appointed OBE and appointed Chief Civil Affairs Officer for the Netherlands East Indies.

Crook suffered a severe injury to his back and returned to England in 1947. After a spell at the War Office, he returned to staff college as an instructor and then rejoined QORWK. With them, he served as a company commander of 1st Battalion in Malaya in operations against the Chinese Communists. He was mentioned in despatches for the third time.

In 1954 Crook took command of 3rd Battalion the Parachute Regiment. He hurt his back again, but showed great determination in passing the medical board and getting his wings. He took 3 Para to Cyprus, where it carried out operations against EOKA, and commanded it for a further year after the Suez invasion.

Crook was appointed head of the Army Airborne Training and Development Centre before becoming commander and chief of staff of the Jamaica Defence Force. He was advanced to CBE at the end of his three-year tour. A move to Aden as security operations adviser to the High Commissioner was then followed by a final assignment as Commander Rhine Area. He retired from the Army in 1971.

Crook was aide-de-camp to the Queen from 1964 to 1967, Honorary Colonel 16 (Lincoln) Independent Parachute Regiment (TA) from 1974 to 1979; Deputy Honorary Colonel 15 (Scottish) Parachute Battalion (TA) from 1979 until 1983 and 4th (Volunteer)

Parachute Battalion, 1984-85. He held the US Bronze Star.

A keen jazz vocalist who had been accompanied by some of the great stars, Crook claimed to have probably been the only person who had sung *Basin Street Blues* in that New Orleans thoroughfare. Paul Crook married first, in 1944, Joan Lewis. The marriage was dissolved and he married secondly, in 1967, Betty Lown (née Wyles), who survived him with a daughter of his first marriage and a stepson.

CAPTAIN DICK ANNAND, VC

Captain Dick Annand (who died on Christmas Eve 2004, aged 90), won the Army's first Victoria Cross of the Second World War while serving with the 2nd Battalion Durham Light Infantry in Belgium in 1940.

On May 15, 2DLI was in a defensive position on the south side of the Dyle river, east of Brussels, with battalion headquarters established in the ominously-named village of La Tombe. The German assault began shortly after dawn.

Annand's platoon, positioned astride a blown bridge, had beaten off a strong attack the previous night and was now facing the main thrust of an enemy determined to cross the river in strength. At 11 am, the Germans launched a violent attack, pushing forward a bridging party into the sunken bottom of the river.

As a second lieutenant, he led a counter-attack.

When the ammunition ran out, he went forward himself over open ground with utter disregard for the mortar and machine-gun fire. Reaching the top of the ridge, he drove out the party below with hand grenades, inflicting more than twenty casualties. Already wounded, he rejoined his platoon, had his wounds dressed and carried on in command.

That evening, the Germans launched another assault, and again Annand went forward armed with hand grenades and repelled it. His platoon sergeant said later: "Mr Annand came to me at platoon headquarters and asked for a box of grenades as they could hear Jerry trying to repair the bridge. Off he went, and he sure must have given them a lovely time because it wasn't a great while before he was back for more. Just like giving elephant strawberries."

At 11 pm the order was given to pull back from the Dyle, and Annand withdrew the remnants of his platoon. There was no transport and anything that could not be carried had to be abandoned. In the early hours of May 16 Annand learned that his batman had been left behind severely wounded. He returned at once to the original position and brought him back in a wheelbarrow before losing consciousness as a result of his own wounds.

For two days Annand jolted through France in a Belgian hospital train without food or water. He no sooner arrived at the hospital in Calais than it had to be evacuated. He was put aboard the first of two hospital ships. The second was bombed and sank. Annand was invested with the Victoria Cross by King George VI at Buckingham Palace on September

3 1940. Air raid warning sirens had been sounded shortly before the ceremony and the investiture was held inside the Palace instead of the quadrangle.

Richard Wallace Annand was born on November 5 1914 at South Shields, County Durham. His father, Lieutenant-Commander W. M. Annand, was killed at Gallipoli the following year. On leaving Pocklington School in East Yorkshire, Dick joined the National Provincial Bank for whom he worked in South Shields then Rugby and London.

Keen to follow in his father's footsteps he became a midshipman in the Tyne Division of the Royal Navy Volunteer Reserve. In 1936, he was promoted sub-lieutenant and attended a navigation course at Portsmouth and a gunnery course at Whale Island. But his application for a regular commission was turned down because of his age, and the following year he was gazetted second lieutenant in the supplementary reserve of the DLI.

Annand landed in France in September 1939 but was invalided home as a result of the wounds received in the action in Belgium in May 1940. He joined the re-formed DLI at Bridlington the following month but then was discharged after losing much of his hearing as a result of rifle practice on the ranges.

From then on he relied largely on lip-reading. He became an instructor at the Commando training centre at Inverailort Castle, Inverness-shire, and then was posted to the Young Soldiers DLI Training Battalion at Brancepeth Castle, County Durham, before moving to Elgin as GS03, training the Home Guard. He was seconded to Gordonstoun School, where he instructed the cadet force in pre-service training, and appointed an instructor at the Highland Fieldcraft Centre in the Cairngorms before being posted to the War Office in Mayfair. He declined a commission in the Pay Corps and in 1948 was invalided out of the Army.

Most of the rest of Annand's life was devoted to helping the disabled. After giving a speech proposing a club for the hard of hearing, he was deluged with letters, and became a founder member of the British Association for the Hard of Hearing (now Hearing Concern). He also helped to set up the Durham County Association for the Disabled, where his role was more than administrative; he provided transport, often carrying members to his car. Believing training the disabled did little good without finding them work, he once loaded four tailors in his car and took them to London, where he found them jobs.

He was president of his local branch of the British Legion, of the Dunkirk Veterans Association and of the St James's Art Society for the Deafened. In 1956 Annand became a Deputy Lieutenant for the County of Durham, and was president of the Durham branch of the Light Infantry Club until 1998. In retirement his main recreation was golf.

Aged 64 in 1979, he saved his wife from drowning in the River Tyne after they had dined aboard the frigate *Bacchante*. The next day one local newspaper paper carried the headline: "War hero rescues wife from drowning". Another had "Durham magistrate falls in Tyne after naval party". Annand confined himself to the gentle observation that perhaps the reporting said more about the newspapers than about himself. Annand married, in 1940, Shirley Osborne.

CAPTAIN GEORGE HEYWOOD

Captain George Heywood (who died on June 2 2005, aged 89) was awarded the Distinguished Conduct Medal in 1944 while serving with the Cheshire Regiment during the Italian Campaign.

On the night of September 29, Heywood was a sergeant commanding a machine-gun platoon of the 6th Battalion in support of 169 (London) Infantry Brigade. He was ordered to take 9 Platoon forward and give supporting fire to a company of 2nd/5th Queen's Royal Regiment, which was holding a position on the Castel Vécchio feature near Rimini.

When it was discovered that the track via La Pièta was impassable to carriers, and would take hours to re-open, Heywood went forward under heavy fire to reconnoitre an alternative route. On his return, he led his men on a 'long carry' of 1,200 yards through intense mortar and artillery fire. Halfway to the Castel Vécchio feature, the platoon was pinned down, but he organised a group of two guns in position before returning for the others. He then brought up the rest with the ammunition, still under fire while resisting all attempts to halt them.

The citation for his award paid tribute to his courage and outstanding leadership in providing supporting fire to a hard-pressed company at a very critical moment. Six weeks later, he was commissioned in the field.

One of eleven children, George Heywood was born at Warrington, Lancashire, on January 5 1916 and educated at the Oakwood Avenue School. When he was 14 he was given a second-hand cornet to play in the Cheshire Lines Brass Band and started work at Wyman's foundry at Warrington, where he met his wife.

Enlisting in the Cheshire Regiment in 1940 he joined 2nd Battalion. Although wounded in the North African campaign, he recovered in time for the invasion of Italy. After transferring to the 6th Battalion, he took part in the Salerno landing, the battles of the Anzio beachhead and the fierce fighting on the Gothic Line.

When he came out of the Army in 1946, Heywood returned to Wyman's foundry where he became assistant manager. After moving to John Hall & Sons, he became managing director and then president of North West Iron Founders. He settled in a Yorkshire village where, aged 65, he learned to cook; he also enjoyed golf, listening to brass bands and going to the opera. George Heywood married, in 1940, Elsie Haddock, who predeceased him; he was survived by their son.

SERGEANT 'SMOKY' SMITH, VC

Sergeant 'Smoky' Smith (who died in Vancouver on August 3 2005, aged 91) was the last surviving Canadian holder of the Victoria Cross.

On the night of October 21 1944, two companies of the Seaforth Highlanders of Canada crossed the Savio River in Italy, and seized a shallow bridgehead in drenching rain. In less than 5 hours, the river rose six feet to become a raging torrent, impassable to supporting tanks and anti-tank guns.

Early next morning, the thinly held right flank of the Seaforths was attacked by three Panther tanks, supported by two self-propelled guns and thirty grenadiers of the formidable 26th Panzer Division. As the tanks ground forward, sweeping the Canadian positions with fire, Private Smith was ordered to go out and 'bag' a few Germans. He led his team, with their PIAT anti-tank weapon, across an open field to a roadside ditch which offered the close range needed to be certain of a kill.

Almost at once, a tank lumbered down the road firing its machine guns along the line of the ditch and wounding Smith's companion. At a range of only 30ft, Smith rose into the enemy's view and fired his PIAT. The bomb stopped the Panther, putting it out of action. Immediately ten German infantrymen jumped out and charged, firing their Schmeissers and hurling grenades. Reacting instantly, Smith sprang on to the road, shot down four of them with his tommy gun and drove the others back.

A second tank, safely beyond PIAT range, now opened fire, covering the advance of another ten enemy grenadiers who began to close in on the two Canadians. With no thought of abandoning his wounded comrade in the ditch, Smith continued to protect him, fighting off the enemy with his sub-machine gun until they gave up and withdrew.

By this time, the Seaforth company, with only light weapons, had knocked out a second tank, the two self-propelled guns, a half-track and a scout car. But the third tank, keeping well back, continued a constant hail of fire on Smith's position.

Despite this, he helped his wounded comrade to take cover behind a nearby building, obtained medical help, then returned to his position to await a possible further enemy attack. Later he reported back, asking what to do next. The Seaforths captured the third Panther, bogged down in a ditch. For the moment the enemy had had enough. ("Even Germans do not like to be shot at," commented Smith.) Before they were ready to attack again, Canadian tanks and anti-tank guns had crossed the Savio, and the bridgehead was secure. Smith had played a vital part in a battle which was crucial to the Eighth Army's advance into the Lombard Plain.

But when the military police came to pick him up "in Naples or somewhere", he would recall with a grin, they put him in jail so that he would be sober to receive his decoration from King George VI at Buckingham Palace on December 18.

The son of a teamster, Ernest Alvia Smith was born at New Westminster, British Columbia, on May 3 1914. He earned the nickname 'Smoky' as a sprinter at Herbert Spencer Elementary School and at the T. J. Trapp Technical High School, where he played basketball, football and lacrosse. He was employed by a building contractor when he enlisted as an infantryman in March 1940. Five months later he sailed for England, where he spent the next three years training with the Seaforths.

In July 1943 he took part with his regiment in the assault on Sicily. Throughout that campaign and the battles which followed in Italy, he fought as a private soldier, being twice wounded. In March 1945, Smith moved to Holland for the final weeks of the war in Europe, but was sent to Canada on leave the day before the Seaforths fought their first action there.

After demobilisation, he worked for a photographic studio in New Westminster, then re-enlisted in the regular Army as a sergeant. But he was exasperated to find himself given a job selling bar supplies instead of being sent to Korea. "Why didn't they tell me before I rejoined?" he demanded.

Smith and his wife Esther later ran a travel agency. Ever wisecracking, he became a firm favourite with a growing circle of admirers. When, aged 84, he attended the service at the Menin Gate in Flanders to commemorate the end of the First World War, the remaining veterans from that conflict insisted that he parade with them as 'the young 'un'.

Retaining a liking for a cigar, a well-aged Scotch and the attention of ladies all around the world, he was level-headed in his recollections of the Savio River after sixty years. "I don't take prisoners. Period. I'm not prepared to take prisoners. I'm paid to kill them. That's the way it is." Smoky Smith was appointed a member of the Order of Canada in 1995, and had a mountain named after him in British Columbia. He was one of ninety-four Canadians awarded the VC since the first at Balaclava in 1856.

MAJOR GEORGE DREW

Major George Drew (who died on October 20 2005, aged 87) helped prisoners to cope with the boredom and deprivations of Colditz Castle by producing potent home-made alcohol. He and his friend Pat Fergusson first tried to brew from the sugar and raisins in Red Cross parcels but failed. Then they realised that there was sufficient sugar for fermentation in the turnip jam supplied by the Germans. Mixing the jam with yeast and water, they used a piece of purloined drainpipe and a large tin, sealed with plaster of Paris from the sick-bay, to produce 'hooch' for such events as St Valentine's and St Patrick's Days.

However, the effects of more than 100 per cent proof alcohol could be severe, even leading to temporary blindness. Dental fillings would fall out. If a man was having obvious difficulty walking and talking in the castle yard it was said that he was 'jam happy'.

When Drew and Fergusson took part in the Channel 4 television series *Escape from Colditz* in 2000, they made their potion for the first time since 1945. Taking the first glass before the camera, Drew said, "Dear God," remarked that the smell was not quite as bad as it used to be, then drank again. "Oh Christ," he gasped. He found a less lethal diversion in carving some forty statues of nude women, though he admitted that there was one trouble: "The memory was lacking."

The son of a moderator of the Congregationalist Church, George Shepherd Drew was born on March

5 1918 and educated at Wellingborough College and Sandhurst before being commissioned into the Northamptonshire Regiment. Young George became a platoon commander with 2nd Battalion at Ballykinler in Northern Ireland, where his untrained bulldog puppies did not win him universal popularity in the mess.

On the outbreak of war in 1939, the Northamptons formed part of the expeditionary force sent to France. Drew remembered wondering dreamily in the relaxed atmosphere of the phoney war whether to win the VC "straight away and get the others later on in the week, or whether to work up to it slowly". They were stationed at the Belgian border, opposite Menin, and moved to near Arras to prevent Rommel driving towards Calais.

After a skirmish in which several men were lost, Drew led a convoy over a canal in Belgium, where they found none of the defensive shelter they had been promised, and were quickly overrun. They were being marched off into captivity when the artillery barrage they had expected finally arrived.

He was taken first by train to a camp at Laufen, in Bavaria, where a dead donkey helped to make up for the lack of Red Cross food parcels. It was while sitting on the ground in the sun that he picked up a small branch and started to whittle away with a knife; to his astonishment, he found that a tiny, misshapen little man emerged from his efforts.

On being moved to Biberach, where he was inducted into the escaping community by being asked to produce a German bayonet scabbard, Drew was transferred to Warburg. He and Fergusson built a tunnel, through which they duly escaped across the battlefield on which the Marquess of Granby had lost his wig in a charge in 1760, and reached a railway line.

After walking several miles, they turned into a wood, and flopped down to hear footsteps. Drew felt something pulling his trouser leg and, turning over to surrender, found that it was a fox. The pair jumped on several trains, which took them to a nearby mashalling yard, and walked along a deserted autobahn before turning into a field and falling into the hands of a German patrol.

Drew used his solitary confinement in a French camp at Soest to read through Hugo's *Italian in Nine Days* and then *Pinnochio* in the original. He then was transferred to Eichstatt, where he worked on a highly professional tunnel escape by sixty-five prisoners.

He and Fergusson reached the Danube, where they found a punt without a paddle and drifted across to the other side. On landing they were challenged and ran into the arms of a policeman. Such inveterate escapers were now deemed suitable for Colditz, where he looked back with a professional eye on the Eichstatt break-out:

Worthy men! and none were pupils,
men prepared to die or do.
Men in fact just lacking scruples –
men like Fergusson and Drew.

On arrival at the castle, Drew quickly became conscious that there was a hierarchy, and that he represented "a very amateurish lower class tunneller", compared with "a professional upper class escaper going through the main gate at will".

He used his skill to carve not only nudes – "I had not mastered how to show drapery" – but fantasy figures for a chess set. The black pieces included Merlin as the king, Hecate as the queen and members of the distilling team as the different pawns; while, among the white, the walrus and the carpenter were the bishops and the gryphon and mock turtle the rooks.

He made fake German belt buckles, and forged an eagle stamp on to a shoe heel, spending months cutting away with a razor blade before it was inked with an indelible pencil and spit to reproduce the right shade of purple ink for stamping on German official documents. But when Hitler ordered fifty men to be shot after the mass breakout from Stalag Luft III, London forbade any more escapes.

Following liberation Drew rejoined his battalion at Brunswick, and, in October 1945, married Mavis Gibson, with whom he had two daughters. He was next posted to Vienna and then Trieste, where he guarded the commander-in-chief, General Sir John Harding. After attending the staff college at Camberley in 1950 he became deputy assistant adjutant general at the War Office, then was posted to 26th King's African Rifles operating against Mau Mau, and earned two mentions in despatches.

Drew then became an inspector for the Ministry of Defence and devoted himself to his smallholding in Somerset, which he described as paradise. Even when blind he enjoyed driving his quad bike around his fields, accompanied by two lurchers. Drew did not believe in an afterlife; but he said that if there was one, he and Fergusson would talk for eternity and try to come home: "On past form we will not quite make it."

CORPORAL BOB MIDDLETON

Corporal Bob Middleton (who died on November 5 2005, aged 84) spent most of the Second World War in German captivity from which he eventually escaped, and won a Military Medal in Korea before being captured again to spend six months in solitary confinement with the Chinese.

Middleton won his MM with the Gloucestershire Regiment in the final phase of the Battle of the Imjin river in April 1951. 1 Glosters were concentrated on a narrow, rocky hill-feature known as Hill 235, where he was a member of the foremost elements of A Company which had the vital task of holding the north-west approaches to the position.

Earlier his platoon had been pushed back and, armed with a Bren gun, Middleton was one of a small counter-attack force which returned to the hill's forward slope to await further attacks. He recalled flares being put up and seeing the Chinese advancing with the density of a Cup Final crowd leaving Wembley. "But," he said, "we held them."

Those in front were armed. Some behind were not, and had to wait for someone to be shot down so as to take over his weapon. In some cases, Middleton noted, men were carrying ovens and cooking utensils with no weapons at all. Having taken up position, his small force was on the receiving end of the Chinese determination to end all resistance so they could celebrate May Day in Seoul.

For the next 9 hours they were under continuous mortar and machine-gun fire. Ammunition was running low, and Middleton fearlessly exposed himself to heavy fire. Completely disregarding his physical exhaustion after three days of the fiercest fighting, much of it hand to hand, he displayed a splendid will to resist, inspiring others by the example he set at a most critical time during the battle. His devotion to duty, his personal skill in battle and gallant conduct of the highest order earned him the MM.

The Glosters, who continued to fight even after ceasing to be an operational unit, finally tried to break out. But Middleton was among those captured who had to endure a three-week march to the Ching-Song prison camp while stragglers were shot. During their daily indoctrination sessions 'Mid-le-ton', as he was called by the Chinese, caused constant disruption, using the writing material provided to make playing cards.

During the first few weeks of captivity, Koreans were allowed to walk through the camp. One, an attractive woman referred to as 'Queen', was whistled at, but not by Middleton who was nevertheless charged with attempted rape. Taken to their HQ, he was given a platinum pen with which to sign a confession. After pointing out that the nib was broken, he refused. There followed six months of solitary confinement.

At first the Chinese offered cigarettes which were accepted but not smoked, before being taken back when there was no confession. They interrogated Middleton in relays, because he was exhausting them with his silence for up to 12 hours a day. He continued to say nothing. Deprived of light, in cramped conditions which made standing impossible and given watered-down food, he was not allowed to wash, becoming infested with lice and covered in sores. The Chinese even tried asphyxiation by tampering with the ventilation system. It got them nowhere. He remained silent, with his testicles becoming the size of peas.

Finally he was released only when the camp was visited by a Communist sympathiser from the West whom the Chinese wanted to impress. On emerging from his ordeal, Middleton looked like Methuselah, according to one fellow prisoner. His voice had become very high-pitched and he was unable to stand, but still unbroken in spirit. When repatriation finally came, it was no surprise that he was kept until last.

One of a chief petty officer's seven children, Robert Leslie Middleton, was born in Portsmouth on December 5 1920. At 14 he joined a printing firm, then switched to an engineering company. In 1938 he joined the Buffs to be captured in France with the 2nd Battalion in 1940.

He was taken to Stalag XXIB in Poland before moving west as the Russians advanced. The Germans, seeing he was circumcised, assumed he was a Jew and put him to work with pigs, with whom he had to sleep. Thereafter, Middleton said, he held pigs in higher regard than Germans. Eventually he escaped after hiding in a farm building covered in manure, and met US forces with a nasty smell. He came home in April 1945.

He spent a year as a POW camp guard in Italy before re-joining the Buffs in Hong Kong as a corporal. He was discharged in 1950 but returned to service, with the Gloucestershire Regiment, for the Korean War. He later served in Kenya where he was badly wounded by friendly fire, his life being saved by the Air Ambulance Service of Doctor Anne Spoerry of the Kenyan Air Ambulance Service whom he greatly admired.

Middleton was medically discharged in 1956 and became a postman. Subsequently he worked at the Royal Hospital Chelsea as office keeper. He retired in 1980 and became an In Pensioner ten years later. Two days before his death he expressed dismay at the destruction of the regimental system, which he believed had sustained him in Korea.

CAPTAIN BILL HELM

Captain Bill Helm (who died on May 19 2006, aged 87) began his career as a doctor treating Allied and German casualties on the battlefields of northern Europe, as his father had before him. Although both arrived at the front as recently qualified 25-year-olds, young Bill had the advantage in Normandy of being able to draw heavily on his parent's experience; Colonel Cyril Helm, DSO, MC, had served on the

Western Front in 1914, and was serving in the north-west Europe campaign thirty years later.

In his diary Bill recalled his own 'baptism of fire' during the brutal fighting at Caen. His advanced dressing station started to receive fifty wounded every 10 minutes, a daunting challenge for someone who had qualified only months before; and he was soon to see 700 wounded in 36 hours.

"I went on duty soon after the German counter-attack started at dawn," he wrote. "Casualties began to arrive in great numbers, and it looked like we might be swamped. There were large groups waiting to be assessed in reception – some already dead, some dying – some in urgent need of transfusions – a group of terrified disorientated lads, jittering and yelling in a corner… Several SS wounded came in – a tough and dirty bunch – some had been snipers up trees for days. One young Nazi had a broken jaw and was near death but before he fainted he rolled his head over and murmured 'Heil Hitler'."

Helm recorded the acute shortage of blood for transfusions, and the immense ignorance among the troops about how best to handle the wounded, particularly those with broken limbs. It seemed to him that the mass of invaluable knowledge gained by his father's generation in the Great War had not been properly passed on. One particularly sad case was a young officer who had been brought in slung over a tank having lost a foot and with both legs broken. Helm tried to transfuse him, but it was too late: "I remembered my father's advice from the 1914-18 war… that it was better to leave a casualty with severe fractures where he lay, until medical help could reach him rather than move him back unsplinted."

Father and son met when Colonel Helm, who had set up 60 General Hospital about seventeen miles away at Bayeux, came to inspect Bill's unit and make recommendations to improve its operations. Later Bill sped off on his beloved motorcycle to see his father, periodically pausing to take cover in ditches as enemy aircraft swooped overhead: "I arrived in a filthy state, and my father was about to reprimand this dirty slovenly soldier in front of a group of top brass colleagues when he recognised me, and I felt there was perhaps a touch of pride in the introduction of his son from a forward unit."

Both doctors kept wartime diaries. Bill described being with 210 Field Ambulance attached to 177 Brigade. His father wrote, with greater skill, about life as a regimental medical officer with 2nd Battalion King's Own Yorkshire Light Infantry, and then 15 Field Ambulance, charged with collecting casualties from the front at night. The manuscripts have striking similarities, demonstrating an eye for countryside and its destruction by war. The father mentions meeting an English nun at a convent, the son being befriended by a small dog in his dug-out.

Each records desperate attempts to find buildings safe from enemy fire in which to treat the wounded, and the worry that lack of sleep would impair their judgment. Both refer to cases that were to haunt them for years, in which they had to make instant decisions to administer morphine to end the lives of the hopelessly wounded.

William Harding Helm was born on August 30 1918 and educated at Bradfield. He grew up familiar with his father's experiences at Ypres, Inverness Copse and Passchendaele and did his medical training at the Middlesex Hospital before joining the Royal Army Medical Corps.

After serving in Belgium and Holland, he returned briefly to London to see the celebrations of the end of the war in Europe, then was posted for two years to military hospitals in India. For his last six months in the country, where he experienced the thrill of big game hunting in the Biligiriranga Hills while on leave, he was the only specialist in charge of several thousand British troops stationed in Bangalore.

At the time he feared that he would miss out on the promotion ladder as the new National Health Service was being born. Following his return to England, he became a thoracic specialist at the Middlesex, the London Chest and the Brompton hospitals, then went to Lancashire and York; his father settled as a GP in the West Country, where he died in 1972.

As a senior consultant with the Leeds Regional Hospital Board, Bill Helm helped to redevelop chest services across most of North Yorkshire, publishing numerous groundbreaking papers on respiratory and other chest conditions. He was a leading expert in asbestosis, treating many patients who had acquired the condition at the British Rail carriage works in York. He served as president of the Yorkshire Thoracic Society and the York Medical Society. In 1971 he became a Fellow of the Royal Society of Physicians.

Helm was also a prominent figure in the sporting life of North Yorkshire as well as a keen fisherman and racegoer. He was a first-class squash player until his mid-fifties, and was later vice-chairman of York City Football Club. He prided himself on creating one of the finest private grass tennis courts for miles around – it was carved out of the hillside at the family home in the Howardian Hills – and was chairman of the Ryedale branch of the Council for the Preservation of Rural England.

On retiring as a consultant in 1981 he studied at the Open University, and produced an acclaimed paper on tuberculosis in the Brontë family, which appeared in *Brontë Studies* (2002). Bill Helm married, in 1949, Diana Beazley. They had two daughters and two sons, one of whom was Toby Helm, *The Daily Telegraph*'s former chief political correspondent.

CORPORAL 'NUTTY' HAZLE

Corporal 'Nutty' Hazle (who died on June 22 2006, aged 87) was severely wounded in the face when he won a Distinguished Conduct Medal as a stretcher bearer in North Africa in 1942, then returned to the front to win another in even worse fighting in March 1944.

He was serving in Italy with the 1st/4th, Essex Regiment, taking on the German 1st Parachute Division who, its own Army joked, had had to murder their parents to be admitted to the elite unit. The fighting was often hand-to-hand with head-butt and bayonet, and involved attacks on hill features where the Germans were entrenched.

These had to be approached, under intense shelling, in difficult terrain where men easily lost touch and sometimes disappeared down the precipitous slopes. The Germans, too, carried out fierce counter-attacks. But so heavy were the casualties on both sides that they sometimes shared cigarettes during the ceasefires negotiated to allow the wounded to be recovered.

Hazle was sent with one of two companies to reinforce a Gurkha battalion on an isolated position 300 yards from the Benedictine monastery of Monte Cassino, known as Hangman's Hill because of a gibbet-like pylon located nearby. Under machine-gun fire, Hazle received a nick across his throat from a piece of gravel, before the companies reached their objective with a combined strength of forty, plus thirty wounded; the Gurkhas were pinned down, also with heavy casualties, and there was little food or water.

As the only medic present, with only a first aid haversack containing some bandages, a bit of morphia and scissors, Lance Corporal Hazle became, in effect, the regimental medical officer, according to his regiment's history.

Working in cramped conditions under constant mortar fire and artillery bombardment, as the empty canisters from smoke bombs caused further casualties when they fell among them, Hazle fearlessly exposed himself to continual fire over six days, dressing wounds, and carrying out an amputation. Even when struggling with fumes from the smoke bombs he continued.

His citation, written by the commandant of the 1st/9th Gurkha Rifles, declared: "The magnificent service rendered by this NCO under the most grim and dangerous conditions; the medical skill he displayed; and his never faltering devotion, bravery and spirit have earned the universal admiration of the whole of the force which was isolated in this position." Hazle's second DCM made him one of only five men to be so decorated during the Second World War; and one of these was another member of his own regiment.

The son of a painter and decorator, Edmund Bryant Hazle was born on November 26 1918 at Hadleigh, Essex. Young Ted was educated locally and went into the printing industry. He joined the 4th Battalion, Essex Regiment (TA), and was mobilised in 1939. As a member of the battalion band he became a stretcher bearer, serving in West Africa, Cyprus and Palestine before moving to the Western Desert.

Hazle won his first DCM during a period of almost continual action between June and July 1942, when Rommel was still threatening to advance on Egypt. His battalion, along with several Indian units, was heavily involved in the Ruweisat Ridge area, south of El Alamein.

During this time Hazle was said to have shown a devotion to duty of the very highest order, never hesitating to go out to dress the wounds of men in forward areas and then carrying them back to safety under intense shell fire.

On July 23, when an attack by 161 Indian Mounted Brigade failed, Hazle went out three times to bring men back. As he went forward on the fourth occasion, to attend an Indian soldier who lay in full view of a sniper, the right side of Hazle's face was completely smashed, and his shoulder was also hit; but he displayed courage that was "an inspiration to all", according to his citation.

MAJOR BRUCE SHAND

Major Bruce Shand (who died on July 11 2006, aged 89) was a gallant soldier, a wine merchant, a master of foxhounds and a discreet member of the Royal Household; late in life, however, he found himself thrust towards the public limelight as the father of the Duchess of Cornwall.

A bluff, shy man who had a Wodehousian penchant for ending sentences "What? What?" Shand proved adept at sidestepping attempts to question him about his daughter's relationship with the Prince of Wales, and advised friends to keep their mouths shut. But there were periodic rumours that Major Shand was becoming exasperated with the hostile publicity his daughter was receiving, as the royal marriage drew to a close and after Diana Princess of Wales died. Some soldierly blunt words were said to have been offered to the Prince on several occasions before he married Camilla Parker Bowles in 2005, an event at which Shand was discreetly present.

In March the Duchess repaid his stalwart support by carrying out an errand for him when she accompanied the Prince to the battlefield of El Alamein. This was to lay posies and cards at the graves of the two soldiers who were killed by his side in his armoured car. The message declared: "The gallantry and sacrifice of two fellow 12th Lancers on 6th November 1942 will never be forgotten by me. Bruce Shand."

Bruce Middleton Hope Shand was born on January 22 1917, the son of Philip Morton Shand, a wine writer and architect whose family owned a Glasgow calico business. Morton Shand first married the daughter of an accountant in Hammersmith. When this marriage quickly broke up, he went on to wed thrice more, giving the boy two half-sisters, one the future Lady Howe of Idlicote, wife of the Tory politician Lord Howe of Aberavon. Young Bruce was sent to Rugby, which he cordially disliked, and from which he emerged with few talents beyond an enthusiasm for riding.

After being sent to France to learn the language, he passed into Sandhurst with high grades, despite becoming imprudently drunk on the second night of the exams. The sergeant major used to bellow at the cadets: "I have had men through my hands from the bogs of Ireland, the moors of Scotland and the claypits of Staffordshire – but none so idle as you gentlemen." Shand thrived on this, and was commissioned into the 12th Royal Lancers, to become a troop leader with A Squadron.

On the outbreak of the Second World War, the regiment landed in France as part of the British Expeditionary Force. Equipped with armoured cars, it was stationed at Foncquevillers for six months, and moved up to the neutral Belgian frontier three times in response to threatening enemy troop movements before finally entering the country when the

Germans invaded on May 10 1940.

During the next eighteen days Shand led patrols to Hazebrouck and St Omer to gather intelligence of enemy dispositions. By skilful and daring manoeuvre, he covered the withdrawal of a column of new lorries and guns under fire from four German tanks, and was awarded an immediate MC.

On being assigned the crucial task of covering the withdrawal at Dunkirk, Shand and comrades took their share of the heavy casualties while acting as embarkation officers during the bombing. In his despatches, Field Marshal Viscount Gort wrote that without the 12th Lancers only a small part of the BEF would have reached the port, where Shand finally boarded a cement ship for Margate on May 31.

After the regiment reformed at Poole, Dorset, he went to Northern Ireland to help with training the North Irish Horse, then spent Christmas in command of HQ Squadron near Reigate, Surrey. In September 1941 he set off with the regiment's armoured cars and a tea chest of books as part of 7th Armoured Division for Libya.

The following January the Eighth Army had advanced more than 300 miles in three weeks, and was at the extremity of its lines of communication when Rommel went on the counter-offensive. As the Germans advanced in considerable strength on Msus, Libya, the 1st/6th Rajputana Rifles were ordered to destroy the supply dumps there and withdraw.

Temporary Captain Shand was in command of a half squadron of 12th Lancers ordered to watch the threatened flank. The enemy advance was so rapid that the situation of the Rajputanas and about 100 soldiers of the Indian Pioneer Company became extremely precarious. Shand's small force came under heavy fire, but he handled it with great skill and coolness, and succeeded in covering the Rajputanas' withdrawal and in evacuating twenty armoured cars.

Loading the Indian Pioneers into his cars and two lorries, he just managed to slip through the gap to the north before the Germans closed it. The recommendation that he be awarded a Bar to his MC described him as a cavalry leader of the first order.

Shand commanded C Squadron in the three days of fierce fighting at the Battle of Knightsbridge, when the Lancers' task was to move behind the advancing armour, infiltrate the enemy lines and destroy their transport. Before the second Battle of Alamein, he found himself introduced to Winston Churchill, who prodded his medal ribbon with approval, commented on how thin he was, and asked if he were getting enough food and drink, before moving on.

A few days after the Germans started to retreat on November 2, 7th Armoured Division was ordered to move to Kalda, south of Mersa Matruh. Shand's squadron arrived ahead of the rest, encumbered with some 100 prisoners. As darkness fell and a slight mist rose on November 7, he was just able to make out a large body of vehicles approaching along the escarpment. By the time he realised that it was an enemy convoy, he was under fire.

His radio operator, Sergeant Charles Francis, slumped dead to the bottom of the car after being hit by a bullet that passed through Shand's cheek. With his mouth filling with blood, Shand ordered his driver, Corporal Edward Plant, to turn the car around, when it received a second blow, killing Plant. As he climbed out of the burning vehicle, Shand remembered being urged to jump on to another car, then being hit in the knee and falling off. He awakened to a buzz of German voices. After his wounds were dressed, a German officer pointed out Rommel, a figure in a long overcoat who was walking towards a plane.

Shand was driven first to Tobruk and later evacuated in an elegant hospital ship which had once been the Tsar's Black Sea yacht. After a month in hospital in Athens, he was told that he had suffered no permanent damage and was taken by train to Spangenberg Castle, near Kassel, where he joined some 300 British POWs.

On emerging from the sick bay he found that General Eisenhower had absolved officers from the duty of escaping because the Germans were unlikely to respect the rules of war. Shand took on such responsibilities as laundry officer and taking down BBC radio broadcasts. The camp was short of food in the later months of the war, but Shand received monthly parcels of books sent out from a shop in Piccadilly, and was able to devote several hours a day to reading history and biography as well as Thackeray and Trollope, for whom he developed a lifelong affection.

As the Allied forces approached in March 1945,

Shand and his comrades were moved out of the castle and marched for two days. Their guards, however, were elderly and tired easily, and he escaped from the column. He hid in woods for two days and nights, "dodging the hair-trigger adolescents of the Hitler Youth", as he said afterwards, until joining up with the American forces.

After being debriefed in Paris he flew back to England, where, in 1946, he married Rosalind Cubitt, daughter of the 3rd Lord Ashcombe and a descendant of Thomas Cubitt, the builder of Mayfair and Belgravia and Bloomsbury. She was also (as their daughter Camilla was to be reminded by the newspapers) the granddaughter of Alice Keppel, mistress of King Edward VII. Like many young men just out of the Army, Shand took some time to find a suitable job, working first for an educational films company then going into the wine business. With a friend, he first took over Block, Grey and Block in South Audley Street, a firm of old-fashioned merchants which supplied Oxford and Cambridge colleges. The firm eventually ran into difficulties, and he joined Ellis, Son & Vidler, of Hastings and London, with which he remained until his retirement.

In time he had a house in Kensington and another at the Sussex village of Plumpton, close to the racecourse, where he and his wife brought up their son, Mark, and two daughters, Camilla and Annabel. This gave him plenty of opportunity to indulge his passion for hunting.

As joint master of the Southdown Hunt in the early 1970s he was driven to declare that some of the people who went out with the hounds were distinctly unkempt. "Nobody can be expected to have a vast wardrobe by Christian Dior, but if they can afford to buy a horse they can afford to keep it and themselves clean. It's offensive to the farmers, you know. One or two have said to me: 'We welcome the hunt, major, but can't you tell some of those blighters to be less scruffy'."

At the same time Shand served as Vice Lord-Lieutenant of East Sussex and worked his way up the Queen's Bodyguard of the Yeomen of the Guard to become Clerk of the Cheque. It was a career, he joked, that involved dressing as if to fight the battle of Waterloo.

In his later years Bruce Shand devoted much of his energy to nursing his wife; she died of the bone-wasting disease osteoporosis in 1994. He also produced *Previous Engagements*, a slim volume of war memoirs spiced with shafts of humour, and reviewed military books for *Country Life*.

BRIGADIER 'BUZZ' BURROWS

Brigadier 'Buzz' Burrows (who died on July 22 2006, aged 75) was regarded as the best commander in the New Zealand SAS with an uncanny ability to think like a terrorist when tracking elusive enemy in the depths of the Malayan jungle.

As troop commander of the Royal New Zealand 1st Rangers, which was on loan to be the newly formed SAS regiment's 4th Squadron in 1957, he learned late on October 17 of two terrorists in a camp six miles away. Despite a foot injury, he formed a patrol and set off with only 2 hours of daylight remaining to struggle through the dense undergrowth and over a ridge 4,000 ft high. At first light, after a journey of 10 hours, much of it on hands and knees while tied to comrades with parachute rigging, they reached their objective. Although he and his men were utterly exhausted, Burrows mounted an immediate attack and killed one of the terrorists. He was awarded an MC.

On August 19 the following year Burrows commanded a patrol operating in the Angsi Forest Reserve when they contacted a group of terrorists, killing one and wounding a second who died. With complete disregard of his own personal safety he charged forward and personally killed DCM Li Hak Chi, the most able terrorist in the region, leading to the elimination of the enemy in the Tampin/Pedas area.

Burrows's endurance, courage and determination throughout the operations were an inspiration to the remainder of the platoon and, in recognition of his services, the Regent of Negeri Sembilan conferred on him the Negeri Simbilan Conspicuous Gallantry Medal. On returning to New Zealand he was an instructor at the School of Infantry before being appointed aide-de-camp to the Governor-General, Lord Cobham, then serving for two years as adjutant with the Nelson Marlborough West Coast Regiment.

On being posted to the Indonesian/Malaysian border in 1965 Burrows commanded a company of the newly reorganised 1st Battalion Royal New

Zealand Infantry Regiment, which built and garrisoned one of four bases forming the main line of defence preventing Indonesian incursions across the Malaysian border with Borneo. He also commanded penetrations into Indonesia to disrupt enemy formations and movements, and later played a key part on the Malaysian Peninsula as New Zealand, Australian and Gurkha forces apprehended Indonesian forces infiltrating from the sea. Burrows was therefore instrumental in cementing the doctrines and operational knowledge of the reformed NZ infantry.

Ian Hamilton Burrows was born on November 11 1930 at Christchurch, New Zealand, the son of Brigadier 'Gentleman Jim' Burrows, a distinguished sportsman with a DSO and Bar. He was said to have been nicknamed 'Buzz' because of his short, fuzzy hair at Waitaki Boys' High School at Oamaru. On going to the Royal Military College, Duntroon, he captained the first XI, played in the first XV and boxed before being commissioned into the Royal New Zealand Infantry.

Command of 3rd Task Force Region was followed by appointments as Commander Land Forces in Auckland and Commander NZ Forces South East Asia. On retiring from the regular Army in 1985, he became Colonel Commandant of the New Zealand SAS for ten years as well as chairman of the Rothmans Sports Foundation in 1987 and president of the Outward Bound Trust (New Zealand) in 1991.

Burrows, who was appointed OBE in 1991, was interested in art from his schooldays, and had a house at Auckland, stacked with portraits he had completed. 'Buzz' Burrows married, in 1959, Judy Jenkinson who survived him with their two sons and two daughters.

LIEUTENANT COLONEL GEORGE STYLES, GC

Lieutenant Colonel George Styles (who died on August 1 2006, aged 78) was awarded the George Cross in 1971 for leading ordnance disposal teams during the terrorist campaign in Northern Ireland and for personally dealing with extremely hazardous devices.

As the senior ammunition technical officer, Styles, a major in the Royal Army Ordnance Corps, was responsible for the supervision of Explosive Ordnance Disposal (EOD) teams dealing with the increasing number of explosive devices used in the terrorist campaign.

In September 1971 the first of what became known as IEDs (Improvised Explosive Devices) was discovered at Castlerobin, Co Antrim. In the course of trying to dismantle it, one of Styles's close colleagues was killed. What the IEDs lacked in power they made up for in ingenuity, and it became clear that their main purpose was to kill EOD members who tried to disarm them. When, eventually, one of these devices was recovered intact, the radiograph showed micro-switches at the top and bottom of the box so that if it was lifted, tilted or the lid opened, the bomb would explode.

Styles gave the order for an identical model to be built with a light bulb substituted for the detonator. He took this device home and worked on it in his kitchen until the bulb lit up. "I would have been dead," he said later. But something that a science teacher had said during a lesson years before came back to him and, after a long night, he believed that he had found a way to deal with the IEDs – at least in theory.

On October 20 1971 Styles was called to deal with a device placed in a public telephone booth at the bar of the Europa Hotel, a twelve-storey building in the centre of Belfast. Having made sure that the military and the police had cordoned off and evacuated the area Styles, assisted by two RAOC officers, took charge of the operation of disarming and removing the bomb.

The radiograph showed that it contained more than 10lb of explosive, and Styles realised that until the electrical circuit had been dealt with, the slightest false move might detonate it. He decided to disarm the bomb in stages, each one requiring meticulous planning and execution before he proceeded to the next.

At last he was able to fix a line around the device and gingerly pull it a distance of some 18ft before drawing it a further 30ft out of the hotel and on to the pavement. The whole operation took 7 hours and was completed successfully.

Styles refused to divulge details of his theory, proved under these testing conditions, but he recalled later how he had felt: "You couldn't avoid the feeling of menace each time you walked towards that telephone box. Inside it was enough energy to blow your head from your shoulders, your arms and legs from your trunk, and your trunk straight through the plate glass windows of the Europa."

He was sure that he knew the identity of the bomb-maker and was just as certain that the man would not take this defeat lying down but try again. Two days later Styles was called back to deal with a bomb containing a charge of almost 40lb of explosive.

After analysing the radiograph, Styles realised that the device had the same circuitry as the earlier IEDs, but this time a jumble of complex wiring and micro-switches had been added to try to confuse the EOD team. Inscribed in small letters on it was "Tee-Hee, Hee-Hee, Ho-Ho, Ha-Ha". Styles's men worked for 9 intense hours until the bomb was disarmed and removed, to the sound of *Some Enchanted Evening* wafting from the hotel's Muzak system.

"Throughout each operation," his citation concluded, "Major Styles displayed a calm resolution in control and a degree of technical skill and personal bravery in circumstances of great danger far beyond the call of duty." Styles was invested with the George Cross by the Queen at Buckingham Palace on March 28 1972.

The son of a bricklayer, Stephen George Styles was born on March 16 1928 at Crawley, Sussex, and educated at Collyer's Grammar School, Horsham. He was called up for National Service in 1946 and after officer cadet training was commissioned into the RAOC (now the Royal Logistics Corps) and posted to the Army's central ammunition depot at Kineton, near Banbury.

In 1949 Styles obtained a regular commission, and was seconded to the King's Own Yorkshire Light Infantry to gain infantry experience. He served with the 1st Battalion in the Malayan Emergency of 1949–51, and was mentioned in despatches. Back home Styles studied for a degree in Engineering at the Royal Military College of Science before being posted back to Malaya to take command of the 28th Commonwealth Brigade Ordnance Field Park Regiment, based at Taiping. A posting to Germany with 1st British Corps followed before Styles moved to Northern Ireland in 1969 as deputy assistant director of ordnance services.

In the year after the operations at the Europa Hotel, teams under Styles's command dismantled more than 1,000 explosive devices in Northern Ireland and destroyed as many more by controlled detonation. Valuable technical information was obtained over this period that would help to save the lives of operators confronted with these devices in the future.

On leaving Northern Ireland in 1972 Styles was promoted lieutenant colonel and appointed chief ammunition technical officer (EOD), responsible for the RAOC bomb disposal teams throughout the world. When he attended a dinner for bomb disposal men back in the safety of the Ordnance Corps' training centre at Camberley, a pudding named Improvised Explosive Delight was on the menu.

After retiring from the Army in 1974 he served on the boards of several companies advising on anti-terrorist measures in an often abrupt manner. For many years Styles campaigned energetically for a change in the design of commercial detonators in order to preclude their use in IEDs.

His expertise in explosives was called upon in other fields. When construction at Dungeness nuclear power station was completed, the cost of dismantling the giant 1,100-ton crane was judged to be prohibitively expensive, and it was decided to demolish it. Because of the proximity to the power station, it was essential that the ground shock of the demolition be kept to a minimum.

Styles recommended collapsing the structure into an area of shingle to absorb the shock and detonating a series of charges to break the rigid joints of the crane while it was still falling. So light was the impact that a cup which had been placed on one of the legs of the crane remained undamaged.

In 1975 he wrote *Bombs Have No Pity*, the publication of which was delayed for several months at the request of the judge in a Birmingham bomb trial. Three years later Styles attracted more publicity when he complained, after taking part in the television documentary *Death on the Rock* about the shooting of three IRA men by the SAS, that it lacked balance.

In retirement, Styles enjoyed rifle and game shooting and cataloguing his repairing of his rifles from the Zulu and Boer wars. George Styles married, in 1952, Mary Woolgar with whom he had a son and two daughters.

LIEUTENANT COLONEL JOHN PINE-COFFIN

Lieutenant Colonel John Pine-Coffin (who died on August 22, 2006, aged 85) had a distinguished and adventurous career in the King's African Rifles and the Parachute Regiment. John Trenchard Pine-Coffin was born in Kashmir on June 12 1921 and educated at Wellington, where he was known as 'Wooden Box'. After Sandhurst, he was commissioned into the Devonshire Regiment and then served with the King's African Rifles (KAR) in East Africa.

His African-born sergeant was not best pleased when Pine-Coffin advised him not to wear medals that had been awarded to him by the Germans, but he quickly won the respect of his men without them. Pine-Coffin subsequently accompanied the KAR to Burma, where stealth was often the key to survival.

One night, while lying low in an attempt to conceal their presence from the Japanese, Pine-Coffin impressed on his African troops the need for complete silence. They had, however, acquired a taste for tea and one of them, in his search, perhaps, for a superior brew, had placed the billycan on a fire piled high with full ammunition boxes.

On another occasion, when a strong Japanese patrol was preparing to attack his unit, his soldiers threw down their arms and disappeared into the darkness. Pine-Coffin and his brother officers had resigned themselves to their fate when the men reappeared from the jungle with rather sheepish faces saying: "We like you too much to see you killed." They collected their weapons, regrouped and helped to beat off the enemy assault.

After the Japanese surrender, Pine-Coffin went to Pakistan to look for his father, who had been a prisoner of the Japanese since the fall of Singapore. He scoured the hospitals treating soldiers from POW camps but was unsuccessful. Eventually his father was repatriated to England.

Pine-Coffin then joined the Parachute Regiment and was posted to the Middle East where he saw action during the Suez crisis. Following a move to Cyprus, he was involved in counter-insurgency operations in the Troodos Mountains.

When he came across heavily bearded men hiding in a monastery, Pine-Coffin suspected that they were EOKA terrorists in disguise and asked his sergeant to give their beards a sharp tug. These all stayed firmly in place and he had to make a swift tactical withdrawal.

During his twenty-eight years with the Parachute Regiment, Pine-Coffin served with all three battalions and in 1961 took command of 1st Battalion. His parachuting career was brought to a premature end when he landed in the dark on a tractor and broke several bones in his feet.

A series of staff appointments followed. In 1963 he was in Nassau when he was ordered to investigate a party of Cuban exiles that had infiltrated Andros Island, part of the Bahamas. His seaplane landed in thick mud and Pine-Coffin decided that his only chance of reaching dry land was to strip off.

On coming ashore, plastered in mud and wearing only a red beret and a pair of flippers, he was confronted by a party of armed Cubans. Mustering as much authority as he could in the circumstances, he informed the group that they were trespassing on British sovereign territory and were surrounded.

The following morning, when the Royal Marines arrived to rescue him they were astonished to find him and his radio operator in a clearing standing guard over the Cubans and a pile of surrendered weapons. He was appointed OBE.

Pine-Coffin attended the Joint Services staff college and the Imperial Defence College before retiring from the Army in 1969. He built up a large farming enterprise in Devon and established a three-star country hotel. He was involved in many local charitable enterprises, including the British Red Cross and the RNLI. In 1974 he was appointed High Sheriff of Devon. John Pine-Coffin married, in 1952, Susan Bennett, who survived him with their son and two daughters.

LIEUTENANT COLONEL DAVID GARFORTH-BLES

Lieutenant Colonel David Garforth-Bles (who died on September 27 2006, aged 96) was the central figure in an episode which must rank highly even in the bizarre chronicles of military field sports.

A young officer in the Guides Cavalry, Garforth-Bles was attending a course at the Army Equitation School in Sagar, Central India, in 1937 when he went pig-sticking with a colleague, Denis Voelker. As he wrote shortly afterwards to his parents: "A sounder [herd] of pig broke between us and the heat on the right.

"There were three rideable boars amongst them and Denis and I were on the largest. Everyone else was chasing the other two and we were quite by ourselves. Denis had a very fast horse and was about ten yards in front of me and just going to spear the pig. Suddenly the pig and Denis and his horse vanished completely."

Garforth-Bles at first assumed that his friend and his quarry had descended into a deep nullah (gully), but he could find no evidence of one. He turned his pony round, and came across a well, which was overgrown with long grass.

"I had a nasty moment wondering what I should find at the bottom," he continued in his letter home, "as most of the wells here are very deep indeed, and some are dry at the bottom. Luckily this was a very wide well and the water was very deep and only about twenty-five feet down from the top, and there were large flat stones sticking out to form steps down to the water."

When he peered down into the gloom Garforth-Bles made out Voelker hanging on to the bottom step; his horse was plunging about in the water, while the pig was swimming round and round, occasionally rushing at the horse and at Voelker and trying to get on to the step.

Garforth-Bles descended into the well to find that his friend had broken his left arm and had a six-inch cut down to the bone of his elbow. He helped the injured man up the steps, then got hold of the horse's bridle, trying to keep the animal's head above water:

"It was rather difficult, as he was terrified of the pig, which kept swimming at him and trying to bite him. Then the horse would rear up in the water, beating with his fore legs, and turn over backwards and sink. I thought that he was certain to be drowned.

"By this time several village people had come up and one of them held the horse's bridle, while I speared the pig several times until it sank. We then got a rope with a stone on the end and lowered it down one side of the horse and brought it up on the other side underneath its belly. I had to dive under the horse to get hold of the rope. We could now keep it from sinking, and there was nothing to do until the others came up. They had killed the two other pigs and arrived at last, seeing the village people round the well."

While Voelker was taken to hospital, Garforth-Bles asked the nearby veterinary hospital to provide one of the slings used for supporting lame horses; when this arrived he returned to the water, and fitted it to his friend's distressed horse.

"It was quite tricky work, as I had to dive underneath it several times and it plunged about a bit. However, in the end, the village people, directed by Griffiths, a Sapper officer on the course, got a strong beam across the top of the well, and hauled the horse out. It came out remarkably easily and was not much scratched, though very exhausted and cold, but recovered in the sun and walked home."

Garforth-Bles added: "General Wardrop, the ultimate authority on pig-sticking, says that it has never been known for pig, horse and rider to fall down a well. Far from spoiling their drinking water, the villagers were delighted. They fished out the pig and ate it!"

George David Garforth-Bles was born on October 5 1909 at Knutsford, Cheshire. He was the grandson of Sir William Garforth, the inventor of the coal-cutter, a safety lamp and breathing apparatus for miners. Garforth-Bles was educated at Rugby, where he played for the first XV and the hockey XI and was Master of the Rugby Rat Hounds (ferrets).

After going up to Jesus College, Cambridge, to read Military Studies and German, he served with the Guides Cavalry (10th Queen Victoria's Own Frontier Force) on the North West Frontier Force from 1931 to 1939; in the latter year, he played in the regimental polo team which won the last Indian Cavalry Polo Tournament.

During the Second World War Garforth-Bles commanded the 4th Battalion 3rd Madras Regiment in fierce fighting against the Japanese in Burma. He was mentioned in dispatches.

In 1948 he retired from the Army and emigrated

to Canada, where he was secretary at the Eglinton Hunt Club in Toronto. On his return to England, he ran a small family business. In retirement, at Farnham, Surrey, he enjoyed fishing and gardening. He was co-author of *Now or Never* (1946), an account of his regiment's experiences in the Burma Campaign.

David Garforth-Bles married first (dissolved), in 1939, Susan Muir-Mackenzie. He married secondly, in 1948, Ann Deshon. She predeceased him, and he was survived by a son and a daughter from his first marriage and by three sons from his second.

COLONEL KEN HARVEY

Colonel Ken Harvey (who died on December 3 2006, aged 80) won a DSO for his part in a daring raid on a German corps headquarters behind enemy lines in Italy. In the spring of 1945 Operation Tombola was launched to harass German troops in their withdrawal. One of the targets was the enemy's 51st Corps HQ which was based at two villas near Albinea, south of Reggio nell'Emilia, and protected by Spandau machine-gun posts sited at strategic points.

The raid by SAS commandos, Italian partisans and escaped Russian prisoners was launched to the sound of *Highland Laddie*, played by a piper in a slit trench. Harvey, a lieutenant attached to 3 Squadron, 2nd SAS, commanded by Major Roy Farran, was ordered to attack the Villa Calvi. After approaching unseen in the moonlight on March 26, Harvey led ten British parachutists against the villa. First, he killed two German sentries on the lawn; then his men burst into the villa after blowing in the front door with a bazooka bomb.

Four more Germans were killed on the ground floor, but others fought back gallantly, sweeping the grounds with machine-gun fire and rolling grenades down the spiral staircase. Confronted in the darkness by a German with a Schmeisser sub-machine gun, Harvey ducked but failed to extinguish his torch. Fortunately a sergeant reacted quickly and fired over his shoulder.

The ground floor was taken. But when Harvey realised that he could not take the staircase in the 20 minutes allowed, he lit a big fire in the operations room with the aid of petrol and explosives. The wounded were evacuated, and the Germans on the first floor were pinned down by bazooka and machine-gun fire until the villa was well ablaze.

The whole area was now in a state of high alarm, with Harvey and his men coming under intense fire as they withdrew. He guided his party, which included two wounded men, through heavy concentrations of enemy troops back to the safety of the mountains.

It was discovered afterwards that the 51st Corps chief of staff was among the enemy casualties and a German general was killed in a raid on the second villa. The citation for Harvey's DSO stated that he had inflicted grievous damage on the German Army from Bologna to Massa on the coast.

The son of a shopkeeper, Kenneth Gordon Harvey was born on December 7 1924 at Bulawayo, Southern Rhodesia, and educated at Milton Junior and Senior schools, where he was acknowledged to be bright but not academic. On leaving, he spent nine months with the Rhodesian Railways, then enlisted as soon as he could. In 1943 he joined the King's Royal Rifle Corps as a private, and served in Egypt and Palestine. He was commissioned into the Seaforth Highlanders and, after a chance meeting with Farran, volunteered to join the SAS.

During Operation Tombola, he escorted seven American airmen who had been shot down during a raid on Bologna, through the German lines to link up with the Allied forces, and then returned to his unit in enemy-occupied territory. He was troubled by the suffering of the SAS wounded who could not be given proper treatment and were often transported on ladders. So he raided a German hospital, and commandeered a Mercedes ambulance and an Opel staff car complete with its driver. He subsequently sold the car in Florence on the black market, and spent the proceeds on a three-day party after his return to England.

After the war ended, Harvey was demobilised and returned to Africa, going to Witwatersrand University, Johannesburg, to read Architecture. His time with the Seaforths had given him a great affection for the bagpipes and Highland dances; as an undergraduate he enrolled in the Transvaal Scottish.

Harvey returned to Bulawayo in 1951 as a partner in an architectural practice, but never completely settled into civilian life. Joining 2nd Battalion Royal Rhodesia Regiment, he saw active service in Nyasaland (now Malawi) in 1959, when he helped to suppress riots against the colony being linked to Northern and Southern Rhodesia to form the Central African Federation. He commanded Operation Wetdawn, a sweep of villages known to harbour African nationalists. This nipped a possible rebellion in the bud, and Harvey was appointed MBE (military) for "loyal and meritorious service". Subsequently he served as honorary colonel of the Rhodesian SAS.

A modest, friendly man, Harvey continued working as an architect after Rhodesia gained its independence as Zimbabwe in 1980 and designed many office buildings in Harare and Bulawayo. He was deputy chairman of the Central Africa Power Corporation for many years. As chairman of the Zimbabwe Legion, he worked hard to help ex-servicemen, particularly those whose savings were destroyed by hyperinflation. In his spare time he was a keen philatelist.

Despite the onset of cancer, he was most reluctant to leave the country, but was eventually persuaded to move to a retirement home in Cape Town, where he struck up a friendship with another resident, Ian Smith, the former Rhodesian prime minister. Ken Harvey married, in 1951, Luna Klopper, who predeceased him; he was survived by their three daughters.

COLONEL JOHN COLDWELL-HORSFALL

Colonel John Coldwell-Horsfall (who died on December 18 2006, aged 91) won a Military Cross in France in 1940, and a Bar to his MC in Tunisia in

1943, when serving with the Royal Irish Fusiliers; while commanding a battalion of the London Irish Rifles the following year, he won a DSO at Monte Cassino.

In May 1940, during the retreat to Dunkirk, Coldwell-Horsfall was commanding his regiment's D Company, which was defending key bridges over the Dender river at Ninove, west of Brussels. The Germans enjoyed great superiority in air power and field artillery and Coldwell-Horsfall's 'warriors' – as he liked to call his men – were for much of the time under heavy fire. When German machine-gun detachments infiltrated his battalion's flank, Coldwell-Horsfall, revolver in hand, led a counter-attack that drove them off with heavy casualties.

Having held the bridges until the forward elements of the British Expeditionary Force had withdrawn across them, he had to extricate his own company and fall back to new positions on the La Bassée canal at Gorre. A believer in aggressive forward defence, he impressed on his men the importance of killing the enemy at the earliest opportunity. His positions on the south side of the canal had great success throughout the ensuing battle, enabling the remnants of the BEF to pass through.

After holding out until the last possible moment, Coldwell-Horsfall burned a number of canal barges that might have been used by the enemy, and withdrew five miles to a position guarding bridges over the Lys river, where he fought yet another holding action. By now the BEF was surrounded, and after fighting their way down the corridor to Dunkirk Coldwell-Horsfall and his battalion were evacuated. For his conduct at the three defence lines during which, in the words of the citation, "he displayed conspicuous coolness and exemplary cheerfulness," Coldwell-Horsfall was awarded his first MC.

By February 1943 Coldwell-Horsfall's regiment was fighting in Tunisia as part of the 38th (Irish) Brigade, with the 78th 'Battleaxe' division of First Army. Near Bou Arada on the night of February 28/ March 1 he led a patrol consisting of his D Company, less one platoon, to harass enemy supply lines. Despite suffering casualties from an enemy machine-gun post, his men took a position close to an enemy-occupied farm and succeeded in ambushing a lorry full of Germans.

Skilfully withdrawing, his patrol captured two men from an enemy fighting patrol which had been sent out to deal with them. On the afternoon of March 2, Coldwell-Horsfall took out a second patrol which he led over mountainous terrain five miles beyond the British front lines. As darkness fell he carried out a thorough recce of the area, bringing back much valuable information. For these two actions he was awarded a Bar to his MC.

Further heavy fighting followed before Axis forces in Tunisia surrendered, and in an attack on the mountainous feature of Kef el Tior, Coldwell-Horsfall was wounded by a grenade. After three months out of the line he rejoined the Irish Brigade in Italy as second-in-command of 2nd Battalion, the London Irish Rifles. The brigade was assembled on the line of the Rapido river at Cassino. The Germans were still holding the monastery, which overlooked the whole battlefield, and it had been decided that the Irish Brigade should try to break through the enemy's Gustav Line up the Liri valley.

The 6th Inniskillings began the assault; 2nd London Irish were to follow up and push through, but the commanding officer was killed on the start line. Coldwell-Horsfall took over command in time to command its attack on the village of Sinagoga on the Gustav Line itself. Supported by divisional artillery and a dozen tanks of the 16th/5th Lancers, his men speedily seized their objectives; but it was only after a four-hour battle, in which the battalion captured many prisoners and knocked out a number of German self-propelled guns, that the position was secured.

By then H Company – which had seized the village – had lost 100 men and was only twelve men strong. When its officer Desmond Woods apologised for losing so many Horsfall replied, "Never mind. You're here, which is what I told you to do – well done!" Coldwell-Horsfall was awarded a DSO for commanding his battalion with great skill, and setting a magnificent example of personal bravery and leadership.

John Henry Coldwell-Horsfall was born in Putney on February 21 1915, and educated at Harrow. A keen shot, he went on to Sandhurst and, in 1935, was commissioned into 1st Battalion, Royal Irish Fusiliers, known as the 'Faughs' from their battle cry "Faugh-a-Ballagh" ("Clear the Way").

In 1936 he went with his regiment to Palestine to help quell the Arab revolt. From 1937 to 1939 they were in Guernsey and Jersey where he devoted his energies to bringing the men up to marksman standard. After a period of intensive training in Scotland – the Faughs took part in Operation Torch, the Allied invasion of North Africa, and the subsequent advance to Tunis.

To help keep his men fit on the ship going out to North Africa Coldwell-Horsfall, a keen upholder of tradition, organised Irish dancing on the upper decks to tunes provided by the regimental pipers. Under fire, one of his platoon commanders recalled, Coldwell-Horsfall would walk about "as unconcerned as if on a stroll in the park". A tall man of aristocratic bearing, he generally wore a peaked cap, only donning a steel helmet when leading an attack.

After the fall of Cassino, he remained in command of the London Irish until the 78th Division was withdrawn to Egypt, when he was appointed to command 1st Royal Irish Fusiliers in the fierce fighting for the Gothic Line before being wounded in both legs during an attack on Casa Tamagnin.

In 1946 he returned to England with his wife Mary, a third officer WRNS whom he had married in Alexandria, to take over the running of the family firm, Webster & Horsfall of Hay Mills, Birmingham. The firm, a manufacturer of Atlantic cable, mining ropes and industrial wire, was in severe difficulties at a time of rising post-war demand.

Coldwell-Horsfall immediately embarked on a programme of modernisation, scrapping old plant, reducing overmanning whilst maintaining good relations with the trades unions, and taking no salary for a year until the firm was back in profit.

He became honorary colonel of the 5th Royal Irish Fusiliers (TA) and later the North Irish Militia, was High Sheriff of the West Midlands in 1976 and a member of the ancient archery society, the Woodmen of Arden. From 1954 much of his life was occupied with running the Dalchosnie estate in Perthshire, which he bought for the shooting and stalking.

Coldwell-Horsfall wrote *Say Not the Struggle* (1977) about Dunkirk, *The Wild Geese are Flighting* (1976) about Tunisia, and *Fling our Banner to the Wind* (1978) about Italy. He also wrote *The Ironmasters of Penns* (1971) a history of Webster & Horsfall. John Coldwell-Horsfall married in 1945, Mary Charlotte Poole, who survived him together with their daughter. Their son was killed while training in Scotland with the Royal Irish Rangers in 1973.

SPECIAL CONSTABLE TERRY PECK

Special Constable Terry Peck (who died on December 30 2006, aged 68) played a dashing role in the Falklands War when he first spied on the enemy in Port Stanley, then escaped to become a scout for the 3rd Battalion Parachute Regiment with which he fought at the Battle of Mount Longdon.

A rumbustious member of the legislative council as well as a former head of the police force, he puzzled locals after the Argentines arrived on April 2 1982 by walking round Stanley with a length of drainpipe. This concealed a Russian camera with a telephoto lens he used to take pictures of enemy anti-aircraft missile sites. They were brought to Army intelligence in London by returning contract workers.

When told that he was about to be arrested, Peck made a hasty exit on a motorcycle. His first stop was a farm where a party was being held for the Queen's birthday. When an enemy unit surrounded the house and conducted a hasty search, Peck locked himself in a lavatory. Next day he convinced a helicopter crew that he was a travelling plumber, but realised that he would be safer in open country.

For more than a week Peck camped out with two naval sleeping bags. But after lighting his first fire to cook a stew, and accidentally knocking it over, he headed for another farm. He was so caked in mud that he was ordered to have a bath, into which the owner tossed a rubber duck; from then on he had the code name 'Rubber Duck'.

Given a haircut and a forged identity card with the name Jerry Packer, he made regular reconnaissance trips. On entering an empty farm kitchen to make a cup of tea he picked up the phone and heard two English voices cryptically discussing his whereabouts. When he then heard a conversation on a short-wave radio mentioning that "a lot of friends have arrived at San Carlos," he knew where to go.

3 Para's intelligence officers grilled him for three days. Although, at 43, he was twice as old as many of their men, they then gave him a rifle and combat gear, and asked him to join a sixty-strong patrol going ahead of the main force to establish the enemy's whereabouts. His first major contribution was to help overcome the severe lack of military transport by ringing a farmer on their route to say: "Rubber Duck here. Can you get as many drivers and vehicles

as possible to meet us?"

Aided by a wagon train of tractors and Land Rovers, the Paras slowly advanced on Mount Longdon, overlooking Stanley. For ten days Peck was sent out at night to identify enemy numbers and select tactical positions. He once opened fire on a Para patrol, though without causing any injury, but was still pugnacious enough to argue with the corporal leading his patrol when a soldier stood on a mine and alerted the Argentines.

Instead of the opposition they had expected, the Paras found themselves confronting a barrage of fire from a battalion, and Peck's cool vanished. "This is supposed to be quiet," he thought. "Why is everyone screaming and shouting?" Clutching his rifle, he scrambled desperately upwards, trying to find cover as bullets spattered the grass. When a man fell near him, he helped to carry him down to a crater which already contained eight wounded men, before scrambling up to find that his patrol leader had been wounded. As dawn broke the men were in a hollow on the other side of the mountain, still being shelled and subsisting on toffees and food abandoned by the Argentines.

Remaining at the summit for a further 24 hours, Peck was stunned by the carnage and the smell. But he had made his mark with 3 Para as "a man of calibre" and, before the year ended, he was decorated with the MBE at Buckingham Palace.

The descendant of mid-19th century emigrants from Norfolk and Ireland, Terence John Peck was born on August 2 1938 and went to school in Stanley, where he boxed and joined the Boys' Brigade. On leaving he joined the Falkland Islands Defence Force and found a job building a freezing plant at Ajax Bay.

After joining the police force, he had a first encounter with Argentine ambitions in 1966 when right-wing hijackers forced a plane to land outside Stanley with the intention of claiming the Malvinas. Assuming that it was in difficulty, Sergeant Peck arrived to help, only to find himself lured on to the plane with the hostage passengers. He eventually escaped in the cloak of an Anglican priest, who was acting as a go-between, before the Argentines surrendered.

Following training at Bramshill Police College in Hampshire, he showed his mettle as head of the islands' eight-man force, making a 10-hour drive to rescue a family whose house had been burned down at Christmas. Ignoring orders, he dived to help rescue the bodies of a doctor and a pilot whose plane had crashed into Mare Harbour. But, even in the Falklands, old-time police methods, where youths received a clip round the ear and drunks were taken home in the back of a Land Rover to be ticked off the next day, were increasingly frowned upon.

Although awarded the Colonial Police Medal in 1975, Peck retired as chief constable when he was accused of beating up a troublesome prisoner in the cells; the resulting inquiry was unable to reach a verdict. A couple of years later he was elected a member of the Legislative Council (Legco); the day before the Argentines arrived he was sworn in as a special constable.

Once the war was over, he soon resumed his role as the islands' enfant terrible. He had sharp words for

Paras who broke into a house, lambasted the British government for its tardiness in providing aid and even criticised Mrs Thatcher for allowing Argentines to visit the graves of their war dead.

Depressed about the future, he resigned from Legco to start a new life in Scotland in 1984. But he was soon back in Stanley, where he failed to win back his seat in an election, but subsequently succeeded. He was the first local chairman of the South Atlantic Medal Association, and ran the local YMCA. In his last years, he suffered from post-traumatic stress. Terry Peck, who was married twice, had two sons, two daughters and two stepdaughters. He was buried with the maroon beret he had been given as an honorary member of the Parachute Regiment on his chest.

COMMANDER PENNY PHILLIPS

Commander Penny Phillips (who died on February 10 2007, aged 91) wrote a vivid diary of her experiences as an ambulance driver during the Fall of France. Then Penelope Otto, she was one of the intrepid British girls with the Mechanised Transport Corps, attached to the French Sixth Army, which arrived with five ambulances to run a surgical field unit near Crouy-sur-Ourcq just before the Germans struck at dawn on June 5 1940.

Her troubles began with the order to retreat. First her ambulance's self-starter jammed so that she became lost trying to follow the others; her chef de médicin complained furiously about "*cette mademoiselle formidable et si stupide.*"

After catching up with the other vehicles she had a puncture, then found that the spare tyre was flat and there was no pump. When they arrived at their destination, the convoy found a steady stream of wounded coming in, but the oxygen masks did not work. The unit spent the night putting the wounded on to hospital trains before being sent off ten kilometres to await orders that never came.

Then it was announced that the bridges over the Marne were to be blown up. She recorded: "Wagons, mules, horses – great straining beasts – three abreast, drunk men on horseback, little children, old women driving their cows, the pathetic household bundles of refugees carried on carts drawn by tractors, fowls in crates slung between the wheels, canaries in cages on prams, panting Alsatian dogs drawing small carts with babies and bundles inside. The noise comes in waves – the roar of camions, tractors and the shouts of men – then silence, and we lie in a field of buttercups while the cuckoo's cry comes gaily out of the emptiness." After finding a French airman playing the organ alone in a village church, she dined with her unit in a farmyard, where she enjoyed brushing Nigger, her unit commander's Labrador.

On the following day Penny Otto drove into the back of another ambulance; then the convoy ran into a Panzer division, which provided it with armed guards who politely attempted to practise their English. As a nearby railway line exploded, her ensign, the South African journalist Marjorie Juta, sauntered through the dark with her arms folded to say: "Girls, this is the moment when I insist that you should wear your helmets."

But when the Germans began to panic, having heard the rumour of a French advance, Penny Otto and Marjorie Juta gave their escort the slip by turning around at a crossroads. They passed back down the German column, without any attempt being made to stop them, even though Penny Otto had to lean out of her cab because the bonnet had swung up to block her view. A contingent of eight French soldiers on bicycles whom they finally met was dubious about their story at first.

When the two drivers finally boarded a cramped and smelly troopship at Arcachon some ten days later, Penny Otto had found hair in her food at five meals in a row, and was exasperated at being made to remain aboard while King Zog of the Albanians disembarked in England first. "A brigand gets away with it," she commented caustically.

A solicitor's daughter, Penelope Ellison Otto was born in Edinburgh on June 5 1915 and grew up an intrepid horsewoman. She went to Allenswood School, Wimbledon, before becoming a hotel management trainee at Ascot and then at the Savoy.

Penny Otto and Marjorie Juta arrived back from France amid much publicity, and were awarded the Croix de Guerre. The South African Prime Minister, General Smuts, suggested the raising of further ambulance units, though the Blitz frequently interfered with their training; a talk by the South African ambassador to a parade in Chester Square was drowned out by anti-aircraft fire. After being first sent to Kenya, Penny Otto arrived in Egypt to join the spirited girls of Motor Ambulance Convoy 502, who would proudly declaim:

We know all the answers, we know all the Gen;
We know when to say "No"; We know when to say "When!"
We like spades to be spades, and our men to be Men.
We're fearfully 5-0-2.

Penny Otto was the overseer of everything connected with the company, ranging from the transfer of the wounded between trains and ships to the running of its popular mess bar, the Rotor Club, and was presented with a black poodle called Pandora as a mascot. She was in hospital with meningitis in 1943 when she received the MBE.

On her return she was appointed group commander, a post in which she was able to cite the unit's accident-free record to obtain it some Austin ambulances. But the fact that the unit had carried more than 89,000 patients and had covered more than a million miles in the desert counted for little on arriving in Italy, and it had to rebuild its reputation afresh. By March 1946, when she flew home with Pandora, Penny Otto was one of the last three original members in 502.

Three years later she married Lieutenant Colonel 'Jumbo' Phillips, a patron of the Rotor Club (he had earlier married one of her comrades, who had since died). They settled in Somerset, where he farmed and was Master of the Taunton Vale Foxhounds.

With a young son and daughter, Penny Phillips

turned down Anthony Eden's suggestion that she become an MP. But in 1955 she agreed to stand for Somerset County Council as a temporary member while a predecessor recovered from illness. In the event she retained her seat for more than thirty years. She supported comprehensive education and took a close interest in social services, but also understood both the hunting and conservation lobbies.

Although popular, her enthusiasm for discipline within Tory ranks when she was leader led some, after they had received a dressing-down, to call her 'the Ayatollah'. Following her appointment as CBE in 1986, Penny Phillips announced that she would retire in three years time because leg trouble meant that she could no longer manage the canvassing.

MAJOR GENERAL ROGER ROWLEY

Major General Roger Rowley (who died on February 14 2007, aged 92) was awarded an immediate DSO for his role in liberating Boulogne during September 1944, and an immediate Bar five weeks later for the capture of Breskens on the Scheldt estuary.

As commanding officer of Canada's Stormont, Dundas and Glengarry Highlanders, he was charged with taking the port, whose 9,500-strong garrison had been ordered by Hitler to hold out "to the last man". Approaching from the east by armoured vehicles, and then on foot to thread through a minefield, Rowley's men advanced so rapidly that they captured the strongly-held chateau of La Causerie, opening the way for two columns of armoured bulldozers, engineer assault vehicles, flame-thrower tanks and flails to seize bridges over the Laine river.

A hair-raising night followed as aggressive tank-hunting teams, seeking Rowley's supporting armour in the town, were fought to a standstill by the Glens without the loss of a tank. Early next morning as Rowley and one company faced the high walls of the citadel, a civilian who could have stepped out of a romance by Alexandre Dumas, offered to show them a secret tunnel.

Churchill tanks were raking the ramparts with machine-gun fire, and engineers blowing in the portcullis, as a Glengarry platoon emerged at the heart of the besieged fort to deliver the *coup de grâce* to the defenders' morale. A host of white flags appeared on the walls and about 200 prisoners were taken.

The Glens next captured thirty fez-wearing Senegalese in a suburb, and swarmed up another hill with bayonets and grenades to take 180 more prisoners. The energetic Rowley arrived with two officers the next morning, when the three of them swung a captured 88mm gun round to fire on a larger hill; they knocked out an 88 still in enemy hands with their third shot, though the return fire drove them to seek cover.

Following the surrender of the German general, who had previously been a scapegoat imprisoned for the failure of Stalingrad and therefore disinclined to follow the Führer's orders to the letter, two Glens arrived at the dock entrance to find a battered pre-war sign reading: "All vehicles for embarkation to

Folkestone report here."

Rowley's citation praised his speed and daring after the heavy bombing of the chateau outside the town, as well as his action under heavy artillery and machine-gun fire as the battalion attacked the citadel: "This officer's leadership, dash, bravery and unlimited energy were an inspiration to his officers and men, and his action was one of the principal factors in the capture of Boulogne."

On October 22 Rowley was ordered to take the port of Breskens, on the Scheldt estuary, which was surrounded by barbed wire, mines and a 20ft anti-tank ditch filled with water 12ft deep. But shortly before the operation was to begin, a squadron of specialised armour refuelling in the field was blown up by an explosion under an ammunition truck, leaving the only survivors deaf or blind. Within an hour of hearing about the tragedy Rowley learned that bad weather prevented his promised bomber support and the operation had been postponed for 24 hours. He settled down to dinner with his brother John, who was commanding the North Shore regiment of New Brunswick.

Less than 2 hours later a signal, said to have been ordered by Winston Churchill, insisted there could be no delay. Within 12 hours Rowley devised a new plan. While the attention of the enemy was concentrated on one company of Glens advancing up the main road to the port, another was racing in single file along the sea wall.

It was so exposed (Rowley claimed afterwards) that the Germans never thought anyone could be stupid enough to approach that way. By noon they held the harbour, and 12 hours later they had opened a route for tanks, leaving the enemy cut off from any hope of aid.

Rowley's citation, signed by Montgomery, declared that, despite the shortage of time, "Lieutenant Colonel Rowley planned and ordered the new attack with such brilliance and led it with such determination that the garrison was quickly overcome and Breskens was captured."

The son of a match company president who died young, Roger Rowley was born on June 12 1914 in Ottawa, where he played football for Ashbury College. His aunt was married to Sir Francis Macnaghten, 8th Bt, who took young Roger and his elder brother John under his wing, teaching them to shoot, cast a fly and be young gentlemen. He introduced them to his London tailor, shirtmaker, hatter and bootmaker, which resulted in the Rowley brothers becoming two of Ottawa's most eligible bachelors. After graduating from Dalhousie University in Halifax, Roger Rowley became a bond trader and was commissioned as a militia officer in the Cameron Highlanders of Ottawa in 1933.

As the north-west Europe campaign opened, he became one of the three commanding officers whom Major General John Rockingham said he played like musical instruments for various tasks. One was quiet and steady. Rowley was the opposite: flashy, flamboyant, always in a hurry and a bit careless about what he left behind him. The third was a cross between them.

After the German surrender Rowley was sent to command an infantry training battalion in the Pacific. When it was no longer needed, because of the Japanese surrender, he attended the staff college at Camberley before joining the Canadian Army Staff in Washington. Appointments at National Defence Headquarters in Ottawa followed. While visiting Fort Bragg, North Carolina, as director of military training, he was asked by a sergeant for his middle initial. On being told that there was none, he was recorded as Roger NMI Rowley (short for No Middle Initial).

He commanded the 2nd Canadian Infantry Brigade Group in Germany, then spent a year at the Imperial Defence College in London before becoming commandant at the staff college at Kingston. He was general officer-in-waiting at the Sovereign's Parade during the Royal visit to Canada in 1967.

Roger Rowley, who was survived by his wife Barbara and a son and a daughter from an earlier marriage, devoted much of his retirement to work for the Order of St Lazarus of Jerusalem. A frequent visitor to London, where he had his suits made and was a member of the Cavalry and Guards Club, he skied until the age of 85 and remained a keen fisherman. He was particularly proud of having a fly for murky water named after him: Roger's Fancy.

MAJOR SIR TASKER WATKINS, VC

Major Sir Tasker Watkins, the former Deputy Chief Justice of England (who died on September 9 2007, aged 88) was awarded a Victoria Cross for his conduct in commanding a company of 1st/5th Company of the Welch Regiment on August 16 1944, when he attacked a German machine-gun post single-handedly while leading a bayonet charge.

The battalion had been ordered to attack objectives near the railway at Bafour, about five miles west of Falaise, as part of the move to trap the Fifth and Seventh German Armies in the Falaise 'pocket'. Watkins's company had to cross open cornfields with booby traps, coming under heavy machine-gun fire from posts in the corn, as well as being targeted by an 88mm gun.

When heavy casualties slowed the advance of the Welch, Lieutenant Watkins found himself the only officer left, and put himself at the head of his men. Although subjected to short-range German fire, he charged two enemy posts in turn, killing or wounding the occupants with his Sten gun. On reaching his objective he found an anti-tank gun manned by a German soldier. At that vital moment his Sten gun jammed, so he threw it into the German's face and shot him with his pistol before the man had a chance to recover. Immediately after this the company, now down to thirty, was counter-attacked by fifty Germans. Once again Watkins led a bayonet charge that resulted in the destruction and dispersal of the enemy.

The battalion had now been given orders to withdraw, but this could not be passed on to Watkins's company as its radio had been destroyed. He and his men found themselves alone and surrounded by enemy in fading light. He tried to lead them back to the battalion by moving round the flanks of the enemy position through the corn. But while going through the cornfield, he was challenged by an enemy post at close range. Ordering his men to scatter, he charged the post with a Bren gun and silenced it. Then the remnants of the company reached battalion headquarters.

Watkins's citation recorded that "his superb gallantry and total disregard for his own safety during an extremely difficult period were responsible for saving the lives of his men and had a decisive influence on the course of the battle". It resulted in the capture of 50,000 German prisoners and 10,000 enemy killed.

He was promoted to major in the field. After recovering in hospital from a leg wound he went home on leave, taking a bus from Cardiff to his home village, near Mountain Ash, Glamorgan. He arrived unnoticed. Interviewed subsequently, all he would say about the action was that the men with him were Welsh, and "I am proud of that".

Tasker Watkins was born at Nelson, Glamorgan, on November 18 1918 and educated at Pontypridd Grammar School. After the outbreak of war he served in the ranks from October 1939 until May 1941, when he was granted an emergency commission as a second lieutenant, Welch Regiment.

In 1943 he attended the Advanced Handling and Fieldcraft School at Llanberis, Caernarfonshire, then worked as an instructor in the rifle wing of the school. He was posted to 103 Reinforcement Group in Normandy and joined the Welch Regiment in July 1944. Watkins received his VC from the King at Buckingham Palace on March 8 1945, then worked as an instructor at 164 Officer Cadet Training Unit.

Demobbed in 1946, he read for the Bar and was called by Middle Temple in 1948 to start practising common law on the Wales and Chester Circuit. After taking Silk in 1965 he moved to chambers at No 1 Crown Office Row in the Temple, where he first spent the night on a camp bed.

An economical and persuasive advocate, Watkins was deputy counsel to the Attorney-General, Sir Elwyn Jones, at the Aberfan disaster inquiry in 1966. In his closing address he observed with force and accuracy that the subject of tip stability had received less consideration than any other aspect of coal mining. He also prosecuted in several cases involving Welsh extremists, including that of the Free Wales Army trial in 1969, which followed the discovery of a plot to attack Caernarfon Castle and assassinate Prince Charles.

As chairman of the Welsh branch of the Mental Review Tribunal from 1960 until 1971, Watkins headed the inquiry into the ill-treatment of mentally ill patients at Farleigh Hospital in Somerset. His report told a grim story of self-satisfaction and set attitudes at all levels of the staff, and recommended a code of conduct for nurses.

Watkins was deputy chairman of Radnor Quarter Sessions from 1962 to 1971, then Recorder of Merthyr Tydfil in 1970-71, when he was also Leader of the Wales and Chester Circuit. Appointed a judge of the High Court in the Family Division in 1971, he released a fraudster from prison after hearing of the man's gallantry in diving into a fast-flowing river to save a 4-year-old girl. He transferred to the Queen's Bench Division in 1974, and was Presiding

Judge on the Wales and Chester Circuit before being promoted to the Court of Appeal in 1980. Two years later he headed a working party which proposed changes to cut the costs of criminal trials.

Watkins was viewed rather as a safe pair of hands with sound judgment than as a great intellectual or law-maker. During his time as a recorder and his early years on the bench, he spoke quietly and rarely appeared ruffled or bad-tempered. In common with many judges, though, he grew less patient as the years wore on.

He tended to say what he thought. In 1984 he described Britain's first woman coroner, Dr Mary McHugh, as a "mistress of discourtesy" and a "very stubborn lady" when she appeared to delay the inquest into the death in Moscow of a British banker. In the same year he declared the film *Scum*, a vivid portrayal of the violence and savagery of life in a borstal, to be "gratuitously offensive and revolting" and strongly criticised the decision allowing it to be shown.

Watkins was appointed Deputy Chief Justice in 1988 and asked High Court judges to fill in time sheets to show how they spent their working days, in an attempt to boost the case for more judicial manpower. In 1991 he sat alongside Lord Lane in the historic appeal case that established that husbands living with their wives can be convicted of raping them.

Two years later Watkins ordered a posthumous conditional pardon for Derek Bentley, who had been hanged in 1953 for allegedly encouraging the shooting of a policeman with the words "Let him have it, Chris" during an attempted burglary.

Watkins retired from the bench, aged 75, in 1993, the year he was voted president of the Welsh Rugby Union after the first contest for the office in the Union's history. Later in the year he chaired the sub-committee which ended up sacking the Union's secretary, Denis Evans, for 'maladministration'.

He was also a member of the TA Association, Glamorgan and Wales; president of the British Legion of Wales from 1947 to 1968; a Deputy Lieutenant for Glamorgan from 1956; and president of Glamorgan Wanderers Rugby Football Club – for which he had played as a young man in its 2nd XV. He was knighted in 1971, sworn of the Privy Council on his appointment to the Court of Appeal in 1980 and appointed GBE in 1990.

In 2001, as Armistice Day approached once more, Watkins was invited to reflect on the award of his VC. "You must believe me when I say it was just another day in the life of a soldier," he insisted. "I did what needed doing to help colleagues and friends, just as others looked out for me during the fighting that summer… I didn't wake up the next day a better or braver person, just different. I'd seen more killing and death in 24 hours – indeed been part of that terrible process – than is right for anybody. From that point onwards I have tried to take a more caring view of my fellow human beings, and that, of course, always includes your opponent, whether it be in war, sport or just life generally." Tasker Watkins married, in 1941, Eirwen Evans, who survived him with their daughter; a son predeceased him.

CAPTAIN KENNETH LOCKWOOD

Captain Kenneth Lockwood (who died on October 8 2007, aged 95) was one of the first six British Army officers to arrive at Colditz Castle in 1940, and remained there to play a key role in many of the escape attempts made during the next four years and five months. Later, as secretary of the Colditz Association for fifty years, he was charged with representing the prisoners' views as the legend mushroomed and became distorted by modern publicity.

A neat, tidy man, Lockwood had a careful way of speaking that could confuse and even demoralise German guards, as when he explained that one escaper had shrunk himself like Alice in *Alice in Wonderland*. Known as 'The Ear', he was the invaluable right-hand man to Major Pat Reid, chairman of the escape committee. He first demonstrated his gift for running things as accounts manager of the prisoners' shop. This seemingly innocent task meant that he had the care of 80,000 unsmokeable German cigarettes which he was able to sell to a guard for 700 Reichsmarks, thereby providing a float for escaping operations.

Whenever escapers needed help Lockwood was on hand, slipping one a 50-Reichsmark note, finding a pair of rubber-soled shoes for another to climb down a wall, or hiding incriminating evidence from constantly snooping guards. When a manhole leading down to the drains was discovered in the shop floor, he arranged for the ever-present German sergeant to be distracted while he swiftly removed the shop's key to take an imprint in some soap; this was then used to fashion a replica that enabled prisoners to enter the shop at night to work on a tunnel.

As twelve prisoners made their break through it, their leader Pat Reid arrived at one end, followed immediately by Lockwood, to find that guards had been posted at both ends. "So we came out and just roared with laughter, and that defeated the Germans completely," Lockwood recalled. "They couldn't understand it at all."

He pretended to be ill in the sick bay so that those working on another tunnel could hide under his bed before continuing with their digging; and he acted as a stagehand for the prisoners' show *Ballet Nonsense* while helping Airey Neave, the future Tory MP, to make his 'home run' back to England.

As news of Lockwood's role in the camp reached London a stream of parcels from supposedly innocent English friends were sent to him by the escape organisation MI9. One consisted of handkerchiefs containing sugared almonds, which revealed instructions for a detailed code when dropped in water; others included money and maps.

Since these were often discovered by the authorities, Lockwood used a skill he had learned at prep school to make maps from jelly. This involved pressing the tracing of a map of Germany, made with an indelible pencil, on to a melted Chivers yellow jelly. When the paper was drawn off the solidified pudding, there was the map. "The system was good for about thirty copies, working rather like a printing press," Lockwood remembered. "And the jelly was never wasted at the end of it. We ate it."

The son of a London stock exchange jobber, Kenneth Lockwood was born on December 17 1911, and went to Whitgift, where he was taught French and German by a master who used to recount his escape as a student from Berlin on the outbreak of the First World War. Lockwood worked for his father's firm, starting as an office boy before becoming a 'blue button' clerk on the floor and a dealer.

In 1933 he joined 22nd London Regiment (Queen's Royal West Surreys), a territorial unit known as the 'Bermondsey Boozers', along with other young men from the exchange. After mobilisation in August 1939 he did training at Yeovil then was sent abroad to Le Mans, where he took the chance to drive a lorry around the famous racing circuit.

To get the men fit the regiment was then marched in full kit to the Belgian border, where Lockwood made himself unpopular with older officers by criticising an order to dig trenches; he pointed out that these had not stopped the German invasion of Poland. Two weeks after the Germans attacked France in May 1940 he was captured during the retreat to Dunkirk.

Lockwood was first sent to Laufen Castle, near the Austrian frontier, where the guards assured the prisoners that the Geneva Convention on the treatment of prisoners did not apply within its walls. He was one of six men who, with the aid of two nails and a stone, spent three weeks digging a tunnel that came out in a wooden shed outside the camp. Dressed as a woman, Reid climbed out first with two others.

The following night three more, including

Lockwood, also disguised as a woman, made their way through the tunnel – he found that the biscuits with which he had filled his bra crumbled as he scrambled through.

But as neophyte escapers, they wore only the crudest civilian clothes and carried no papers. They split into two groups. Reid's was captured first. Lockwood's took a train, which turned out to be going in the wrong direction, so they had to double back, and were arrested on the road to Switzerland where they were mistaken for burglars.

All six men were threatened with execution for stealing bicycles that were the property of the Reich, for possessing a compass and cutting up a German Army blanket. But after a week in solitary confinement they were despatched to Colditz, the sinister medieval fortress on the Mulde river in eastern Germany.

As they were marched into the courtyard the six wondered uneasily if they were about to be shot. But when some Polish prisoners suddenly appeared in their quarters with bottles of beer and accounts of exploring the castle's 700 rooms, the 'Laufen Six', as they were called, cheered up. By early the next year they realised that they were in a camp for bad boys – those who had tried to escape from elsewhere – and started to make new plans.

In April 1945 Reid had made a successful break, but Lockwood was still at Colditz when an American relief force finally arrived – and was deterred from shelling the castle only by signs hung out by the prisoners. Although his incarceration was hardly comfortable, Lockwood realised how much harder the war had been for some others when he was with an American patrol which entered a nearby concentration camp.

The Hungarian Jewish inmates had manufactured ceramics until they were shot by the SS. When four of the Jews who had survived by hiding under the bodies were found, the American doctor in charge told Lockwood to give each man a sip of water only, lest too much killed them. He also ordered a captured German to fetch more water. The German refused – so the doctor called him out into the street and shot him.

With such memories, Lockwood settled back into his father's firm on the stock exchange before moving to run an office on Jersey for almost ten years. But he realised how much he had appreciated the prison-camp camaraderie at the launch party for Reid's bestselling book, *The Colditz Story* (1952); this was to lead to the successful film of the same name, in which John Mills played Reid and Lockwood was portrayed by Richard Wattis.

The former prisoners decided to form an association for regular meetings, and Lockwood, who had no wife, agreed to become the painstaking secretary responsible for organising reunions and keeping contact with members at home and abroad.

By the 1980s, what had been only one of a large number of wartime servicemen's organisations had turned – thanks to an aura of schoolboy bravado nurtured by the flood of books, films, television dramas and documentaries – into an unrivalled symbol of the wartime generation's spirited, frustrated, yet upright youth.

While uneasily accepting his steady evolution into 'Mr Colditz' in the public mind, Lockwood retained his dogged common sense. At first he denied that his members would ever agree to revisit the castle, but eventually admitted that he would like to go back to see what escaping opportunities they had missed when it became clear that others were similarly tempted. If he sometimes changed his mind he was keenly aware of the dangers of distortion by reporters, desperate for new angles on a familiar story.

He found himself rebutting suggestions that the association would be glad to contribute to the restoration of the castle as a hotel, or that the German guards had really been the prisoners' friends, whatever grudging respect had occasionally been shown by both sides.

He was particularly exasperated by an ITV drama, *From Colditz with Love* (2005), which showed the prisoners too well dressed, too well fed and being made to beg for their lives on their knees before a German firing squad. Lockwood was appointed MBE in 1990.

The importance of his role was shown in the Channel 4 documentary series *Escape from Colditz* (2000), in which survivors returned to the fortress for the cameras. He retraced his first steps through the gate into the castle's courtyard, inspected the spot in the lawn where he and Reid had emerged from their tunnel to meet waiting Germans, and demonstrated how he had made maps from jelly.

At the launch of a full-sized model of the glider which the prisoners had been building in the eaves of the castle when the Americans arrived – long considered an apocryphal story – Lockwood was among those who watched it fly at an airfield in Hampshire.

In his last years Kenneth Lockwood was unable to hear those who spoke to him face to face, but he kept in touch with his dwindling membership through a special telephone which he used in bed at his Gloucestershire cottage. By the time the association was wound up in 2006 he concluded that enough had been written about Colditz.

MAJOR GENERAL HARRY GRIMSHAW

Major General Harry Grimshaw (who died on November 1 2007, aged 96) won a DSO in Burma and saw repeated front-line service, which ranged from the North-West Frontier of India in 1932 to the EOKA operation in Cyprus in 1956.

Grimshaw accompanied 161 Indian Infantry (Mechanised) Brigade (161B), part of 5th Indian Division, to Burma in 1943 and fought in the first successful operations against the Japanese in the Arakan. Hurriedly withdrawn from the front line, the brigade was flown to Dimapur on the northern front to hold the Japanese at Kohima.

During the siege, Grimshaw took command of 1st Battalion 1st Punjab Regiment (1/1PR) which played a notable part in the fighting and the pursuit of the Japanese 33rd Division in monsoon weather through the wild country to the Chindwin river. Awarded a DSO and promoted in the field by

General Sir William Slim, he returned to 161B for the final advance to Rangoon. At 33 he was one of the youngest brigade commanders.

Ewing Henry Wrigley Grimshaw (always known as Harry) was born on June 30 1911 in India, where his father was serving with 1PR, and educated at Brighton College and Sandhurst. He was commissioned into his father's regiment in 1931, and saw service in the tribal territories of the North-West Frontier and later against terrorists in Bengal. He loved this period of his service which indulged his passion for fishing and big-game shooting in the Himalayas.

In 1939 Grimshaw rejoined 1/1PR as adjutant and moved with the battalion to Iraq and then Libya. Following the withdrawal to Gazala in 1941, his battalion transferred to 161B and, after the final battle of Alamein, he went to Burma with the brigade.

Following the Japanese surrender, he accompanied it to Java where trouble had broken out at Surabaya, but returned to India in 1946 before going home to Ireland the following year after almost nine years' continuous service overseas. When India gained independence, Grimshaw transferred to Royal Inniskilling Fusiliers which went to Malaya at the beginning of the campaign against the terrorists.

In 1952 he commanded 1st Battalion in the Canal Zone before taking them to Kenya to help put down the Mau Mau insurrection. Two years later a large terrorist gang entered the Fort Hall area when Grimshaw ordered his men to engage and pursue them. Through his skilful control of the operation and the tenacity of his men, the terrorists were virtually exterminated.

A fortnight later, when a district officer was ambushed and killed near Battalion HQ, he and three soldiers rushed to the scene to find a police inspector surrounded by insurgents and fire coming from the Home Guard post which they had captured. Armed only with a revolver, Grimshaw led a spirited four-man charge up the hill whereupon the terrorists, some twenty in number and well-armed, took to their heels. He was appointed OBE.

His next posting was Northern Ireland as chief of staff, but his tour was interrupted by the Suez crisis in 1956. At four-days' notice he took command of 19 Infantry Brigade, part of 3 Division, bringing it to battle-readiness. Eventually he was the last British soldier to leave Port Said after handing over to the UN force commander and being awarded a CBE for his part in the operation.

In 1958 he took his brigade to Cyprus, where it was deployed in the hunt for the terrorist General Grivas. His final staff appointment was as deputy director of movements at the War Office. In 1962 he became GOC 44 Division (TA) and Home Counties District, then appointed Deputy Chief Constable of Dover Castle and appointed CB. He was Colonel of Royal Inniskilling Fusiliers from 1966 until the Irish regiments amalgamated two years later when he became Deputy Colonel of the Royal Irish Rangers.

Harry Grimshaw married, in 1943, Hilda Allison, who died in 1993. He was survived by a son and a daughter; his elder son, Colonel Ewing Grimshaw, died in 1996.

MAJOR GENERAL LORD MICHAEL FITZALAN HOWARD

Major General Lord Michael Fitzalan Howard (who died on November 2 2007, aged 91) earned an MC in north-west Europe during the Second World War; later he became Marshal of the Diplomatic Corps, responsible for easing the tensions and uncertainties in ambassadors and high commissioners as he escorted them in the State landau to present their credentials to the Queen at Buckingham Palace.

Tall, dignified and supremely elegant in cocked hat with white plumes, he had an easy, suggestively ducal manner that led many who saw them together to believe that he, not his elder brother Miles, was the 17th Duke of Norfolk. The brothers were only fifteen months apart in age, and maintained a friendly rivalry throughout their military careers. Both won their MCs in 1944, and they climbed up the promotion ladder to become colonels in 1958 and brigadiers in 1961 until Miles attained the rank of major general in 1968, three months ahead of his younger sibling.

Michael Fitzalan Howard was born on October 22 1916, one of four boys and four girls, all of whom were given Christian names beginning with M by their parents, the 3rd Lord Howard of Glossop and the 11th Baroness Beaumont. The children grew up in an atmosphere of piety and frugal economy at Carlton Towers, their mother's ancestral seat in North Yorkshire, which is said never to have been bought or sold since the Conquest. If guests came to lunch the children were not allowed to use napkins, but were told to leave them by their plates to save on the laundry bill. On rainy days Miles and Michael would run round the table in the nursery, pretending to be the Flying Scotsman and shunting their sister Marigold, a goods train, into a corner that represented a siding.

The two boys went to Ampleforth before Miles went up to Christ Church, Oxford, and Michael to Trinity College, Cambridge. Miles was commissioned into the Grenadiers, and Michael into the Scots Guards. After the declaration of war they knelt before their mother as she made the sign of the cross on their foreheads; she retained vivid memories of other brothers departing for the First World War and not returning.

In August 1944 both men were tank officers at Caumont, aiding the breakout from Caen in Normandy. Miles was brigade major of 5th Armoured Brigade and Michael a squadron leader with the 3rd Scots, while their younger brother, Martin, was a tank commander with the 2nd Grenadiers.

As Miles's brigade became embroiled in a four-day duel with tough SS troops holding an isolated position at La Marvindière, Michael and Martin were (unknown to each other) engaged a few miles to the south in the same battle. An attack on the hamlet of Estry met with unexpectedly fierce resistance from troops under orders to fight to the last man, and Michael was ordered to make the final assault of the day on the crossroads. Maintaining his squadron in the closest formation to secure the objective, he provided firm support for the Highland Light Infantry and the remnants of a Gordons unit, until finally ordered to withdraw under intense mortar fire at 3 am. Martin then took the lead in an attack on Viessoix, just past Estry, in which his hands and face were badly burned when his tank was hit.

Five miles away, on the same day, Michael was ordered to support a Welsh Guards attack on an observation post, which involved using deep ravines that made the going all the harder under heavy fire as they moved up to capture a vital ridge near Chenedolle. In both his Estry attack and in this action, the citation for his MC declared, "Major Fitzalan Howard's cool leadership and undefeatable determination contributed more than any other single factor to the obtaining of those objectives".

Shortly afterwards, Michael became brigade major of 32nd Brigade, alongside Miles in the Guards Armoured Division, for the advance on Brussels. With Miles on the left and Michael on the right, Major General Sir Allan Adair gave them the objective of capturing Brussels, seventy miles away, declaring that the city's railway bridge was to be the winning-post in the fraternal race. Michael won.

Later Michael broke through to Eindhoven, where Miles took over from him. Michael's men then paused for rest and refuelling, and his game book recorded some partridge shooting in the rain before the division pushed on to the Elbe. Looking back on a campaign that covered 1,500 miles and cost 956 killed and 545 missing, Adair wrote: "Special mention must be made of the two brigade majors – the Fitzalan Howard brothers."

After the war Michael Fitzalan Howard was best man at Miles's wedding in 1949. He was brigade major with the 1st Guards Brigade in Palestine, instructed at the Haifa and Camberley staff colleges and was second-in-command of the 1st Battalion Scots Guards, in the Suez Canal Zone. He received command of 2nd Battalion, then became chief of staff, London District, and later commander, 4 Guards Brigade.

In 1964 he was the first commander of the Allied Mobile Force in Europe, then Chief of Staff Southern Command, and, finally, GOC London District, and major general commanding the Household Division. He was colonel of Lancashire Regiment from 1966 to 1970, then of Queen's Lancashire Regiment until 1978.

In retirement he became Marshal of the Diplomatic Corps in 1982 and, after the assassination of Earl Mountbatten in 1979, Gold Stick in Waiting and Colonel of the Life Guards for the next twenty years. He was also chairman of the Territorial Army and Volunteer Reserve Council. In the mid-1980s he was involved in the Royal Commonwealth Ex-Services League as the driving force behind Prince Philip's appeal which raised almost £3 million for those who had fallen on hard times.

He was appointed MVO in 1953, CBE in 1962, CB in 1968, KCVO in 1971 and GCVO in 1981. On his brother's succession to the dukedom of Norfolk in 1975 he was granted the title and precedence of a duke's son. In 1999 he became an extra equerry to the Queen. Michael Fitzalan Howard was a devout Catholic with an unassuming manner and a deep love of the countryside.

He married, in 1946, Jean Hamilton-Dalrymple, daughter of Sir Hew Hamilton-Dalrymple, 10th

Bt; but she died a year later, shortly after the birth of their daughter. In 1950 he married Margaret Meade-Newman, daughter of Captain W. P. Meade-Newman; they had four sons (three of whom were called Tom, Dick and Harry) and a daughter. After Margaret's death in 1995 he married Victoria Baring, widow of Sir Mark Baring.

MAJOR SIR PETER LAURENCE

Major Sir Peter Laurence (who died on November 26 2007, aged 84) was serving as a diplomat in Berlin in 1968 when his nephew spotted a two-page picture story in a children's comic recounting how he won the MC in Italy during the Second World War.

The boy, who was home from Marlborough, told his parents – who then informed Laurence of this unusual piece of publicity in *The Victor*. In the first frame Lieutenant Laurence of the 11th Battalion, King's Royal Rifle Corps, was shown wondering whether the enemy was occupying an isolated house, known as 'The Apostle', near Ponte in December 1943. Then, in broad daylight, he and a Corporal Angus crept up close, to find themselves under fire from a hole in the wall. "You spray the windows while I pop a visiting card through the hole," Laurence was shown saying, before he threw in a grenade and Angus fired his tommy gun up at the first floor window.

Simultaneously the remainder of his platoon opened up on the other side of the house with two

Bren guns, also putting down two-inch mortar fire which enabled the two men to withdraw. "It was indeed one of those rare occasions in war when everything went according to plan," commented the caption below the final frame.

Having developed such a sure technique Laurence went on to use it again. Charged with raiding a house near Vasetti on the night of April 18/19 1944, he manoeuvred his patrol to within ten yards without attracting the attention of the sentries, then fired a PIAT (projector infantry anti-tank weapon) before going forward alone. Finding the ground floor entrance barred, he climbed up to enter by an upper floor window. As he prised open a trap door, enemy machine guns opened up from three directions at close quarters, sending two bursts straight through the room.

Laurence called out for the PIAT to be handed up to him so that he could engage one of the German positions. When this proved impossible, he carefully recorded the exact positions of the enemy, and returned to his patrol. Two nights later he raided another house, shooting two sentries, then hit the building with three PIAT bombs. Withdrawing his men about 100 yards, he went forward again from a new direction, even though Very lights were illuminating the ground, to fire his last PIAT bomb and direct his Brens on to the enemy before bringing out invaluable information about the enemy defences. During these operations, his citation declared, "This officer has shown outstanding qualities of leadership."

Laurence's last taste of action was when his

regiment was sent to Greece, where a void left by the Germans' withdrawal was being filled by a bitter civil war. As the British entered Athens every crossroad seemed to come under sniper and machine-gun fire until the situation was finally brought under control in Constitution Square, where Laurence was slightly hurt in the leg by shrapnel; two of his fellow officers were killed.

The son of a Dean of Leicester, Peter Harold Laurence was born on February 18 1923 and won a Classics scholarship to Radley, where he fenced and played the piano before going into the 60th Rifles.

After the war he went up to Christ Church, Oxford, where he came top in the entrance exam for the Foreign Office, which insisted he join straight away without waiting to obtain his expected First. Laurence's postings were to reflect the growing awareness of the Cold War. He was first sent to Athens, where the civil war had ended, and then became an assistant political adviser in Trieste, still under an uneasy four-power administration.

His next posting was Prague, where he was arrested counting tanks in the Tatra Mountains and was even considered a target for espionage. But a report in the files of the StB, the Czech security service (which believed he had been in the Royal Navy), declared that Laurence had "huge self discipline" and was "in no way the kind of person who could be swayed by pressure". His career took a different turn after the Suez crisis when he was sent to Cairo; although he knew no Arabic, he got by with his French. A spell as a political adviser in Berlin, still administered by four powers, was followed by a year as a visiting fellow at All Souls, Oxford, where he wrote a technical book on Ostpolitik.

Laurence then became an inspector of diplomatic posts before achieving a longstanding ambition by ending his career as ambassador to Turkey. A fluent Turkish speaker, he arrived in Ankara in 1980, in time to see a period of familiar turbulence leading to the establishment of a military government. His posting was made easier by the friendship he established with a former diplomat who was appointed foreign minister by the generals.

Peter Laurence was appointed CMG in 1976 and KCMG in 1981. On retiring he moved to Devon, where he took on a host of unpaid tasks. He was chairman of the Community Council of Devon, a member of the Exeter Cathedral Music Trust, which helped to raise money to save the organ and choir. He was also *custos* of Grenville College, Bideford, and chairman of the Council of the British Institute of Archaeology at Ankara. He was appointed a Deputy Lieutenant of Devon in 1989.

Peter Laurence married, in 1948, Elizabeth Way, with whom he had two sons, and a daughter who predeceased him. Among Laurence's sterling qualities as a diplomat was his sharp eye for potential embarrassments. When his eldest son, Charles, arrived in Ankara as *The Daily Telegraph*'s correspondent in the 1980s he was informed that he would be welcome at the embassy – after he had completed his journalistic work.

LANCE CORPORAL 'OZZIE' OSBORNE

Lance Corporal 'Ozzie' Osborne (who died on December 10 2007, aged 85) showed exceptional courage in two attacks on the Normandy village of Le Plein while serving with 3 Commando on D-Day. His unit landed on Sword Beach at 9.10 am as part of Lord Lovat's 1 Special Service Brigade, which was tasked with linking up with 6 Airborne Brigade further inland.

Approaching the beach, they were met by accurate shell fire, the first shell landing just left of Osborne's landing craft, the second taking the radio-aerial away. A third scored a direct hit on another landing craft, leaving twenty of 3 Commando unaccounted for. Although opposition on the beach was less intense than earlier in the day, the Commandos were hampered by having to carry folded bicycles and three mortar bombs, each weighing 3.5 kilos.

On moving quickly inland they were pleasantly surprised to be met by Lovat, also riding a bicycle. Because the ground was wet and the bicycles covered in mud, they thought it seemly to clean them before they pressed on.

As the brigade's leading unit, 3 Troop was ordered to go to the assistance of the remnants of 9 Battalion Parachute Regiment, who were hard pressed in the area near to the Château d'Amfreville, where the Germans were holding Le Plein. A recce was quickly made and no time was wasted in putting in an attack. But on the road to Amfreville they faced intense fire from automatic weapons in the open without cover.

One casualty was caused by a bullet penetrating

a sergeant's helmet, leaving him with "a parting down his scalp" according to a fellow Commando. The troop leader, Captain Roy Wesley, was also hit. When it became obvious that a quick withdrawal was essential, Osborne made it his business to kill the German who had shot Wesley before engaging the others. Showing exceptional courage and devotion to duty, he continued firing until all the wounded were evacuated.

Determined to clear Le Plein of Germans, the troop's remaining officer decided to go forward again, taking Osborne with him. Finding a row of houses to provide cover and a good view of the village, they called for low-angle mortar support. This enabled the troop to move up, one section being ordered to clear some houses of Germans and giving fire while another went into attack, capturing some thirty Germans. Again, Osborne showed such bravery and initiative that he was recommended for the DCM. When he received the MM his troop commander invited him to dinner as part compensation.

Vincent Arthur Osborne was born at Chester on June 1 1922, one of a large family, whose father had served in the Royal Navy in the Great War and had died when Osborne was only four. He enlisted in the Welch Regiment in May 1941 and volunteered for the Commandos because it was part of 'a new concept in soldiering'. Fifty per cent of his comrades also volunteered.

Posted to 3 Commando he was on the Dieppe raid and then saw service in North Africa, Sicily and Italy until returning to the United Kingdom to prepare for D-Day. He was twice wounded during the advance through the Low Countries. He then trained for the Far East but was posted with the Welch Regiment again to the Yugoslav border, being finally discharged in 1946.

After working as a window-fitter and serving in the Malay Police in the 1950s, Osborne joined the Royal Hospital Chelsea after his wife's death and was much appreciated for his good nature and sense of fun. In four years of almost continuous action, he never saw a Commando knife used. "Why use a knife if you can shoot him?" he would ask.

REGIMENTAL QUARTERMASTER SERGEANT JOHN PROTT

Regimental Quartermaster Sergeant John Prott (who died on February 22 2008, aged 88) was awarded two Military Medals for unusual courage and unfailing presence of mind during the fighting in north-west Europe. He won the first as a gunner with the Ayrshire Yeomanry, which had been converted to a Royal Artillery field regiment. On July 19 1944 Prott was driving a tank serving as an artillery observation post for 3rd Royal Tank Regiment at the village of Bras, on a ridge south of Caen, when his commander was shot in the face by a sniper and the tank caught fire.

Although still under small arms attack, Prott tried to douse the flames before helping down the officer and two other wounded. He then climbed back up to rescue another crew member, only to be hurled to the ground when the turret exploded. On recovering he found some SS soldiers with automatics standing over him, and was taken with his wounded crewmen to a building, which the Germans soon abandoned as 3RTR approached.

After dressing his comrades' wounds Prott prevented them from dashing outside in front of the German snipers and went to an upper floor, from where he identified them for the Rifle Brigade, which was coming up in support. Finally Prott led his wounded out of the building, which was now ablaze, summoned medical orderlies to load them on to a tank and returned to his unit on foot.

He won his Bar on May 2 1945, the last day of the war, when his observation-post tank confronted German units tenaciously holding a wooded area around Lasbeck-Dorf, near Lübeck, on the Baltic. He and his co-driver were wounded by bombs which exploded above his head and knocked out the tank's gun.

But although suffering from shock Prott drove skilfully through the enemy gunners as they tried to finish off his tank. On being ordered to halt two miles down the road, he was found to have shell splinters all down one side of his face and body.

The citation declared that he had saved both the tank and its crew from being destroyed; it also noted that this was the third time that a tank driven by Prott had been hit by anti-tank weapons, yet he had never lost his nerve and was always cheerful under fire.

The son of a grain storeman, John Prott was born on November 13 1919 and went to Lady Jane

Hamilton School, Ayr. He began an apprenticeship as a glazier, but never completed it because of a disagreement with his employers. On the outbreak of war he mobilised with the mounted Ayrshire Yeomanry, which found him a cheering presence. Such was his physical strength that it was said of him in the sergeants' mess: "That's no' a man, he's a horse."

While billeted in a country house before the invasion he and a comrade found a comfortable sleeping place beside a large fireplace. But its warmth attracted so many others that the two tossed a bulging sandbag on to the fire, saying "There, boys, that'll give you heat", and then watched the room being rapidly vacated as two dozen thunder flashes went off.

Back in civvy street after the war Prott settled down with his wife Nancy to have a son and three daughters. He worked as a lorry driver delivering timber to collieries before becoming shaftsman at Rankinston and then going to Barony colliery, which he left to look after his wife in her last years. Outside work he gave much of his free time to the regiment, which valued him for his fund of stories and his recitation of *Tam O'Shanter* in his guid Ayrshire at Burns suppers.

Prott was a sergeant in the guard of honour when the Queen visited Ayr in 1956, and finally rose to regimental quartermaster sergeant. At home he enjoyed marching round his house to a recording of pipes and drums accompanied by his children (and later his grandchildren), one on his shoulders and the others following behind.

SERGEANT DOUGIE WRIGHT

Sergeant Dougie Wright (who died on February 29 2008, aged 88) earned a Military Medal and a legendary reputation as a fighting soldier with Lord Jellicoe's 1st Special Boat Squadron in the Greek islands. In April 1944 he distinguished himself in a close-quarter attack on an enemy post on Ios, which resulted in no SBS losses but five enemy casualties. He was also involved in two dramatic attacks on a radio station on Amorgos. In the first he found himself under the command of Captain Anders Lassen (a Dane later to win a posthumous VC) who hated Germans and usually killed them; but on this occasion Lassen did a deal with a captured wireless operator by which he took the man's dog as well as the station's code books, while Wright took the German's Greek mistress.

When the second attack was made, the station had been reinforced to be the Germans' local headquarters. Wright, a left-hander who had taught himself to become an expert with a Bren gun, was given the crucial task of providing cover. He positioned himself with twenty magazines of ammunition on a flat rooftop to await the signal to fire: a Greek officer throwing a grenade through the station's middle window. Although nearly 300 yards away, Wright opened up with such accuracy, that the enemy became too demoralised to respond. Six of them were brought down as they fled the building, and he later counted five more. The resulting success of these actions was "to a very great extent due to the work of this NCO", according to his citation.

Wright consolidated his reputation for conduct of the highest order during further operations on Naxos between May 16 and May 26 when, weak from a serious relapse of malaria, he refused help carrying his heavy equipment during a fifteen-mile march over mountainous country. It was due to his determination that the patrol was spared an extra day's waiting in an area heavily patrolled by the enemy, the citation concluded.

Douglas Wright was born on March 11 1919 at Macclesfield, Cheshire, one of nine children; his father had been in the Pioneer Corps during the Great War. Young Dougie worked for a baker, as a butcher's boy and on a farm before enlisting in the Grenadiers in 1938; he was posted to the King's Company, where the shortest man was 6ft 3in tall. During the Dunkirk retreat he recalled coming under fire as the Grenadiers arrived on the beaches and were ordered to march to attention. They wondered "what the hell was going on" until the "eyes right" was given, and General Alexander returned their salute. Then "some silly bugger forgot to give the halt," Wright recalled, "so we ended up in a foot of water."

Following service in North Africa, Wright volunteered for the SAS, then joined the SBS. He took part in raids on Sardinia, Crete and Yugoslavia as well as on the Greek islands, where he was said to have strangled nine Germans with his bare hands. No written evidence for this exists. As an in-pensioner at the Royal Hospital, Chelsea, he had no family photographs on the wall of his bunk, only the bayonet he had carried at Dunkirk. Once, when the pensioners were (unusually) recalling how many enemy they had each personally despatched, Wright brought the discussion to an abrupt end by saying: "Sank a troopship once."

After the war he was discharged because of his malaria, but re-enlisted in the Grenadiers ten years later to serve on Malta and then Cyprus, where he became the pioneer sergeant. While trying to procure some badly needed cement for a tennis court, he was searching company stores out of hours when a guard dog went for his throat. "Having worked with farm animals, I wasn't having that," Wright recalled, "so I bit the bastard back." The dog yelped, and ran off.

Later, back with the battalion in London, he took a mentally deranged soldier to Millbank Hospital, where Wright ended up swearing at a psychiatrist whose white coat concealed that he was a brigadier. This earned Wright a severe reprimand, and lost him his Long Service and Good Conduct Medal. But he went on to see further service in the Cameroons, Germany and Sharjah, being finally discharged in 1970 after more than twenty-one years' service.

He then worked as a butcher and a security man before joining the prison service. Entering the Royal Hospital in 1995, he reverted to out-pension for family reasons in 1997 but returned the following year. Dougie Wright was twice married and divorced, and is survived by three children from each of his marriages.

LIEUTENANT GARRY MAUFE

Lieutenant Garry Maufe (who died on April 6 2008, aged 86) earned an MC for his relief of a besieged unit at Mezzano in Italy.

Given to shouting "Aren't we having a lovely time?" at tense moments, Maufe enjoyed perhaps more than his fair share of good fortune. He crossed the Marano river under attack from 'moaning minnie' rockets; took a shot in the back which inflicted only a severe bruise; and once saw a shell land near his feet, only to sink into the mud before exploding ineffectually.

While he recalled being shaken by the sight of the blackened faces of dead Germans in the sun and a pig eating the remains of a peasant woman, he enjoyed a young man's vicarious pleasure in watching a Canadian tank driving in one end of a house and being applauded as it came out of the other. He later reflected: "It has to be fun for young men to be encouraged and clapped for being such vandals."

At around 4.30 am on January 4 1945, Maufe was woken by German activity near his farmhouse headquarters at Mezzano (which he had reached in a Bren carrier despite being ordered to approach on foot). A sergeant from his former platoon then came on the wireless, saying that they had lost two men and pleading for badly-needed ammunition. As the commander on the spot, Maufe's duty was to remain at his headquarters; but he decided to go himself, borrowing a despatch rider's round helmet.

Setting off in a carrier at dawn with a driver and Rifleman Walker, who had extra grenades in the back, he sprayed and killed the grey figures of enemy bazooka men in the ditches on either side of him as they hurtled 600 yards down a narrow cart track.

After skidding round a blind corner the carrier sped on, with Maufe emptying the contents of another magazine into more men on his right. Only when he reached the sergeant did he learn that towards the end he had been firing on the very men he had come to rescue – who were now swearing and laughing at his failure to hit any of them.

Later, when he was shooting from an upstairs window at a limping German, Maufe found his rifle pushed aside by a rifleman who said: "Give him a chance, guv, the poor sod's wounded." "Well enough to fight again," thought Maufe; but he remembered the man ever afterwards. Following a restorative brew-up of tea, he and Walker (who was awarded an MM for their exploit) went out for "a swan around looking for a bit of loot"; instead they joined some Canadians flushing out some seventy Germans, who fled back to their lines.

The day the Germans surrendered, May 2, Maufe entered Austria to be confronted in the road by a Mark III tank which had run out of petrol. Climbing up to the turret, he found inside a black-uniformed SS officer commanding a 75mm gun and a large machine gun trained on Maufe's carriers. But noting the man's Afrika Korps medal ribbon, Maufe assured him of their kinship as desert soldiers and after 30 minutes persuaded him to surrender.

After Maufe had driven the officer off to headquarters, the men of both armies retired to a local inn. When the Germans were eventually led off to captivity nobody noticed one soldier climbing back into the tank, where he blew himself up.

Garry Humphris Maufe was born on May 28 1922 at Ilkley, West Riding. The family name was originally Muff, and Garry's father owned the Bradford department store Brown Muff, known as 'the Harrods of the North'. In response to their rising fortunes the family had left Bradford and changed their name to Maufe, thereby inspiring the local ditty:

In Bradford 'tis good enoof
To be known as Mrs Muff
But in Ilkley by the river Wharfe
'Tis better to be known as Mrs Maufe!

Young Garry had an unhappy time at Uppingham before leaving to learn about farming. He joined the Royal Norfolk Regiment on his 18th birthday, and was on guard duty with another private who shot himself in the shoulder to get out of the Army but dropped dead after the bullet ricocheted off his shoulder into his heart. Maufe started to train as an artillery officer but switched to 1st Battalion, King's Royal Rifle Corps, after seeing the regiment's dashing green uniforms. His first posting was to North Africa.

On returning home from the war Maufe took up 500 acres on Lord Leicester's Holkham estate at Burnham Thorpe, Norfolk, where he planted wheat, barley and sugar beet. He also started a successful commercial plum orchard, despite being assured that the trees could never bear fruit so close to the sea, and planted two extensive areas of mixed hardwood trees which he knew he would never see reach maturity. In 1949 Maufe met, and within six weeks married, Marit Børstad, a Norwegian au pair with whom he had four daughters.

A passionate Europhile he encouraged Germans to visit Norfolk and employed Eastern Europeans to work on the farm. Before setting off for a month-long motoring holiday in Europe at the end of the harvest, he would give his foreman one day's notice and leave him blank cheques with which to pay off the eighteen helpers. One year the family was trapped on the Greek island of Thassos during the colonels' rule; on another they drove down dried-up riverbeds in Yugoslavia after the Skopje earthquake of 1963.

There was a summer sailing at home in a dinghy and in a lifeboat named *The Centipede* (which had been designed by Uffa Fox to be slung beneath a Lancaster bomber) as well as skiing in the Alps during the winter. When Maufe, a keen reader of Russian classics, finally had to give up these activities he became an enthusiastic bookbinder.

In his later years he also compiled a handwritten 200-page folio, *Miscellany of a Family at War*, which recorded his detailed comments on the history of the Rifle Corps; it includes family letters and gallantry citations for five of his kinsmen, including his uncle 'Squash' Maufe of the Royal Garrison Artillery, who won the VC during the First World War, aged 19, and died in an accident while serving in the Home Guard during the Second.

Garry Maufe, who was survived by his wife and three of their daughters, started laying down port in the early 1950s to be drunk at a rate of a dozen bottles a year; he had enough to last him to the age of 90.

GENERAL SIR FRANK HASSETT

General Sir Frank Hassett (who died on June 11 2008, aged 90) fought in North Africa and served in New Guinea during the Second World War before commanding 28th Commonwealth Brigade during the Malayan emergency and finally rising to become Chief of the Australian Defence Staff.

Hassett's greatest success was the capture of Maryang San, an imposing 650ft hill north of the Imjin river in Korea. In October 1951 he was commanding officer of 3rd Battalion, Royal Australian Regiment, when it was charged with clearing a series of peaks in order to strengthen the Allies' hand in peace negotiations.

Two American advances had been repulsed by the well-entrenched Chinese, and the Australians were under strength and short of experience. So Hassett decided to deceive the enemy by sending one company to take an enemy post on the lower slopes of an eastern range, and then dispatching two others on to a ridge higher up to their right.

The operation began in darkness, which gave way to thick fog, forcing each man to hold on to the scabbard of the one in front. Two of the company commanders ran into one another, discovering that they were both lost. Hassett, who had moved his Tac HQ to the lower objective, told one of them to remain where he was and directed the second to drive the enemy from four knolls; this involved close fighting that included rifle butts, fists and even teeth.

When one member of the company declared, "This is no bloody place for a white man," Captain Reg Saunders, then the only Aborigine officer in the Australian Army, replied: "It's no bloody place for a black man either."

Then, as they slowed with exhaustion, Hassett sent the still fresh third company racing through them to take the peak. It turned out to be abandoned, but shells were soon raining down. After night fell three attacks had to be repelled before Hassett ordered the second company to fix bayonets and capture a further peak in order to relieve the flagging Royal Northumberland Fusiliers nearby. When the Chinese appeared to collect their wounded, the Diggers let them do so unhindered.

Throughout the battle the sight of Hassett's tall, erect figure calmly directing fire support and talking to his company commanders filled his men with confidence. But when he appeared at critical points under fire they asked: "Are you sure you ought to be here, sir?"

Hassett was awarded an "*immediate* immediate DSO" by Major General James Cassels, commander of 1st British Commonwealth Division. The other awards included another DSO, nine MCs, two DCMs, nine MMs, one MBE and fifteen mentions in dispatches. Yet the action, which is considered Australia's finest in Korea, was largely forgotten for the next thirty-five years.

The son of a railway yard manager, Francis George

Hassett was born in Sydney on April 11 1918 and went to Canterbury High School, where he boxed. After a first job as a clerk, Frank won a place at the Royal Military College Duntroon, arriving, aged 16, so puny that the RSM would tell him during drill practice: "Staff Cadet 'Assett, your rifle seems a bit 'eavy for you."

But he grew three inches and captained the XV, once scoring a try on the wing while playing for the Australian Capital Territory against the All Blacks. On passing out he was posted to the Darwin Mobile Force; his most frightening experience occurred when, lost and separated from his men, he came across a crocodile in a mangrove swamp.

Posted to North Africa with the Australian Imperial Force after the declaration of war, he first saw action in the attack on Bardia, in Libya, when, as adjutant of 2nd/3rd Battalion, he pushed into the centre of the battle to find himself under air and tank attack.

At Tobruk he found a weak point in the Italian front line and started laying white tapes for a start-line; but in a desperate effort to complete the task before dawn he began to walk instead of crawling and prodding for mines; they duly blew up. He hobbled back with a shrapnel wound in his foot, and earned a mention in despatches.

After a staff course at Haifa alongside the future Field Marshal Lord Carver, Hassett was exasperated to be embedded in staff work in Melbourne and then New Guinea, receiving another mention and being appointed OBE. He was next made GSO1 of 3rd Division at Bougainville, where swamp and jungle were severely slowing Allied progress. While the surrender talks with the Japanese were going on, Hassett decided to fly to Buin, where the enemy still seemed strong and belligerent.

When it was time to leave, the pilot asked Hassett to take the throttle while he turned the propeller, and the plane immediately pitched on to its nose. The pilot ingeniously shaved down the propeller, enabling the aircraft to take off – but without its passenger, who had to await rescue while contemplating his impetuousness in proposing the trip. As they flew off again the pilot confided he would rather not report the full story.

On returning from Korea Hassett became director of military art at Duntroon. The cadets were in awe of his aloofness until one day he marched into a saleroom and bought a lime-green sports car. When the Queen came to Australia he received his DSO on one day and the MVO for his services as marshal of the royal tour on the next.

Hassett's last active service appointment was as commander of 28th Commonwealth Brigade in Malaya, where he was bemused to find that his brigade major was the New Zealander Ron Hassett, who went on to become his dominion's Chief of the General Staff. Since both had similar cultivated accents and answered the phone "Hassett", there was confusion until callers started asking which one they were addressing.

Realising that the French and South Vietnamese had failed in Indo-China because of outdated tactics, Hassett decided to investigate. Unable to obtain permission to visit Laos, he flew in pretending to be a middle-ranking officer on a social call – though the disguise was compromised by his supposed seniors addressing him as "sir".

Back in Malaya he set up models of runways and Viet Minh villages for training purposes, and impressed General Sir Walter Walker, who forcefully declared that, as a brigade commander, Hassett was "in a class of his own". With this recommendation he was next sent to the Imperial Defence College in London before returning home with a CBE to become a robust Deputy Chief of General Staff.

In London again, as head of the Australian Joint Services Staff, he became a gentleman usher to the Queen and smoothed away the Labour government's unease at the award of Australian VCs in Vietnam. He also warned Canberra about the coming British withdrawal from east of Suez.

By the time Hassett became Chief of the Defence Force Staff in 1975, he was suffering from longstanding stomach problems. After a year he retired to become colonel commandant of the Royal Australian Regiment, run a farm and enjoy his fox terriers, Batty and Ratty. Frank Hassett, who was appointed AC in 1975 and KBE in 1976, married, in 1946, Hallie Roberts, who survived him with a son and two daughters; another son died in a car crash.

MAJOR JACK ALPE

Major Jack Alpe (who died on July 8 2008, aged 87) was an ammunition officer whose career took him from the North African desert to Hitler's bunker in Berlin. In 1944 Alpe found himself at the heart of the battle of Normandy in command of twenty lorries carrying 25lb shells to advance gun positions at the village of Démouville, outside Caen. As his unit was being directed by field telephone and despatch riders toward their gunners, it was spotted from a tower by the enemy, who unleashed a rain of 88mm fire at Alpe's soft-topped vehicles. Casualties mounted, and Alpe was wounded in the head by shell splinters as he was going to the aid of one of his sergeants.

After his men had dressed his wounds, Alpe insisted on moving his forward ammunition point to avoid further loss of life and equipment. Only then did he consent to going to a dressing station; after he had been taken to hospital, he quickly discharged himself in order to return to his unit.

The citation for Alpe's immediate MC declared that "his behaviour was an excellent example to his men, who were considerably shaken, and through his coolness and courage the ammunition point continued to function".

Jack Gerald Alpe was born on July 25 1920, the son of the founder of Alpe & Saunders, a firm of Rolls-Royce coachbuilders in London, which specialised in hearses. After being educated at St Paul's, where he distinguished himself as a boxer and on the rugby field, he joined the Territorial Army and arrived at Suez as a captain in the Royal Army Service Corps.

In his first taste of action Alpe transported troops of 4th Indian Division in the advance on Tobruk and then escorted a convoy of Italian prisoners to Alexandria. When he was ordered to cordon off some unexploded Italian thermos anti-personnel bombs, he decided that it would be easier to fire on them with a .303. He was wounded by the shrapnel from the resulting explosion.

The arrival of Rommel with the Afrika Korps in late 1941 brought an end to the Allies' run of good fortune, sending the Eighth Army into retreat for 1,000 miles under constant fire from Stuka dive-bombers.

During these attacks Alpe sometimes managed to slip under his Jeep, but even afterwards he felt uneasy when he considered that this had prohibited him from rescuing drivers who had been injured and immobilised in their vehicles before the ammunition they were carrying exploded.

As the Eighth Army regained control at Alamein, Alpe started to make a photographic record. His pictures showed abandoned Italian trucks being looted, Arab horsemen racing in the desert, and Vivien Leigh performing in a Roman amphitheatre.

From his truck he also photographed the entry into Salerno under enemy fire and then the slow move up the length of Italy. After being sent home to England, he was next to see action in the Normandy campaign.

Later, on crossing the Rhine, Alpe was again injured when his Jeep overturned, but he was back with his men when they were stationed in a large country house, which turned out to have been serving as a brothel for senior German officers. The girls were still in residence, posing a problem under the Army Council rules against fraternisation; Alpe endeavoured to solve this by placing a visitors' book in the entrance hall.

Following the German surrender he was one of the first British officers to enter the Reich Chancellery in Berlin. Although the Russians had removed Hitler's remains, he could see the ashes where his body was said to have been burned. Since the Russians present showed no interest in what he did, Alpe removed a dinner party invitation from the Führer (dress code: tailcoat or uniform) and took a photograph of a vast chandelier in ruins.

On being demobbed he married Lorraine Owen, with whom he was to have two daughters and a son. He worked for the family firm in Marylebone High Street before starting his own firm selling Rolls-Royce and Bentley cars.

Like many veterans, Jack Alpe disliked discussing his war service. But he co-operated with his son Jeremy in producing *My War*, a slim, handsome volume of recollections and pictures, which was completed just before his death.

LIEUTENANT 'BUSTER' SWAN

Lieutenant 'Buster' Swan (who died on November 24 2008, aged 88) won an immediate Distinguished Conduct Medal as a sergeant in the Essex Regiment during some of the fiercest fighting of the Italian campaign. After the crossing of the Sangro river just before Christmas 1943, Swan commanded the leading platoon in an attack on the village of Villa Grande, near Ortona, which was barring the Allied advance. Unknown to 5th Essex, this position was defended by a German 1st Parachute Division determined to fight to the end.

A covering party for Swan reached some outhouses about 100 yards from the village, unaware that these were their objective, and then pushed on to encounter fierce defensive fire. Swan's Z Company was then caught in the open between the outhouses and the village and took many casualties before being pinned down as the ground was swept by enemy machine guns firing on fixed lines.

On reaching the village after dark he and his men cleared Germans from twelve buildings during the course of the night – "a most unpleasant time", according to the regimental history. When the enemy counter-attacked, Swan's platoon was reduced to five men beside himself. But he still managed to break out of his position to inflict heavy casualties as he rejoined his battalion.

The following day, when the assault on the village was renewed, Swan insisted on leading his platoon in person. With total disregard for his own safety he defied intense grenade and mortar fire to prevail in the fiercest hand-to-hand fighting with the enemy. Few of the Germans surrendered, and those who did were wounded.

Once his objective had been achieved, Swan found his new position surrounded on three sides.

He quickly organised it for defence, consolidating the gains of the night while still under heavy fire. After leading his platoon for five days of continuous action he was severely wounded on Boxing Day. The slaughter had been such that at noon on Christmas Day the Germans raised a Red Cross flag to allow the wounded to be evacuated. Swan's citation declares, "he was an inspiration to all who saw him because of his determination and powers of leadership".

The elder of a builder's two sons, William John Swan, known as 'Buster', was born on September 14 1920 at Saffron Walden, Essex. He did well at primary school and passed a scholarship to go to Newport Grammar School, but to help the family he gave it up to become a delivery boy with a fruit and vegetable merchant named Frank Bacon.

In November 1937 young Bill joined 5th Battalion, Essex Regiment TA. He went to Egypt and the Middle East before finally seeing action in three major Italian battles, which cost the Essex more than 500 casualties in 1943.

Swan was discharged in 1947. He briefly rejoined his old employer, then was a postman before becoming a security officer with the engineering firm Ciba-Geigy for twenty years. From 1952 until 1955 he held a commission as a second lieutenant in the TA, when he was much valued as an instructor in the cadet force.

Despite his time in action, he considered meeting the King to receive his DCM the most terrifying experience of his life. To the end of his days he preferred to salute those he met rather than say goodbye. 'Buster' Swan married, in 1947, Rose Gale, who predeceased him, and is survived by a daughter.

LIEUTENANT COLONEL ERIC WILSON, VC

Lieutenant Colonel Eric Wilson (who died on December 23 2008, aged 96) was awarded a posthumous Victoria Cross for his gallant defence against a large Italian force in Eritrea, during which he was thought to have been killed in August 1940; some months later, he learned of his award from a fellow prisoner who was surprised to meet the 'late' Captain Wilson in a prison camp.

The Italians, with 350,000 troops in Abyssinia and Eritrea, had invaded British Somaliland, which was defended by 1,500 men, threatening control of the entrance to the Red Sea and British positions from Aden to Suez. As they headed for Berbera, on the coast, a meagre Allied force began to search for a defensive position. Most of the terrain was flat, but parallel to the sea lay the rugged Golis Hills, with an 8,000ft pass, where the Allies made their stand.

Wilson, an acting captain with the Somaliland Camel Corps, was given the vital task of siting the corps' machine guns on four small hills of the Tug Argan Gap – named Black, Knobbly, Mill and Observation – though they were too widely separated to cover their entire vista. Placing himself on Observation, which commanded the widest arc of fire, he was tremendously exposed on a position well known to Italian truck drivers who had driven past it daily before the declaration of war.

As two battalions of Blackshirts, with three brigades of colonial troops and artillery, appeared on all sides on the morning of August 11, Wilson's machine gun received a hit which knocked it off its mounting – though he and his three Somali gunners soon had it back in action. Then another shell came straight into the embrasure of their post, killing the Somali sergeant standing next to Wilson, as well as severely wounding Wilson himself in the right shoulder and left eye; his spectacles were broken, and the fragments could be seen under his skin ever afterwards.

Repairing and remounting the gun, he poured down fire on enemy troops advancing on Mill in the afternoon. This inflicted such heavy casualties that the Italians brought up a pack battery to within 700 yards which fired back over open sights until it was hit in turn by the defenders' only artillery, 1st East Africa Light Battery.

A heavy downpour of rain brought a respite. But next morning the Italians began to work their way in small parties up through the scrub, concentrating their field artillery on Wilson's position. On August 13 the enemy overran the artillery position on Mill. An order to withdraw was sent to Wilson's company but never arrived. Next day, two of the other machine-gun posts were destroyed, yet Wilson, now suffering from malaria as well, kept his own post in action until finally overrun at 5 pm.

On recovering consciousness he emerged from the crevasse which had sheltered the gun to find dead bodies all around, including that of his terrier.

Walking down he met a white NCO, with whom he was then captured by the Italians.

When news of the action reached London, Wilson was believed to have been killed in the final assault, and his VC was gazetted two months later. But after medical treatment, he was put in a prison camp at Adi Ugri in Eritrea, where a surprised RAF officer informed him of the award. Some weeks later preparations were almost complete for a mass escape by tunnel when the prisoners woke up to find all their captors but the commandant gone before the arrival of British troops.

A tall, shy, nervous man whose mother had described him as "such a dear boy and so timid" and had sold his dress sword, Wilson received his medal from King George VI at Buckingham Palace; he said he did so on behalf of the men with him at the Tug Argan Gap.

Eric Charles Twelves Wilson, the son of the rector of Hunsdon, Hertfordshire, was born on October 2 1912 at Sandown on the Isle of Wight. His interest in East Africa was kindled by his grandfather, who had founded the Church Missionary Society in Buganda.

At Marlborough, where Eric was a fine athlete, he discovered a statue of Richard Corfield, who had perished fighting with Somalis against the 'Mad Mullah' in 1913. He decided on a military life and, despite wearing spectacles, passed the Sandhurst entrance exam while still at school.

In 1933 he was commissioned into East Surrey Regiment. Four years later he volunteered for King's African Rifles, supporting the colonial administration upcountry in Tanganyika and becoming a Nyassa speaker.

In 1939 Wilson was delighted to be ordered to form seventy-five Somali conscripts into a company of machine-gunners with Somaliland Camel Corps; the Somalis considered camels too precious to ride, keeping them for their milk and for transporting the Vickers machine guns. He formed the deepest admiration for his three NCOs, particularly Sergeant Omaar Kujoog, who was to be killed beside him.

After recovering from his wounds at Tug Argan, Wilson served in North Africa as adjutant of the Long Range Desert Group, demonstrating a knowledge of the desert which greatly aided its work behind German lines. He then served in Burma as second-in-command of 11 KAR in the advance down the Kabaw valley to the Chindwin. But after contracting scrub typhus he spent the rest of the war commanding an infantry training centre in Uganda.

Wilson retired from the Army in 1949 and joined the Colonial Service in Tanganyika (now Tanzania), where he became fluent in four Bantu languages, which enabled him to dispense with interpreters. In 1961 he retired with the granting of independence, and the following year was appointed deputy warden of London House, the foreign students' residence, of which he was warden from 1966 to 1977.

He was honorary secretary of the Anglo-Somali Society from 1972 to 1977 and organised relief for the famine that struck Somalia in 1975. He remained greatly attached to the Somali people, whom he would "back against all comers for cheerful toughness, natural aptitude and fieldcraft and the ability to stand up to a bad climate".

His youngest son, the photographer Hamish Wilson, maintained the family link with the Somalis, fighting in 1991 in the war to establish a separate state of Somaliland in the north of the country. As the only European present at the liberation of its capital, Hargeysa, he made a television programme about it, visiting the same places as his father, and fighting alongside the children of men his father had known and fought with.

A keen countryman, Eric Wilson retired to Dorset, where he published *Stowell in the Blackmore Vale* in 1986. He married first, in 1943, Ann Pleydell-Bouverie; they had two sons. After a divorce in 1953 he married Angela Gordon, with whom he had another son.

In retirement Wilson found himself increasingly sought after as the oldest VC. He told Private Johnson Beharry, of 1st Battalion Princess of Wales's regiment, who won a VC in Iraq in 2005: "It will not make a difference to your life. You might get a few drinks, though." On being invited to attend the pageant for the Queen Mother's 100th birthday he refused to be cowed when Irish terrorists disrupted London's transport network and, aged 87, insisted on walking from Waterloo station to the parade ground at Horse Guards.

Eric Wilson kept a manila envelope containing his cuttings which ranged from a sober obituary in *The Times* to a lurid tale in the *Daily Sketch* with three headlines "Another Rorke's Drift", "First Africa VC Dies" and "Last Stand in the Desert". There was also a dramatic eyewitness account of the action published in *The Daily Telegraph*, which was full of circumstantial assumptions from the original citation. "People talk about the fog of war, but I am beginning to wonder what was lost in it," he would say.

COLONEL DAVID SMILEY

Colonel David Smiley (who died on January 9 2009, aged 92) was one of the most celebrated cloak-and-dagger agents of the Second World War, serving behind enemy lines in Albania, Greece, Abyssinia and eastern Thailand. After the war he organised secret operations against the Russians and their allies in Albania and Poland; then as Britain's domination in the Arabian peninsula drew to a close, he commanded the Sultan of Oman's armed forces in highly successful counter-insurgency campaign operations.

Later he organised with MI6 royalist guerrilla resistance to a Soviet-backed Nasserite regime in Yemen. Smiley's efforts helped to force the eventual withdrawal of the Egyptians and their Soviet mentors, paved the way for the emergence of a less anti-Western Yemeni government, and confirmed his reputation as a post-war military Arabist.

In more conventional style, he commanded the Royal Horse Guards (the Blues), riding alongside the Queen as commander of her escort at the Coronation in 1953. During the Second World War he was parachuted four times behind enemy lines. On one occasion he was obliged to escape from Albania in a rowing boat. On another mission, in Japanese-controlled eastern Thailand, he was stretchered for three days through the jungle with severe burns after a booby trap meant for a senior Japanese officer exploded prematurely.

As an assistant military attaché in Poland after the war, when the Soviet-controlled Communists were tightening their grip, he was beaten up and expelled as a spy after an operation he was running had incriminated a member of the politburo. He next headed the British side of a secret Anglo-American venture to subvert the newly-installed Communist regime in Albania led by the ruthless Enver Hoxha. But Kim Philby, who was secretly working for the Russians, was the liaison between the British and Americans; almost all of the 100 agents dropped by parachute or landed by boat were betrayed, and nearly all were tortured and shot. This failure haunted Smiley for the rest of his life.

Smiley's exploits led some to suggest that he was, along with several other candidates, a model for James Bond. It was widely mooted that John le Carré, albeit unconsciously, had taken the name of his hero from the real-life Smiley.

Born on April 11 1916, David de Crespigny Smiley was the youngest son of Major Sir John Smiley, 2nd Baronet, and Valerie, youngest daughter of Sir Claude Champion de Crespigny, 4th Baronet, a noted jockey, balloonist, all-round sportsman and adventurer famed for his feats of derring-do.

After Pangbourne Nautical College, where he excelled in sport, David went to Sandhurst in 1934. He served in the Blues from 1936 to 1939, based mainly at Windsor, leading the life of a debonair man about town, owning a Bentley and a Whitney Straight aircraft. Before the outbreak of war, he won seven races under National Hunt rules. In his first point-to-point with the Garth Hunt, he crashed into a tree, suffering serious injuries.

Over the years Smiley was to break more than eighty bones, mainly as a result of sport; on two occasions he broke his skull, once in a steeplechase and once when he dived at night into an almost-empty swimming pool in Thailand. And after the war, he held the record for the most falls in one season on the Cresta Run in St Moritz; and, bizarrely, represented Kenya (where he owned a farm) in the Commonwealth Winter Games of 1960.

When war broke out in 1939, the Blues sailed for Palestine, where one of Smiley's first jobs as a lieutenant was to shoot his troop of forty horses when it became clear they were of no use in modern combat. His introduction was against the Vichy French in Syria. For his nocturnal reconnaissance work in ruins near Palmyra he was mentioned in despatches.

Later in 1940 Smiley joined the Somaliland Camel Corps, arriving at Berbera the very day it was decided to evacuate British Somaliland. Returning in frustration to Egypt, he persuaded General Wavell, a family friend, to recommend him for the newly-formed Commandos, in which he became a company commander with the rank of captain. Sneaking from Sudan into Abyssinia, Smiley operated for the first of many times behind enemy lines.

The following year he returned to his regiment

to command a squadron of armoured vehicles being sent from Palestine to raise the siege of Habbaniyah, sixty miles west of Baghdad in Iraq, where the king and regent had been overthrown in a pro-German coup led by Rashid Ali. Under Colonel John Glubb, he led in full cry a charge alongside Bedouin levies, which he called 'Glubb's girls', because of their long black locks. After helping to capture Baghdad, Smiley's squadron was sent to Mosul with the task of capturing the German ambassador, who escaped.

His squadron then moved east, to capture the Persian capital, Tehran, followed by "two weeks' celebration with plenty of vodka, caviar and women". After a spell in Palestine, Smiley led a Blues squadron of dummy tanks into the Western Desert pretending first to be British Crusaders and then, on a further foray, American General Grants, which were repeatedly attacked by Stukas. When Rommel broke through, they withdrew to Cairo. Three months later Smiley commanded a squadron of armoured cars at the battle of El Alamein – his last bout of conventional warfare.

After training at a school for secret agents in Haifa and taking a parachuting course with his friend David Stirling and his Special Air Service (SAS) near the Suez Canal, Smiley joined the Special Operations Executive (SOE), the organisation set up "to set Europe ablaze" by helping local partisans sabotage the Nazis' infrastructure.

He was parachuted with his life-long friend Neil 'Billy' McLean into the mountains of Albania, occupied by the Italians and later by the Germans. For eight months he organised the fractious partisans in a series of ambushes and acts of bridge demolition, sometimes by climbing under them at night while German troops were patrolling above: a Smiley trademark. He was awarded an immediate MC.

In early 1944 Smiley was again parachuted into Albania, with McLean and Julian (later Lord) Amery, to liaise with the royalist guerrillas loyal to King Zog. After leaving Albania, where his activities brought a Bar to his MC, he was transferred to the Siamese section of SOE, Force 136, where he liaised with guerrillas operating against the Japanese who ruled the country through a proxy government. It was then that he was injured by the premature explosion of a booby trap meant for a Japanese officer.

After recovering at Government House in Calcutta, where he consorted with both Nehru and Gandhi, he was parachuted behind enemy lines into eastern Siam. After the dropping of the atomic bombs and the surrender of Japan, he organised the liberation of several prisoner-of-war camps, including the one on which the film *The Bridge on the River Kwai* was based. Though only a major, he personally took the surrender of the 22nd Division of the Imperial Japanese Army.

On Lord Mountbatten's orders, Smiley re-armed a Japanese company and led them against the Communists of the fledgling Vietminh (who later became the Viet Cong) in French Indo-China. Among other exploits, he freed 120 French women and children held hostage by the Communists. The only British officer in an area the size of Wales, he then took the surrender of Vientiane, Laos's capital, from another Japanese general. For his activities in

Siam and Indo-China Smiley was awarded a military OBE. He later ruefully noted that, at the time, the Vietminh were backed by the American OSS, the CIA's forerunner, which had a naïve enthusiasm for proclaimed democrats and hostility to the British and French empires.

After his early post-war exploits in Poland and then his efforts to roll back communism in Albania were betrayed by Philby, Smiley returned to more conventional duties in Germany and at home. In 1955 he was appointed military attaché in Sweden, from where he made surveillance trips with his young family along the Russian border with Finland and Norway. But the pinnacle of Smiley's post-war career was his three-year tenure as commander of the Sultan of Muscat and Oman's armed forces during a civil war which threatened to bring down one of Britain's more reactionary allies in the Gulf.

By now in his early forties, Smiley ran a gruelling counter-insurgency which gradually drove the guerrillas back from the scorching plains into their mountain retreat, the 10,000ft high Jebel Akhdar, which had never been successfully assaulted. With two squadrons of the SAS under his command, he led a classic dawn attack on the mountain fastness, finally crushing the enemy. After leaving Oman in 1961, Smiley was offered command of the SAS, but retired from the British Army to file occasional reports for Raymond Postgate's *Good Food Guide*.

He was not able to relax for long. Within two years he had been persuaded to help bolster royalist forces in Yemen. Liaising with King Faisal of Saudi Arabia and MI6, who arranged for former SAS and other mercenaries to accompany him, Smiley made thirteen trips to Yemen between 1963 and 1968. Often disguised as a local, he travelled on foot or by donkey for weeks at a time across Arabia's most rugged terrain. He won the admiration of his colleagues, both Arab and British, for his toughness, bluntness, and shrewdness as an adviser. King Faisal, whom Smiley greatly admired, personally expressed his appreciation.

After ending his Arabian career, Smiley moved to Spain, where, for nineteen years, he grew olives, carobs and almonds, and continued to advise Albania's surviving anti-Communists, by now all in exile, before returning to live in Somerset and then Earl's Court. To Smiley's delight, he was welcomed back to Albania in 1990, as the Communist regime, which had sentenced him to death in absentia, began to collapse. He forged a friendship with the country's first post-Communist leader, Sali Berisha.

Smiley was appointed LVO, and Knight Commander of the Order of the Sword in Sweden and Grand Cordon of the Order of Skanderbeg in Albania. In 1947 he married Moyra, daughter of Lord Francis Scott KCMG, DSO, the 6th Duke of Buccleuch's youngest son, and was survived by his wife, two sons, a stepson and a stepdaughter.

LIEUTENANT COLONEL RICHARD HEAVEN

Lieutenant Colonel Richard Heaven (who died on January 10 2009, aged 89) was the last officer-cadet to be given the Sword of Honour at the Royal Military Academy Woolwich before it closed in 1939, and was later awarded a Military Cross as a mountain battery commander in Italy.

In November 1943 Heaven landed at Naples with 479 Light Battery, which had 3.7in guns that split into eight pieces to be transported by mules. These (he recalled in his memoirs) were beautiful, placid, broad-backed beasts, which were drilled to prepare for action by standing in a circle looking outwards, with a smaller, pivot mule at the centre. The unit would march six days a week between dawn and around 6 pm, halting every 2 hours for a 20-minute break. The animals would then be unloaded and watered, have their girths slackened and their hooves inspected for repair, if necessary, by the farrier sergeant using a portable anvil.

Though the battery trailed well behind the front-line troops as it marched north, it none the less amazed infantry battalions by its average speed of five miles an hour and the way the animals held their heads down with their ears flopping backwards and forwards in a way that suggested a happy acceptance of their lot.

Heaven proved an efficient officer, refusing to allow the men to drink water before lunch because it made them drowsy, and not letting officers ride unless they were sick or checking the rear of the column. He was involved in several skirmishes with stragglers from the retreating German Army before he earned his MC supporting some Gurkhas on August 26 1944, near Bologna.

The action took place on a hill that was the

Gurkhas' headquarters, which had little more than one depleted company. As the brr-brr of German machine guns drew closer, Heaven agreed to start continuous firing, but finally had to turn to the Gurkha colonel, saying he could do no more to hold off the enemy.

"At that moment we heard whoops and cries and shouts of joy," Heaven recalled, "and up the hill came these two Gurkha companies with their kukris out. I have never seen such alarm and dismay in the German faces before or since, and there were very few of them left alive." As a tiny Gurkha ran towards him, waving a kukri streaming with blood, the colonel said: "Don't worry, Richard, he is just telling you he has killed three German soldiers. He has been bloodied, it is the first time he has done it, and he is going to carve three notches on his kukri. And what a splendid warrior he is."

According to his citation, Heaven "performed services with his battery in intimate support of infantry of the very highest order. He has himself been constantly under shellfire at observation posts and in forward positions; and has continued to direct the work of his observation posts and his guns to the best possible effect."

Richard John Gyde Heaven was born on July 9 1919 in Bristol, the son of a solicitor whose family had owned Lundy Island from 1836 to 1917. After his father's early death he was educated at Clifton, where he captained the 1st XV and played in the 1st XI cricket team. He was also a Senior Rover Scout, and remembered having tea with Lord Baden-Powell in 1937, on the 25th anniversary of the founding of the school's troop.

Heaven then captained the 1st XI and excelled at boxing and rugby at Woolwich before being commissioned into the Royal Artillery. He was on a course at Larkhill, where the declaration of war was greeted by cheers in the mess. Following a posting to 456 Light Battery for training in Scotland, he landed at Algiers as part of 78th Division of the First Army in November 1942, and was in action a week later supporting the Royal West Kents and the Argyll and Sutherland Highlanders.

When the Germans mounted a strong attack on Sedjenane the following March, Heaven's battery supported 2nd/5th Sherwood Foresters until the guns ran out of ammunition and the order was given by the battery commander to "spike guns" so they could not be of use to the enemy. Five days later he was promoted major and took command of his battery.

After eight months' battle experience in Tunisia he landed on the southern tip of Sicily, where he had a successful rendezvous in front of a lighthouse. After three sleepless nights, however, he overslept and missed an appointment with his superior, who told him: "My dear Heaven, you can't go to sleep in the middle of a battle."

After the war Heaven had several postings in East Africa, was on the staff at Sandhurst and served in Germany for six years before retiring from Larkhill in 1971. He then started a successful trout farming enterprise with his three sons and son-in-law. Richard Heaven married, in 1942, Peggy Loring, who survived him with their five children

CAPTAIN BILL BELLAMY

Captain Bill Bellamy (who died on March 18 2009, aged 85) was the author of a classic account of a naïve young tank commander's introduction to campaigning in north-west Europe.

Landing with 8th Royal Irish Hussars on June 8 1944 aged 20 and unsure whether he should be wearing a tin helmet, he tried to halt his echelon of fifteen vehicles, only to be told by an angry beach marshal: "Not on my beach, sonny." When he sped off to report the regiment's arrival, Major General George Erskine replied: "God, man, I don't want any more bloody tanks. Give me 131 Brigade" (the divisional infantry which had not yet landed).

Leading his fuel and ammunition lorries around the uncertain front line near Bayeux during the next few days, Bellamy was forced to take his vehicles into a ditch to make way for 131 Brigade, but earned unexpected praise for finding the regiment's new headquarters. On getting up from cover after some intensive shelling, he found himself next to the colonel, who said: "Ah, John. You're here. Well done" – a flattering compliment, even if the name was wrong.

The day Bellamy took charge of his own troop of three Cromwell tanks, he impressed his men by extricating the dead and wounded from two armoured cars which had been hit. Sick with the stench of death he accepted a sympathetically proffered tea.

When his colonel approached on foot, he saluted, but then launched into a tirade about those who thoughtlessly walk through fields to disclose their men's whereabouts. He was quietly silenced with a terse "That's enough". But the colonel never forgot to call him Bill again.

On October 22 Bellamy earned an immediate MC at the village of Doornhoek in southern Holland while advancing as part of a screen for infantry. His book, *Troop Leader* (2005), recounts how he led his men through trees to find the enemy firing from three cottages so that machine-gun bullets pinged on his tank and sprayed his face with particles of molten lead. A jerry can of petrol was spilt. His bedding caught fire. He narrowly avoided running his tank over a Teller mine.

Bellamy's citation explains that for 3 hours until the infantry arrived, he stood up in his turret, attracting heavy small arms, mortar and artillery fire as he manoeuvred to avoid enemy bazookas while directing his tanks: "On three separate occasions he went forward beyond his position and overran infantry posts." The citation does not mention the two bullet holes he found in his beret afterwards.

By now Bellamy was becoming 'bomb happy' – overkeen to face danger. He was sent home for the funeral of his mother, who had been killed by a V-2, then sombrely rejoined his men in the devastation of defeated Berlin.

The son of a salesman and a dressmaker who had separated, Lionel Gale Bellamy was born on December 1 1923 and educated at Blackfriars School, Laxton, near Kettering, where he attended

Mass at 6 am every day before taking a four-mile run. He became head prefect and captain of rugby.

On being called up he announced on arriving at Bovington Camp, Dorset, that his name was Bill. He was sent to North Africa, where he contracted dysentery before returning home for the Normandy invasion.

After the war Bellamy made a pilgrimage to Lisieux, the home of St Teresa, which he had watched being shelled, to give thanks for his deliverance. He spent four years in Germany then returned to England, and was preparing to leave for Korea when he contracted jaundice.

Coming out in 1955 he joined a shoe components firm, rising to managing director until retiring in 1983. He then became a parish councillor at Great Brington, Northamptonshire, and took a close interest, as a Knight of the Holy Sepulchre, in the Christian Arabs of Palestine. Bill Bellamy married, in 1950, Ann Burbury, with whom he had four sons and a daughter; after her death in 2001, he married Felicity Sidders.

LIEUTENANT COLONEL BILL BECKE

Lieutenant Colonel Bill Becke (who died on April 3 2009, aged 92) earned an immediate DSO in the assault on the Gothic Line in Italy, and nineteen years later was appointed CMG after facing down a raging mob in Jakarta.

As an acting major with the Sherwood Foresters

on the night of September 5/6 1944, Becke led his company through the cemetery to a church in San Savino, Tuscany, under considerable enemy fire, and entered the main door to be wounded in the head by a grenade thrown from inside.

After withdrawing to reload his tommy-gun, he returned to account for at least four of the enemy while receiving further wounds in the shoulder and arm. Then, backing out again, he went to the aid of a section under fire in some houses behind the building, and was wounded in the leg as he silenced an enemy machine gun.

Becke next fired his gun through the window at the back of the church to provide covering fire for a further assault on the main door, in which one of his section commanders was killed. Finally collapsing, he continued to give orders for the capture and evacuation of the enemy prisoners, who included a battalion commander and some fifty men, before handing over to his second-in-command.

On September 16 1963, Becke demonstrated archetypal British pluck when, monocled and with moustache bristling, he defied a mob trying to sack the British embassy in Jakarta while his deputy as military attaché, Major 'Rory' Walker, marched up and down playing the bagpipes.

Exasperated by the British decision to bring Sarawak and North Borneo into the new Malaysian federation, the rioters, with banners declaring "Smash Malaysia" and "Smite the British imperialists", hurled stones at the two attachés in front of the building. The mob could not force their way inside, but tore down the Union flag (which Becke had restored to the flagpole) and burned the ambassador's car.

The unflinching conduct of the two soldiers was complemented by the calmness of the ambassador, Andrew Gilchrist. After meeting representatives of the mob, he airily remarked that it was a pity the Indonesians did not play cricket as some had demonstrated "their ability to handle stones with great credit".

Two days later the mob announced its return by hurling stones through the already broken windows, then tore down the wire fence and set the building on fire. Most of the embassy staff by then were elsewhere, but Becke and Walker forced their way through to join the ambassador in taking a stand on British sovereign territory to prevent the strong room being forced open. Becke then supervised the evacuation of some 3,000 Britons. He and his wife had lost everything (except their dog's rubber ball) when their house was burned down; even his monocle was smashed.

Rigby, the Australian cartoonist who was later to work for *The Sun* in England, was impressed. He drew a picture of the musical defence of the embassy, following it with another showing two replacement monocles being brought in the diplomatic bag to the embassy by a bowler-hatted Foreign Office official. In the New Year's honours list that followed Becke was appointed CMG and Gilchrist KCMG for a display of confidence that was to become increasingly rare in British public life.

William Hugh Adamson Becke was born in Worcestershire on September 24 1916, the son of Brigadier General John Becke, CMG, DSO, AFC, a Free Forester who became a Royal Flying Corps officer. Bill was brought up at Edzell, Angus, and sent to Charterhouse and then Sandhurst before being commissioned into the Sherwood Foresters in 1937.

Having lost the ring and little fingers of his right hand in a motorcycle accident as a boy, he was the cause of some confusion when he saluted a general with a similar injury who shouted "snap" in recognition. Despite his injuries, Becke continued to play high grade hockey until the age of 40.

After serving in Palestine until the outbreak of war he was signals officer of 1st Battalion in Cyprus and Egypt and at Tobruk until shortly before it fell. He commanded a company of 11th Battalion in Iraq, Syria and Algeria then landed in the bitter fighting for the Anzio beachhead.

After marrying in 1945 Mary Richmond, an Australian who had been nursing in Scotland, Becke was assistant adjutant-general to the British military mission in Athens, where the Greeks were puzzled as his brother-in-law, married to Mary's identical twin, had preceded him in the post. It was a source of confusion for strangers who met them in years to come.

From 1957 to 1959, Becke was assistant military adviser to the British High Commission in Karachi, later keeping in touch with their bearer, Abdul Shakoor, who wrote touching letters of gratitude and received in return a collection of Becke's extenuated squiggles that would have made any doctor proud.

In 1974 Becke and his wife drove most of the way from Scotland to Australia, where he became private secretary and comptroller to the last British Governor of Victoria, Major General Sir Rohan

Delacombe, and demonstrated a fascination with procedure and a notable attention to detail during the Queen's visit in 1981.

After retiring from the post he became personnel officer for the Victorian Gas and Fuel Corporation but continued as an honorary ADC. For twenty-two years he was senior marshal for Melbourne's Anzac parade. In later years he exchanged his monocle for spectacles. He was survived by his wife.

MAJOR DICK NORMAND

Major Dick Normand (who died on April 29 2009, aged 97) was awarded an MC during the last month of the Second World War, and achieved celebrity in old age by playing competitive golf into his nineties. His first offensive action came in early January 1945 when, as a member of 5th/9th Royal Scots, he was ordered to mount a night attack near Heinsberg, in Germany. Fifty yards from buildings manned by enemy soldiers he found himself in a minefield, where nineteen of his men were injured and two officers killed.

His company later emerged unscathed from a bloody attack on the town of Heinsberg. But as the Germans were pushed back, it came under constant fire from snipers, machine-gunners and 'moaning minnie' mortars. When Normand established a company headquarters his wireless operator, batman and the gunner officer co-ordinating artillery fire were wounded. A second-in-command who joined him was soon shot through the head beside him.

On the night of April 17/18 1945, Normand was given the task of leading his men around the left flank of the town of Soltau in Lower Saxony. There was no time for reconnaissance. The company advanced through the streets under sniper and anti-tank fire. But, according to the citation for his MC: "With complete disregard for his own safety Major Normand moved from platoon to platoon organising his advance. Whenever enemy resistance was met he was always on the spot directing operations." The citation directly credited him with the capture of "a total of ten officers and 228 enemy other ranks". In the midst of the excitement Normand stopped to loot a shop, picking out some underwear for his wife, which he stuffed down the front of his battledress before continuing the battle.

Richard John Normand was born on January 28 1912 in Johannesburg, the son of a Scots emigrant who took part in the Jameson Raid and became governor of the Transvaal prison service. After going to a local prep school Dick was sent to Fettes and then Edinburgh University, where he read Law. He became a Writer to the Signet with the firm Shepherd and Wedderburn, enjoyed tennis, squash, shooting and fishing, and was commissioned as a territorial in the Royal Scots in 1935.

After arriving in France as part of his battalion's advance party in June 1940, he was reprimanded for wearing a kilt and Tam O'Shanter instead of battledress and a tin hat. When the battalion arrived as part of a vain hope of creating a last line of defence behind the Seine, he accompanied it in a fifty-mile advance towards Paris and then in its rapid retreat back to Cherbourg.

After meeting his future wife, Audrey Green, a Waaf, while guarding a Norfolk airfield, Normand was posted to West Africa, where he was given responsibility for censorship before returning home to his regiment in Britain. By the time he embarked for France after D-Day he had been trained for mountain warfare, seaborne landings and air-portable landings. At the end of the war he returned to the Law, working as a family solicitor with Cowan and Dalmahoy and then Lindsays.

In his later years Dick Normand devotedly nursed his wife, with whom he had three daughters, until her death in 2000, and remained a fiercely competitive golfer. He went round the Royal and Ancient course at St Andrews in 86 while carrying his own clubs, aged 90, and continued to play to a handicap of 21 at Muirfield, where he registered the largest recorded number of club matches and a hole-in-one at all four of the course's par-three holes.

MAJOR MARTIN CLEMENS

Major Martin Clemens (who died on May 31 2009, aged 94) was the district commissioner responsible for supplying American 1st Marine Division with intelligence as they dislodged a 30,000-strong Japanese force from Guadalcanal Island in the Pacific.

Aided by some 300 islanders, policemen and planters, he established a hideout on Mount Austen. It was not as high up as he would have liked, and mist affected his transmitter. Nevertheless he and his men had a good view of both Tulagi, the Solomon Islands' capital twenty-five miles across the straits, and the airfield, which the Japanese were frantically trying to build beneath them.

General Archer Vandegrift's marines landed on August 7 1942, capturing Guadalcanal and renaming it Henderson Field. A week later, Clemens came down to meet them. Although cutting an unprepossessing figure – gaunt, bearded, dressed in rags and wearing a specially donned pair of tight winklepickers – he formed his scouts into two ranks and marched them with rifles at the slope as they carried the Union flag towards the astonished American sentries. He was appointed British liaison officer to US XIV Corps.

As commander of the Solomon Islands Defence Force, Clemens never wore uniform but his unit proved invaluable to the Americans who lacked combat experience and kept becoming lost. They detected an enemy attack being launched along the Tenaru river which was duly annihilated, and accompanied Colonel Merrit Edson's men in the heaviest fighting of the campaign on what is known as 'Bloody Ridge'. Clemens's gallantry was recognised by an MC and the American Legion of Merit.

The son of an organist of Moravian missionary stock, Warren Frederick Martin Clemens was born in Aberdeen on April 17 1915. He won a scholarship to Bedford School and then to Christ's College, Cambridge, where he read Agriculture and Natural Sciences and had the novelist C. P. Snow as his tutor.

Clemens was one of the notorious 'night-climbers of Cambridge', whose feats included capping the pinnacles of King's College Chapel with chamber pots and hauling an Austin 7 above the Senate House. Although he narrowly missed a rowing Blue, he was a reserve for the winning Eight at the Empire Games in 1938, the year he joined the Solomon Islands Protectorate Service.

When war was declared the following year his reserved occupation meant that he was refused permission to join the Army. But as a member of the Coast Watching network set up by the Australians after the First World War, he was ordered to move missionaries, planters and native inhabitants to Guadalcanal. Since it was clear that the Japanese were coming, he paid off the staff in his government station at Aola with several months' advance salary.

Then, exuding characteristic self-confidence, he sat down in a circle of sympathetic tribesmen, who feared that he was going to leave until he assured them in pidgin that he would remain and that their only hope of deliverance was to stick together. Encouraged by his promise and happy at the thought of returning to their traditional occupations, such as headhunting, they set about gathering information, working mostly at night and keeping him constantly on the move to avoid Japanese patrols.

One of his major problems was food. He persuaded his scouts to bring a large crate containing tins of assorted meats, and on the first night was delighted to find one with his favourite scallops, which went well with wild yams. But it soon became clear that the crate contained nothing else, with the result that he ate scallops fried, smoked, boiled, curried and cold until he could not face another. There was one welcome present of a duck. By the time he came down from the mountain he had lost four stone.

Clemens remained district commissioner in the western Solomons until the end of the war, then was sent to Samaria and Gaza during the British withdrawal from Palestine, where he learned to speak Arabic in a month. After being transferred to Cyprus as district commissioner in Nicosia, he arranged with Sir Hugh Foot, the governor, to demonstrate their confidence by walking the length of Nicosia's Ledra Street – the 'death mile' where British forces were murdered periodically by sharpshooters; he considered the experience more hazardous than his Guadalcanal exploits.

After being promoted to the islands' defence secretary, Clemens was offered a post in Sarawak. But his wife, Anne, had been left a house in Australia. So he resigned and emigrated to Melbourne, where he became pastoral superintendent of her family's grazing property in Queensland. Highly gregarious, he was president of the Australia-Britain Society, initiating the Plain English Speaking Award, and continued to visit Henley as a member of the Leander Club.

But he never forgot his beloved 'fuzzy wuzzies', particularly Sergeant Major George Vouza, who was tied to a tree and repeatedly bayoneted and left to die before crawling back to the American lines. Clemens successfully recommended him for a George Medal and, in 1979, a knighthood; he then raised money for a statue.

His memoir, *Alone on Guadacanal*, containing

excerpts from his diary with some sharp judgments on the Americans, was published in 1998, some forty years after he had written it. Five years later he was shown in a video game, *Medal of Honour, Rising Sun*, erroneously speaking with a Scottish accent.

Martin Clemens was appointed OBE in 1956, CBE in 1960 and OAM in 1993. His wife died several months before him, and he was survived by their three daughters and a son. At his funeral the congregation sang *Onward Christian Soldiers*, just as his men had done while they removed the bodies of seventeen marines and 450 Japanese killed on Bloody Ridge.

PRIVATE TED KENNA, VC

Private Ted Kenna (who died on July 8 2009, aged 90) won the Victoria Cross on May 15 1945 while serving with 2nd/4th Australian Infantry Battalion in New Guinea. He was the last surviving Australian recipient of the VC in the Second World War.

Japanese troops had established a defensive line in rugged terrain south of Wewak, and were shelling the Australians from the missionary station at Wirui. After a sharp battle on May 14, 2nd/4th had captured all but the north-western spur. The only position from which supporting fire could be obtained was continuously swept by heavy machine-gun fire, making it impossible to bring artillery or mortars into action.

On May 15, Kenna's platoon was ordered forward

to deal with three enemy machine-gun posts. He moved his support section as close as possible to the bunkers in order to provide covering fire for a flank attack by the rest of the platoon. Two sections of the platoon attacked, but as soon as the enemy spotted them they were pinned down with heavy automatic fire from a position which had not previously revealed itself.

With several of the men already wounded, Kenna endeavoured to bring his Bren gun to bear on one of the bunkers but was unable to bring down effective fire because of the difficult ground. On his own initiative and without orders, he stood up in full view of the enemy less than fifty yards away and engaged the bunker, firing from the hip.

As fire was returned bullets passed between his arms and around his body but somehow missed him. Undeterred, he continued shooting until his ammunition was exhausted. He then discarded his Bren gun, called for a rifle and despite intense machine-gun fire killed the enemy gunner with his first round. When a machine gun opened up on him from a second position, Kenna, who had remained standing, killed this gunner with his next round. The bunker was captured without further loss, the company attack went forward and the enemy position was carried.

The citation declared: "There is no doubt that the success of the company attack would have been seriously endangered and many casualties sustained but for Private Kenna's magnificent courage and complete disregard for his own safety." Kenna was invested with the Victoria Cross in Melbourne by the Governor-General of Australia, the Duke of Gloucester, on January 6 1947.

Edward Kenna, always known as Ted, was born on July 6 1919 at Hamilton, Victoria, the fourth child of a family of seven. He went to St Mary's Convent, Hamilton, but left at 14 and worked as a plumber to look after his mother when his father fell ill. He was an accomplished sportsman and a keen cyclist.

Kenna served in the Citizen Military Forces before enlisting in the Australian Imperial Forces in 1940. He was initially in 23rd/21st Battalion but was posted to 2nd/4th in 1943. In October 1944 he embarked from Cairns with his unit bound for New Guinea.

In June 1945, three weeks after the attack on the Wirui Mission feature, Kenna was taking part in a similar operation when he was hit in the mouth by an explosive bullet and evacuated. When told he was likely to die he simply exclaimed: "Pigs". He recovered, and in December 1946 was discharged.

Kenna returned to work in Hamilton at the borough hall and then as curator of the Melville Oval. He was presented to the Queen when she visited the newly-restored Hall of Memory at the Australian War Memorial in Canberra in March 2000, and appeared on a postage stamp in the same year. Kenna's portrait by Sir William Dargie hangs in the borough hall. Ted Kenna married, in 1947, Marje Rushberry, who nursed him in hospital. They had two sons and two daughters, one of whom predeceased him.

PRIVATE HARRY PATCH

Private Harry Patch (who died on July 25 2009, aged 111) is considered the last surviving British soldier to have gone into action on the Western Front, an experience about which he retained bitter memories.

When the television documentary makers started to interview the small corps of centenarian veterans at the end of the 20th century they found that several retained vivid memories of the trenches. But Patch was the one who burned with the strongest indignation – at the constant danger, the noise, the rats, the lice and the biscuits that were too hard to eat at Passchendaele.

He remembered the fear and bewilderment of going 'over the top', crawling because walking meant the certainty of being mowed down by the German machine guns. As his battalion advanced from Pilckem Ridge, near Ypres, in the summer rain of 1917 the mud was crusted with blood and the wounded were crying out for help. "But we weren't like the Good Samaritan in the Bible, we were the robbers who passed them by and left," said Patch.

As his unit came across a member of the regiment lying in a pool of blood, ripped open from shoulder to waist, the man said: "Shoot me". But before anyone could fire, the man died with the word "Mother" on his lips. "It was a cry of surprise and joy," recalled Patch, "and I'll always remember that death is not the end."

When they reached the enemy's second line three

enemy stood up, and one ran forward pointing his bayonet. Patch shot him in the shoulder. The man kept on coming. With only three rounds left in his revolver, Patch wondered what to do. Then with "Mother" ringing in his ears, he deliberately fired at him below the ankle and above the knee.

At 10.30 pm on September 22 Patch's five-man Lewis gun team was crossing open ground single file on the way back to the support line when a shell exploded, blowing the three carrying the ammunition to pieces. Patch was hit in the groin, and thrown to the ground. Waking in a dressing station he realised that, although very painful, his wound was little more than a scratch.

The following evening a doctor explained that he could remove a two-inch piece of shrapnel with a jagged edge, but there was no anaesthetic available. After thinking over the prospects Patch agreed to have the sliver removed, and had to be held down by four men as it was extracted with tweezers. The operation took 2 minutes, during which he could have killed the doctor.

The son of a master stonemason, Henry John Patch was born at Combe Down, near Bath, on June 17, 1898, and educated at the local Church of England school. On leaving at 15 he was apprenticed to a plumber. One of his brothers, a sergeant-major in the Royal Engineers, had been wounded at Mons, so young Harry knew enough to have no wish to go when called up at 18.

Sent for six months to 33rd Training Battalion near Warminster, Wiltshire, he learned to lock up his kit after his boots were stolen, and earned his crossed guns badge for marksmanship, which came with an extra 6d a day.

On landing in France in June 1917, Patch became a Lewis machine-gunner with C Company of 7th Battalion Duke of Cornwall's Light Infantry at Rouen, and he was in the trenches on his 19th birthday. He did not go into action that day, but saw the Yorkshires and Lancashires climbing out of their dugouts to be mowed down before reaching the German line.

While watching through his firing aperture two dogs scrapping for a biscuit, he found himself wondering why he was fighting for "19d a flipping day". Nevertheless there were some compensations, such as the comradeship and learning to smoke with his pipe upside down so that there was no glow at night, or by getting under a groundsheet to ensure no smoke showed by day.

He would receive occasional parcels from home, though one containing a slice of his brother's wedding cake and an ounce of tobacco had become so jumbled that it had to be thrown away. There was also the respite offered by Talbot House behind Ypres, where there was a sign "Abandon all rank ye who enter here" and the Reverend 'Tubby' Clayton offered games and led the singing.

After being evacuated to England, Patch was sent to a series of hospitals; he met Ada Billington, his future wife, when he knocked her over while running past a cinema at Sutton Coldfield. By the time he was fully fit again, the Armistice had been declared, and he only wanted to forget.

He never watched a war film, or talked about his

experiences, even to his wife, with whom he had two sons. Instead he concentrated on returning to plumbing. He did not go back to his old firm because the foreman insisted that he must complete the final two years of his apprenticeship, though a lawyer told him that the contract had been broken when the firm failed to release him from his indentures in 1918.

After flirting with the idea of joining the police, Patch spurned an offer of his old job back at a full rate and worked on a housing scheme at Gobowen, Shropshire, before being invited to work on the Wills Memorial Tower being built at Bristol University.

With financial help from his boss, he passed the exam to become a member of the Institute of Sanitary Engineers and was made manager of his company's branch in Bristol, to which he cycled twelve miles each day from his home during the General Strike. After ten years he bought his first car, an Austin Seven, and set up his own business.

At 41 Patch was too old to be called up for the Second World War, but he joined the Auxiliary Fire Service in Bath, and was trained to use a Vickers machine gun if the Germans arrived. Called out to deal with the results of the 'Baedeker raids' he found himself fighting fires all night, not only in Bath but also in Bristol and Weston-Super-Mare. The pumps ran out of water because the drains were fractured, and he remembered diving under his fire engine as it was sprayed with bullets from a low-flying plane.

When three of his plumbers were called up, he sold his business and moved to Street, in south Somerset, after seeing an advert for a sanitary engineer to service military camps. He bought a partnership, and found that the job meant that he knew about all troop movements, except the launch of the Normandy invasion. Returning to camp one morning he found plenty of food and the fires still burning. The Americans had left behind large amounts of equipment which, after finding no-one prepared to take it, he sold.

Starting up again after the war, he had ten plumbers and eighteen fitters when he reached 65, but was adamant that he was going to work no more. He and his wife enjoyed ten years of retirement before she died, and a few years later he married Jean with whom he was asked to visit the Normandy battlefield by a friend who had two seats going in his coach. He was driven to tears on Omaha Beach, thinking of the Americans he had known, and had no desire to go again.

But at 92 he was asked to don a hard hat and dungarees to guide geologists from Bath University underneath Combe Down, where the disused quarries had been causing increasing concern about safety. He had not been down for seventy years, but was able to lead the way to one, which had been completely forgotten by the local council.

It was after the death of his second wife and his admission to an old people's home, aged 100, that the light outside his room prompted, as he lay in bed, a recurring nightmare about the flash of the bomb that hit his unit.

By now there were television crews eager for interviews. While agreeing to appear in Richard van Emden's *The Trench*, in which veterans talked about their experiences and a group of today's young men relived their hardships, he still voiced doubts to the camera: "You can make the programme, you can imitate a shell burst by a thunderclap firework ... you can improvise everything, except the fear."

Roundly declaring that anybody who claimed not have been afraid at the front was a liar (pronounced in his defiant West Country burr), he expressed thanks that he had never killed a man. No war was worth the loss of a couple of lives, let alone thousands, for what was nothing but 'a family row', he said, though he admitted he would have shot the Kaiser and Hitler to save millions.

As one programme followed another Patch became a new phenomenon of the age, a centenarian celebrity. He had a cider, Patch's Pride, named after him, and was awarded an honorary degree by Bristol University, where he had worked on the Wills memorial eighty years earlier. He also received the Legion of Honour from the French government and was induced to meet an Alsatian who had fought on the German side at Passchendaele. He found him "a very nice gentleman"; they exchanged gifts of a bottle of cider and Alsatian biscuits then attended the Last Post ceremony at the Menin Gate. He found in the old people's home a girlfriend in her eighties but the thought of the fuss the press would make put him off marrying again.

It was the loss of his three friends on the night of September 22 almost ninety years ago that haunted him. "Those chaps are always with me. I can see that damned explosion now," he would say.

LIEUTENANT COLONEL MAUREEN GARA

Lieutenant Colonel Maureen Gara (who died on October 19 2009, aged 93) had an exacting and adventurous career in wartime field hospitals and afterwards was a distinguished military nurse. As a nursing officer with 79th General Hospital she and her colleagues were cheered in towns and villages as they were driven to Southampton on June 14 1944 to help set up a large field hospital at Bayeux in Normandy.

After a sleepless night on a troopship, she clambered down a scramble net into a landing craft, only to find that rough seas prevented the vessel from reaching shore for four hours. She spent her first night on land in a trench with a 24-hour ration pack for sustenance as battle raged outside Caen and the ground shook beneath her.

At 10 am the following day, she was taken by lorry to the site for the hospital, which was already buzzing with troops – Pioneers, Reme, Sappers and Royal Army Service Corps. The marquees were up, generators were humming, boiling water was bubbling in huge cauldrons; kitchens had been assembled and trenches dug. Crates were unpacked and an enormous Red Cross laid out. By 4 pm, the first casualties were arriving. Four hundred came in that night.

Mary Anne Gara, known as Maureen or Mo, was the eldest of seven children in a family of subsistence farmers. She was born in rural Ireland, near Carrick, Co Donegal, on January 18 1916. Her mother died suddenly and Maureen's aunt took over care of the family, leaving the girl free to pursue her ambition to become a nurse.

Gara went to a convent school and won a scholarship which enabled her to continue studying beyond the age of 14. After qualifying at a training school in Manchester, she volunteered to join the reserve of Queen Alexandra's Imperial Military Nursing Service (QAIMNS) and, in December 1943, was sent to 79th General Hospital at Watford.

It was a mobilisation unit housed in the dreary, dark buildings of a St Agatha's orphanage. She was met by a woman in full battledress, boots and gaiters who trained the nurses in military medical procedures, tentage and drill. The first task was to make up 600 bed rolls in readiness for deploying as a field hospital at the front.

In April 1944, Gara moved to Peebles Hydro, Scotland, where she trained in chemical warfare and mountaineering. In May, the hospital moved to East Anglia with a large concentration of troops ready for D-Day. In her spare time, she and other nurses were sent out on to the lawns to sew a huge red cross made out of hessian.

The surgeons in the hospital in Normandy, she said afterwards, were the best that Britain could provide. Casualties had to be kept moving so trestle tables were always available. There was an airstrip nearby and an efficient evacuation system was organised.

Penicillin was regarded as the new miracle drug but in emergencies there was no time to test patients for allergic reactions. On one occasion, a soldier that she was treating had a violent reaction to the drug and reached for a scalpel to kill himself. Only with great difficulty did she prevent him doing so.

The alarm was raised one night when movement was spotted in bushes near the sleeping quarters. The hunt for a German prowler was called off when the culprit, a stray cow, poked its head into Gara's tent.

While in Normandy, she used to watch the Luftwaffe bombers flying overhead on bombing raids. They deliberately avoided bombing the hospital area, and one particular aircraft with distinctive markings always dipped its wing as it passed over. Some years later, at an event in Germany, Gara mentioned this. One of the pilots present said: "Madam, that was my plane."

In September, she moved with the hospital to Holland for the battles of Arnhem and the Rhine crossing. On the way, she stopped in Brussels for her first proper bath since leaving England.

After the war, she joined the Regular QAIMNS, later designated the Queen Alexandra's Royal Army Nursing Corps (QARANC), and was posted to India. She subsequently served in the Middle East, in Singapore and at the Commonwealth Hospital at Terendak in Malaysia, where she was deputy matron.

In 1967, she was promoted lieutenant colonel and posted to the QARANC training centre as chief instructor. Two years later, she was awarded the Royal Red Cross for excellence in military nursing and moved to the Queen Alexandra Hospital, Millbank, as matron. She retired in 1971.

Settling in the Aldershot area, she became involved with the Normandy Veterans and Queen Alexandra Associations and served as a trustee and subsequently chairman of the latter for a total of eleven years. She never lost her love of her native Ireland and its traditional music – her father and two of her brothers played the fiddle. She also enjoyed travelling and went on several world cruises.

In 2004 a stamp of St Vincent and the Grenadines was printed with her picture to commemorate the 60th anniversary of D-Day. Maureen Gara never married.

COUNT RALPH SMORCZEWSKI

Count Ralph Smorczewski (who died on October 20 2009, aged 84) fought in the Warsaw Uprising with the Polish Resistance before joining the Eighth Army in Italy and then making his home in England.

By early 1943, Poland had been under German occupation for more than three years. Smorczewski, aged 18, contacted the Polish Resistance and was sworn into the ranks of the Armia Krajowa (AK), the Polish Home Army, and subsequently graduated from the Infantry Officers' School.

The following year he moved with his parents from their estate at Tarnogóra, south of Lublin, to a flat in Warsaw as units of the Red Army drew near. The city was run by two opposing factions: the SS and police, and a section of the Polish government in exile, based in London. German rule was ruthless; arrests and executions were part of everyday life. The Resistance forces retaliated, and assassinations of the most notorious agents of the SS and the German security service were ordered by courts meeting in secret, then carried out by squads from the AK.

In July 1944, as the Red Army approached Warsaw, the German civilian authorities began to leave their offices. At 5 pm on August 1, the centre of the city was enveloped in clouds of black smoke, followed by the rattle of machine-gun fire and hand grenade explosions.

Smorczewski was playing bridge. Horrified that the uprising had begun before he had been alerted and sent to his starting position, he threw down his cards and ran down the street towards the sounds of fighting. Meeting one AK unit comprising about twelve well-armed men, he was given a handgun and two grenades. Crouching under cover of a railway embankment, he moved eastward with the group.

A unit of German police approached with the intention of taking control of the railway line. As their heads appeared over the embankment, the AK unit opened fire with its machine gun. The Germans pulled back, leaving their dead or wounded on the railway line as the AK took up defensive positions in an allotment.

Smorczewski, who was nearest to the embankment, found himself pinned down by machine-gun fire and on the receiving end of German hand grenades which exploded near him, showering him with earth and potatoes.

One burst was so close to him that he was knocked out and wounded in the leg. When he recovered consciousness, he found that he was alone when dawn was breaking. He made his way to the Palace of Wilanów, a miniature Versailles occupied by the

Branicki family. To the German guards, he muttered an apology for "returning home so early in the morning" and went inside.

The building was in uproar. The Germans had discovered that a small hospital had been secretly prepared there in readiness for the uprising. The Branicki family was being subjected to a vicious cross-examination, and during the next few days Smorczewski watched, appalled, as groups of captured young Resistance fighters were brought in and executed in the park.

The Germans took over the makeshift hospital, and Smorczewski was recruited as the surgeon's assistant. They had to make do with a few bottles of ether and the most basic of tools, including a garden saw and an old cut-throat razor. One girl was brought in with an arm smashed above the elbow and, with the risk of gangrene setting in, he had to assist in an amputation. Next day, she asked where her ring was and he had the gruesome task of finding the severed arm and retrieving it.

Three weeks later, after a futile attack by the Resistance on the well-guarded palace, Smorczewski was interrogated by two German officers. He was carrying papers showing him to be a Hungarian, but his story was not believed and he was driven to the small town of Zyrardów, strip-searched by the SS and locked in a cellar.

He shared it with three others: a German deserter; a Pole who had been caught acting as a courier; and a teacher who was also a member of the Resistance. His companions knew that they would leave only to face an execution squad or receive a bullet in the back of the head.

The floor was concrete. He slept on bare boards. As the weather grew colder, the nights found him shivering in a lightweight suit as the sleet blew in through the small barred window. Between interrogations by SS officers he was allowed into the garden. There he usually encountered an SS corporal, a powerfully-built man who would point out heavily-bandaged prisoners with a wink and a smile and boast: "My work – yesterday".

Just after dawn on a wet and windy morning, two guards and an SS officer woke him and took him into a courtyard. He was placed with his back to a wall and told that he would remain there until he was ready to give them all the details of his involvement in the Resistance. The alternative was left to his imagination. After a short time, paralysed by cold, he slid to the ground, where he remained in a stupor until he found himself back in his cell being revived with black coffee.

Smorczewski probably survived because his captors failed to get any useful information from him and because he spoke fluent German. His eventual release, however, was due to the intervention of a Hungarian colonel, to whom Smorczewski's mother had appealed for help.

Count Ralph Stanislas Sergius Smorczewski was born at Lwów, Poland, on October 24 1924. The title was granted to his great-grandfather by Pope Leo XIII in 1892 in recognition of the considerable risks that he had run in protecting from Russian persecution the Greek Catholics (known as Uniates) on his estates.

Ralph and his brother, Mark, had idyllic childhoods on the family estates. After the outbreak of war, the railway line nearby became a target and the Germans billeted both houses, confiscated the family's firearms and put artillery pieces on the lawns.

In 1942 transports of Jews from Germany and Austria started to arrive in the area. There was not enough food and many of them were starving. Smorczewski's father applied for the maximum quota of Jewish workers, notionally to work in the fields but in fact to provide them with food and decent living conditions. In the autumn, however, they were all rounded up and packed into goods trains, bound for the camps. Those who resisted were shot.

The Germans closed all the schools, and Smorczewski completed his secondary education under military occupation at special courses organised by the Polish underground movement. The uprising ended with the surrender of the Resistance in October 1944 after two months of fierce fighting, in which more than 15,000 Resistance fighters had been killed; and more than 200,000 civilians had died of wounds, disease or starvation.

Smorczewski joined units of the AK in the forests near Czestochowa. As second-in-command of a troop, he was involved in sabotage, ambushes and the elimination of German SS units, police posts and collaborators. No quarter was given or expected.

One afternoon the whole company was in a small hamlet deep in the forest when a group of Ukrainians in German uniforms appeared. They belonged to the notorious Kaminski Brigade, which had perpetrated the worst atrocities of the uprising.

They frankly confessed as much, and said that they had had enough of the Germans and had deserted to join the Resistance.

Smorczewski and his comrades listened in silence and, after giving them a strong, home-made alcoholic brew, directed them to a shed at the edge of the village in which they could spend the night. Before dawn they were overpowered and soundlessly despatched.

In October, as the Germans threatened to encircle them, their position was spotted by a Fiesler Storch liaison aircraft, and Smorczewski took part in a four-day battle against SS and police near the village of Krzepin. A few weeks later his regiment was disbanded, and he and his family – now homeless refugees – moved to Kraków.

By mid-January 1945 spearheads of the Soviet forces were approaching the city, and Smorczewski and his family succeeded in getting passes which took them by train to Vienna, where they joined a convoy of refugees fleeing west. A German officer, unaware of their nationalities, acted as escort. Eventually the family reached Italy, and Smorczewski joined the Polish II Corps, part of the Eighth Army.

Posted to the 7th Horse Artillery Regiment, based near Macerata, he graduated from the Artillery Officers' School in June 1946 and, that autumn, arrived in England with other units of the Corps possessing little more than his uniform. Smorczewski studied at the Architectural Association from which he graduated to work at Stillman & Eastwick-Field until starting his own practice in 1972 and retiring twenty years later.

In 1965 Smorczewski joined the Polish Knights of

Malta Association, and supported SOS Poland, which helped the persecuted and needy. He cultivated rhododendrons at his Sussex home and hunted wild boar in Poland. In 1968 he married, the beautiful but handicapped, Isabel de la Vega Benjumea, and was grief-stricken by her death in 1997. He was survived by his son and daughter.

STAFF SERGEANT OLAF SCHMID, GC

Staff Sergeant Olaf Schmid (who died in Afghanistan on October 31 2009, aged 30) was killed defusing an improvised explosive device (IED) the day before he was to return home after an exhausting three-month tour.

IEDs represented one of the principal threats to coalition troops and national security forces in the Helmand valley, a land of flooded fields, irrigation ditches and sprawling compounds, where coalition soldiers could be drawn into a maze of footpaths, dirt tracks and alleyways planted with such devices.

None of the situations Schmid encountered was identical, with every device needing to be rigorously assessed. Some were so primitive that a loose wire could cause a short circuit; while the movement of animals, humans or vehicles could also cause the components to degrade.

Schmid added to these dangers by choosing never to wear an explosive ordnance disposal protection suit. He cited the sweltering heat and said that, tactically, it was a mistake to advertise himself unnecessarily as a high-value target. Working in these exacting conditions called for almost superhuman concentration and unwavering nerve.

Olaf Sean George Schmid, known as Oz, was born in Truro, Cornwall, on June 11 1979. His father was Swedish and his mother German. He went to Penair School and was head chorister at Truro Cathedral before joining the Royal Logistic Corps in 1996.

He spent nine years qualifying and working as an ammunition technician in Royal Logistic Corps regiments before completing the commando course. Then, for three years, he served at 3 Commando Brigade where he provided close ammunition technical support to the commando units.

In April 2008 he was selected for promotion to staff sergeant and posted to 11 Explosive Ordnance Disposal Regiment, Royal Logistic Corps (RLC). As an ammunition technician senior NCO at Alpha Troop, he provided IED disposal support to Special Forces and police tactical firearms teams. He had a natural aptitude for the work and, having passed the necessary course, was qualified to operate in Afghanistan.

On arriving in theatre in June 2009 he immediately participated in Operation Panther's Claw, one of the largest air operations of modern times, which was aimed at establishing a lasting coalition presence in one of the main Taliban strongholds.

At Babaji, in July, after heavy close-quarter fighting, the enemy pulled back, littering the valley floor with IEDs. Schmid and his team methodically cleared one compound after another. There was much apprehension, he admitted later though he was deeply aware of the importance of appearing calm.

In August he was involved in clearing a mile of dirt track lined by compounds with high mud walls known as Pharmacy Road. It led from Sangin district in the south of the country to a forward operating base. Several British soldiers had been killed there, and previous attempts to clear the road had failed.

Royal Engineer search teams, flanked by riflemen, moved up the road under cover of darkness. They found the wreck of a mechanical digger blocking the way with IEDs all around it. Two remote controlled vehicles were sent out. Both were blown up. Keenly aware of the expectation and anxiety of comrades and commanders, Schmid approached on foot.

He cleared a route to the digger, which was then hauled away, and within 24 hours, found thirty-one devices on another route. In addition, Schmid also had to assemble the forensic evidence needed to trace the insurgents who manufacture and plant the devices. Evidence during his tour led to the arrest of a number of bomb factory operators and smugglers. During this period, he rendered safe sixty-four devices and made eleven finds of bomb-making equipment.

Men who served with him said that with his tousled hair and engaging grin he radiated confidence, and was ready to make fun of himself; but while a complete professional the pressure showed.

He was working with an advanced search team on routine bomb clearance near a forward operating base when the device he was defusing exploded. He died instantly. Praising his courage his commanding officer said he stood taller than the tallest under the relentless IED and small arms attacks. Olaf Schmid was survived by his wife, Christina, and stepson Laird, aged six.

BRIGADIER THE REVEREND DAVID WHITEFORD

Brigadier the Reverend David Whiteford (who died on February 21 2010, aged 91) was chaplain to the Black Watch and then the Scots Guards during the gruelling north-west Europe campaign of 1944-45.

After landing at Arromanches, Whiteford realised the resolution of the German resistance when, in a field hospital, he was confronted by a young SS officer who, with blazing eyes, pulled out the tubes for his blood transfusion because nobody could assure him that it did not contain non-Aryan blood.

Posted to 5th Black Watch at Caen, Whiteford was introduced to the officers at the battalion HQ then directed to sleep at an aid post but there was no room. Next morning he learned that many of those he had just met there had been killed by an enemy shell. Surveying the carnage, the pipe major told him: "This is nae job for young pipers, padre. You and I will just have to do this ourselves."

After the dead had been buried with prayers, Whiteford saw the battalion liberate a German wine store and locals shave the heads of women collaborators, who were then tarred and feathered. On transfer to 2nd Scots Guards just before the

Rhine crossing, he came under such fierce fire during the attempt to reach Arnhem that roadside funerals had to be carried out at night; and he sometimes had to take cover by jumping into the grave while conducting a service.

Later he was shaken by the starving faces staring through the wire as the battalion passed Belsen, as incoming enemy fire rained down from just two fields away. Whiteford's war ended at the high kirk of Stade ("a county town not unlike Haddington"), where he preached at the thanksgiving service.

David Hutchison Whiteford was born at Lockerbie on December 16 1918, a son of the manse and the brother and nephew of Church of Scotland ministers. He went to George Watson's College, Edinburgh, where he was a second-row forward in the First XV for two years, and then Edinburgh University. He interrupted his Divinity studies to volunteer as aircrew with the RAF; when this scheme was cancelled he joined the Army as a licensed minister.

Whiteford was first posted to the 1st Searchlight Regiment, RA, in Kent, and shortly before D-Day married Mary Simpson. On Sunday June 18 1944, the young couple set off for the Guards Chapel near Buckingham Palace, but their train was delayed. They missed the V-1 bomb attack which killed 121 people attending the service there.

Staying on in the Scots Guards after the war, Whiteford saw three years' service in the Malayan emergency, which convinced him that insurgencies could be defeated by the right methods. He was then sent by the Foreign Office on a three-month speaking

Above: Penny Phillips.
Right: Brigadier Paul Edwin Crook CBE, DSO, MA, USA Bronze Star.
Below: Denny Whitaker organised a game of US football at White City, London in February 1944; with the Canadian Mustangs beating the US Pirates 16-6. Here, captains Frank Dombrowski (left) of the United States and W. Drinkwater of Canada shake hands.

Opposite top left: Dick Annand.
Opposite top right: Tony Hunter-Choat.
Opposite bottom: David Smiley. (Taken from the book *Arabian Assignment* by David Smiley)
Above: David Rose (right) of 1BW in Korea, with General Collins, US Army Chief of Staff at The Hook. (Museum of the Black Watch)
Below: Henry 'Tod' Sweeney being presented with the Military Cross by Field Marshal Montgomery for rescuing a member of his platoon while under heavy fire on June 7.

Left: Amedeo Guillet in full dress uniform of the Guards cavalry, 1935.

Below: Cartoon by Australian cartoonist Paul Rigby depicting the riots at the British embassy in Jakarta, 1963. Lieutenant Colonel Bill Becke and his military attaché Rory Walker defied protesters whilst playing the bagpipes. (Peter Rigby – Rigby Transmedia)

Opposite top: Amedeo Guillet with the Spahys di Libya during the Italian invasion of Ethiopia 1936.

Opposite below left: David Garforth-Bles.

Opposite below right: Sir Michael Gow. (Crown Copyright (OGL))

Opposite top left: John Pine-Coffin.
Opposite top right: Michael Ross with his wife Giovanna, who was the daughter of his protector whilst in Bordighera.
Opposite bottom left: Maureen Gara.
Opposite bottom right: Hugh Pond.
Above: Jumbo Hoare.
Top right: Bruce Shand with Rosalind Cubitt on their wedding day, January 2 1946.
Right: Dare Wilson.

Top left: Henry Metelmann.
Top right: Jim Fraser on a visit to Libya in 2006.
Right: Martin Clemens with his beloved 'fuzzy wuzzies'.
Below: Bill Millin playing the pipes at Dawlish Warren, near his home in Devon.
(*Les Wilson*)

tour of America, talking to military establishments, universities and church groups.

Back at Sandhurst he was schooled by Grenadier drill sergeants to take part, as the only Church of Scotland minister, in the 1953 Coronation parade; the torrential rain during a thirteen-mile march reduced the chaplains in their ceremonial sashes and white gloves to "a row of drowned crows", he recalled.

In the following years Whiteford was in the chaplains' department at Bagshot Park, then posted to Berlin. By now the training drills, which included jumping off landing craft into the Clyde, were losing their appeal. He had begun a PhD on the reactions to Jacobitism in 18th century Scottish ecclesiastical life when he was unexpectedly promoted Deputy Chaplain General and appointed honorary chaplain to the Queen.

On coming out of the Army with a CBE in 1972, Whiteford was appointed minister at Gullane, East Lothian. As a member of the General Assembly of the Church of Scotland, he proved a sharp critic of its espousal of unilateral nuclear disarmament and a keen campaigner for ministers to receive a minimum stipend at a time of rising inflation.

When he became a district councillor after giving up his appointment he did not disguise his Conservatism, roundly declaring that attempts to undo the Union involved "a mammoth misreading and a monstrous understanding of our past history".

David Whiteford's last years were devoted to caring for his wife, who died in 2008. He was survived by two daughters and a son.

LIEUTENANT COLONEL PETER DURIE

Lieutenant Colonel Peter Durie (who died on March 2 2010, aged 84) was awarded a George Medal after prising his sergeant's hands from a truck to which he had become affixed by an intense electric current of 20,000 volts.

On June 14 1951 Durie, then a captain, and a party of signallers had halted off a road at Reddingen, Germany, when the sergeant went over to the wireless truck, unaware that its aerial was touching an overhead high-voltage cable. By putting his hands on the tailboard, he earthed the cable and was stuck to the vehicle as sparks could be seen passing from his body to the ground.

Durie knew that he could save the sergeant's life only by endangering his own, but succeeded in dragging him down to the ground. By then the sergeant had stopped breathing, and Durie had suffered burns. He immediately arranged for the sergeant to be given artificial respiration while he phoned for a doctor and ambulance.

"That the signal sergeant did not lose his life was due entirely to the prompt and very gallant action of Captain Durie," declared the citation. "There can be little higher praise that can be said of a person than that he was prepared to risk his own life to save his comrade's."

The son of an artillery officer, Thomas Peter Durie was born on New Year's Day 1926. He was a sickly child, and did not go to school until he was eight – having taught himself to read by using the Stanley Gibbons stamp catalogue.

At Fettes, however, he was in the First XV and the shooting VIII. In 1945 he was commissioned into the Royal Horse Artillery which was due to fight in the Far East but was instead despatched to India's North-West Frontier. After staff college Durie was made brigade major in Cyprus at the height of the EOKA troubles, for which he was appointed MBE in 1958, and served with the Airborne Division before joining the directing office at the staff college.

When his wife fell ill Durie resigned his commission and joined the brewers, Courage, as a senior management trainee. He designed a fifteen-month training programme, which included working as a drayman, barman, barrel-washer and salesman. Later he was appointed a local director in Kent and Sussex and then in the West Country, before eventually reaching the main board.

After taking demotion because of his wife's continuing ill health, he left the company after twelve years and became chairman of the Bristol and Western Health Authority, in charge of constructing the city's children's hospital, for which he was appointed OBE. He was Master of Bristol's Society of Merchant Venturers in 1988/9. Peter Durie's first wife, Mary Bowlby, died in 1982. He later married Constance Linton, who survived him with a son and daughter of his first marriage.

LIEUTENANT COLONEL CHARLY FORBES

Lieutenant Colonel Charly Forbes (who died on May 19 2010, aged 89) was a French Canadian officer appointed a knight of the Dutch military order of Wilhelm, an honour likened to the Victoria Cross, for his part in some of the toughest fighting in the Netherlands.

In early November 1944 German heavy guns on Walcheren Island, at the mouth of the Scheldt estuary, were preventing the port of Antwerp being reopened. So the Royal Marines and the navy launched attacks on the west and south coasts while Canadian units were ordered to advance along a mile-long causeway from the mainland.

The Canadians were to create a distraction, but their operation plan was over-optimistic, poorly planned and unlucky. First a company of Black Watch was halted with substantial losses by German fire. The Calgary Highlanders established a bridgehead only to be pushed back. Forbes then led one of three depleted platoons of Le Régiment de Maisonneuve to make a third attempt.

On reaching the causeway he handed a Bren gun to a middle-aged Belgian civilian volunteer, who said he had never fired one before. "You're a big man," said Forbes. "If you can't fire it, carry it." As the Maisies advanced he ordered his men to fire on some armed men running towards them in the dark. A shell burst revealed they were Calgaries retreating from a bomb crater where they had been stranded since the day before.

Sweeping past casualties without a thought, Forbes captured a German anti-tank gun which was firing down the causeway, and took up a defensive position to await promised relief while nursing a wounded wrist. At daylight he realised that he had gone 900 yards past his rendezvous point, and was now behind German lines. With eight men left from his forty-man platoon which first saw action at Caen three months earlier, he sat listening to the rain and the big guns until a German column approached.

Hiding beside the raised embankment up to his chest in water, he waited until the first German was 10ft away then, shaking with cold and fear, fired his revolver. In the scrap that followed some dozen Germans were hit and nine captured before the two groups cowered on either side of the road firing sporadically at each other. Finally, at nightfall, a Belgian runner appeared and helped the Maisies escape along a nearby dyke back to the causeway.

Despite the intensive enemy machine-gun fire, all survived though Forbes pulled a piece of shrapnel from between two vertebrae in a private's back. "Doctors told me later that I shouldn't have done that," he recalled. "But the guy was paralysed before and was fine after I removed it."

Forbes was infuriated to find that his battalion had not waited for him before withdrawing. His war ended a few months later when his eye was injured by a bomb that hit a Jeep, killing the driver.

He received no gallantry awards from his countrymen. But on December 8 1945 he was dubbed by Queen Wilhelmina of the Netherlands on receiving the rare Knight's Cross, 4th class, in recognition of "acts of exceptional bravery, leadership and loyalty". While this attracted little interest in Canada or Britain, he became a Dutch hero for the way he had prevented the retreating Germans from destroying dykes and drowning thousands of civilians.

A military march was named after him and his picture appeared on commemorative plates. For the next sixty-five years Dutch primary schoolchildren were agog to hear him speak on his frequent visits to their country for ceremonies of the Wilhelm Order.

Jean Charles Bertrand Forbes was born on March 19 1921, the descendant of an Aberdonian soldier who served in the 78th (Fraser's) regiment with General Wolfe on the Plains of Abraham. His father ran a lumber business at Matane, a small town on the St Lawrence River, where Forbes claimed to have spoken only French at home. At 15 he was sent to Victoriaville College, where he acquired fluent though heavily accented English.

On the outbreak of war he was wondering whether he might become a violinist, a painter or a lawyer when the local priest asked what toys he liked as a child. When he replied "lead soldiers", the priest said: "You are a natural soldier, a natural leader, and there is a war going on." Forbes went to the Royal Military College at Kingston, Ontario, and arrived in Britain, with a violin (which was to stop a bullet in action) and joined Le Régiment de Maisonneuve in Brighton.

He first distinguished himself at Quilly in Normandy when he ducked a grenade and lobbed back three more, wounding one German, severely injuring another and taking a third prisoner. When he saw how young they were, and that one had been unarmed, he burst into tears.

At Ossendrecht in the Netherlands, he encountered small arms fire from some Germans in a home for the elderly that was painted with a red cross. Infuriated by this flouting of the Geneva Convention, he threatened to shoot them until an elegant German officer claimed they had no weapons, and superciliously asked if this was the Canadian way of treating prisoners. Forbes lifted one soldier's cap to find a clip of five rounds, which he scraped across the man's face. He then removed the officer's shiny boots before sending them all into the prison cage.

On returning home in 1946 Forbes married his first wife, with whom he had two sons and a daughter who died. But he felt lonely and depressed in civilian life. He founded a Legion branch and worked in his father's mill until it folded. He next became a radio announcer, but lost the job for swearing on air.

Two years later he joined up again with 2nd Battalion Royal 22e Regiment ('Van Doos'). On being sent to Korea, he played his violin on Christmas Eve and was answered by a festive song broadcast by the other side. His toughest experience was in command of a mortar platoon near Hill 355, which fired 15,000 rounds during a four-day battle when the tubes became too hot to handle and threatened to burst. Afterwards a nearby American ordnance officer thanked him by sending a new set of mortars. Forbes was mentioned in despatches.

But he did not care for peacetime soldiering on returning to Canada. His drinking increased, his marriage broke up, two others followed. After serving in Cyprus and as a parachute instructor in the Arctic he came out of the Army in the 1960s.

This time he gradually settled down, selling mutual funds and working for Hover Industries, which manufactured hovercraft. In retirement he sailed in the St Lawrence and kept a rifle by his bed. He also took up sculpting and painting landscapes and portraits, including one of the Queen. With his tall, impressive figure and well-honed tales, he became a popular after-dinner speaker.

But at the start of every November his wife noticed how he was increasingly haunted by nightmares until the parade at the Cenotaph in Quebec City on Remembrance Day. He would then join 'his boys' for a glass of Johnny Walker at the Legion club.

GENERAL AMEDEO GUILLET

General Amedeo Guillet (who died on June 16 2010, aged 101) was the Italian officer who led the last cavalry charge faced by the British Army.

Early in 1941, following outstanding successes in the Western Desert, the British invasion of Mussolini's East African empire seemed to be going like clockwork. But at daybreak on January 21, 250 horsemen erupted through the morning mist at Keru. They cut through 4th/11th Sikhs, flanked the armoured cars of Skinner's Horse and then galloped straight towards British brigade headquarters and the 25-pound artillery of Surrey and Sussex Yeomanry.

Red Italian grenades – "like cricket balls" – exploded among the defenders, several of whom were cut down by swords. There were frantic cries of "Tank alert!", and guns that had been pointing towards Italian fortifications were swivelled to face this new threat.

At a distance of 25 yards they fired, cutting swathes through the galloping horses but also causing mayhem as the shells exploded amid the Sikhs and Skinner's Horse. After a few more seconds the horsemen disappeared into the network of wadis that criss-crossed the Sudan-Eritrean lowlands.

It was not quite the last cavalry charge; the unmechanised Savoia Cavalry regiment charged the Soviets at Izbushensky on the Don in August 1942. But it was the last one faced by the British Army, with many soldiers declaring it the most frightening and extraordinary episode of the Second World War.

Amedeo Guillet was born in Piacenza on February 7 1909 to a Savoyard-Piedmontese family of the minor aristocracy which for generations had served the dukes of Savoy, who later became the kings of Italy.

He spent most of his childhood in the south, and remembered an Austrian biplane bombing Bari during the First World War. After following the family tradition he went to the military academy at Modena. He joined the cavalry and began training at Pinerolo, where Italian horsemanship under Federico Caprilli had earlier in the century won world renown.

Guillet was selected for the Italian eventing team to go to the Berlin Olympics in 1936. But Mussolini's invasion of Ethiopia in 1935 interrupted his career as a competition rider. Instead, using family connections, he had himself transferred to the Spahys di Libya cavalry with which he fought repeated actions.

He witnessed aerial gas attacks on the Emperor Haile Selassie's lightly armed warriors, which appalled world opinion, but claimed they were largely ineffectual against an unentrenched enemy which could flee. Fighting with horse, sword and pistol, he used the hilt of his sword to dislodge an Ethiopian warrior who had grabbed him around the waist at Selaclacla; but he received a painful wound to the left hand when a bullet hit the pommel of his saddle.

Decorated for his actions, he was flattered to be chosen a year later by General Luigi Frusci as an aide de camp in the 'Black Flames' division, which was sent to support Franco in the Spanish Civil War. It was the first post Guillet had been offered without family influence.

There he suffered shrapnel wounds and helped capture three Russian armoured cars and crews. But the atrocities he witnessed on both sides were a sobering experience, and Guillet deplored what he saw of Italy's German allies during their intervention.

No longer an uncritical, puppyish subaltern, he returned to Italy and Libya, and echoed the views of many in disapproving of the pro-Nazi alliance of the regime and criticising the absurdities of the anti-Semitic race laws.

With growing disgust for the war in Europe, Guillet asked for a posting to Italian East Africa, where another family acquaintance, the royal prince Amedeo, Duke of Aosta, had been appointed viceroy to replace the brutal and inept Marshal Graziani. By this time Guillet had also become engaged to his beautiful Neapolitan cousin Beatrice Gandolfo, and their intention was to make a life for themselves in Italy's new empire.

Mussolini's decision to enter the war on the side of Germany in May 1940 ended these dreams, cutting off Italian East Africa, which was surrounded by the territories of its enemies, and separating Amedeo from his fiancée, who remained in Italy.

Aosta gave Guillet command of the locally recruited Amhara Cavalry Bande as well as 500 Yemeni infantry – approximately 2,500 men. With almost no armour, the Italians used Guillet's horsemen to delay the advance of the British 4th and 5th Indian Divisions when they crossed the Eritrean frontier in January 1941.

Guillet's actions at Keru, and subsequent hand-to-hand fighting at Agordat, helped to give the Italian Army time to regroup at the mountain fortress of Keren, where it mounted its best actions in the entire war. After nearly two months, however, the British broke through, and the road to Eritrea's capital, Asmara, lay clear.

Most of the Italian Army surrendered, but Guillet refused to do so. Aosta had ordered his officers to fight on to keep as many British soldiers as possible in East Africa, while Rommel, the new German commander in the Western Desert, sought to reverse the earlier Italian disasters.

For nine months Guillet launched a series of guerrilla actions against British troops, plundering convoys and shooting up guard posts. At his side was his mistress, Khadija, an Ethiopian Muslim, for he never believed he would ever see Italy or Beatrice again. Two curious British intelligence officers pursued him: Major Max Harrari, later an urbane London art dealer who would become Guillet's close friend, and the driven intellectual Captain Sigismund Reich, of the Jewish Brigade, who was eager to get on with the task of killing Germans.

Despite their attentions, Guillet managed to escape across the Red Sea to neutral Yemen, where he became an intimate friend of the ruler, Imam Ahmed. He sneaked back to Eritrea in 1943 in disguise, and returned to Italy on the Red Cross ship *Giulio Cesare*, where he was reunited with Beatrice. The couple married in April 1944, and he spent the rest of the war as an intelligence officer, befriending many of his former British enemies from East Africa.

In the post-war world, Guillet joined the diplomatic service and, with his fluent Arabic, served in the Middle East. In 1950s Yemen, he and Beatrice were the only non-Muslims permitted to live within the walls of Sana'a and Taiz.

British visitors were struck by his easy friendship with his neighbours in the souk, as well as the incongruity of foxhunting prints decorating his walls. Guillet later served as ambassador in Jordan and Morocco, and finally India. In 1975 he retired to Ireland, where he had bought a house fifteen years earlier to enjoy the foxhunting.

A generous, giving man, with a disarming innocence to his character, Guillet would frequently liken himself to Don Quixote, but say that those who found him ridiculous were the true fools.

He always said he was the luckiest man he knew – surviving British and Ethiopian bullet wounds, Spanish grenade fragments and a sword cut to the face, as well as numerous bone fractures from riding accidents.

He celebrated his 100th birthday in Rome in 2009 at the Army officers' club in the Palazzo Barberini, where the royal march was played and friends gathered from Ireland, the Middle East and India – as well as those members of the Italian royal family still on speaking terms with each other. Amedeo Guillet was survived by his sons Paolo and Alfredo. Beatrice predeceased him in 1990.

SERGEANT ERIC BATCHELOR

Sergeant Eric Batchelor (who died on July 10 2010, aged 89) was one of New Zealand's most highly decorated soldiers, twice earning an immediate Distinguished Conduct Medal.

A canny countryman known as 'the Ferret' for the swift, silent hunting skills he had learned in boyhood, Batchelor was commanding a forward platoon of 23 Battalion NZ when the advance to Florence was checked by enemy concealed in some houses at San Donato on July 21 1944. He cleared them out on his own initiative, taking five prisoners single-handed while his men took another four, thereby permitting the advance to continue.

A short time afterwards Batchelor led a successful attack against a German strongpoint dominating the Strada ridge, despite coming under heavy machine-gun and artillery fire. Then, on suspecting that a house at Sant'Andrea was occupied by the enemy he left his party outside, and went in alone to capture two German snipers. The outstanding leadership and selfless bravery he showed in a long operation against a seasoned enemy were recognised by the award of his first DCM.

On the night of December 14, Batchelor was part of a forward company in the assault on Celle, south-west of Faenza in Italy, when he took over from his wounded officer on the start line to show great skill and personal bravery as his platoon liquidated three enemy strong points, killing eight, wounding eleven and capturing twenty prisoners.

The following night he was ordered to take three men to rendezvous with a senior officer at a company headquarters. But he mistakenly brought them to a house which smelt of sauerkraut and had a sentry in a German helmet on the door. When the sentry went in Batchelor followed to find about thirty Germans. He opened fire on all who offered resistance and, with his comrades covering the exits, engaged in a shot-for-shot duel with one German NCO.

Five enemy were killed, four were wounded, and nineteen prisoners were taken back to New Zealand lines before daylight by men carrying their enemies' guns because their own weapons had run out of ammunition.

Batchelor received a Bar to his DCM, but with typical New Zealand understatement accepted the awards with a grunt and "I was just doing my job". He resisted pressure to accept promotion, saying he wanted to remain with his mates from South Island.

The son of a farm labourer, Eric Batchelor was born at Waimate, near Canterbury, on August 29 1920 and went to the local school, where, he admitted, he had never been considered 'very bright', preferring to shoot rabbits in the hills and raid apple orchards at nights.

He joined the Territorials at 16 and worked as a dairyman before joining 5th Reinforcements in 1941, with which he landed in North Africa to be wounded by shrapnel at Sidi Rezegh in the attempt to relieve Tobruk and then again in the third battle of Alamein, where his worst moments were lying face down in the sand close to the start line while men on either side of him were killed in a shell burst.

While famed among his comrades for sneaking up on the enemy from behind in the dark, he knew how to react when he and a comrade were caught by a German patrol. "They told us to surrender," he recalled. "That was a mistake for them. They missed and I didn't." It was no surprise that officers would be frequently asked by General Freyberg and General Kippenberger "How's 'the Ferret' getting on?"

On being discharged with an additional mention in despatches Batchelor returned to the street where he had grown up, and in 1948 married Thurza Hardwick. He worked as a taxi driver, ran a delicatessen and wine shop before driving a school bus in retirement.

He remained in touch with the Army and, unlike many veterans, was happy to talk about the war. He was part of the New Zealand contingent at the Victory and Coronation celebrations in London and also attended the 50th anniversary commemorations at Monte Cassino in 1994 and the 60th at Alamein in 2002.

At the latter he and three comrades were ordered to leave a covered grandstand reserved for Italian veterans. Three moved. Batchelor, happy to be out of the hot sun, remained where he was.

LIEUTENANT COLONEL JOE SYMONDS

Lieutenant Colonel Joe Symonds (who died on August 15 2010, aged 95) took part in twenty-two attacks in the north-west Europe campaign and was awarded an MC and Bar.

The 4th Battalion, Dorset Regiment, landed at Le Hamel, Normandy, on June 23 1944, and on July 10 Symonds was in command of B Company in the battle for Eterville, a village south of Caen. After an approach march beginning at midnight, his men arrived in the forward assembly area in the early morning.

A lance corporal sounded the charge on his bugle, and the battalion overran a German platoon and advanced to the edge of the village, where Symonds gave the signal for a final assault which he led with great dash on to the objective. They mopped up and took seventy prisoners, but other German soldiers – who had been subdued by the weight of supporting fire and were concealed among the thick bocage – then began to mortar and shell his company. Symonds was digging his own slit trench when he was hit and thrown into it, losing consciousness. He was awarded a Military Cross.

Giles Symonds, always known as Joe, was born at Frome St Quintin, Dorset, on June 28 1915. He was educated at Blundell's and, in 1938, was commissioned into the Dorset Regiment. The following year he led the Evershot platoon to war.

While being evacuated home on a stretcher, an alert nurse discovered that his water bottle only contained Calvados. After surgery and convalescence, he returned to France and his unit.

On February 15 1945, Symonds was in command of A Company during the battle of the Ardennes. They were east of the Forest of Cleve where it was estimated that the enemy had more than 300 guns in support of the sector. Their objective was some fortified farm buildings at the top of a dominant feature. As the Dorsets formed up, they came under very heavy fire.

Afterwards their CO wrote: "I shall always carry a vivid picture of the tall figure of Major Symonds standing up, blowing his whistle, and bowling his steel helmet in the direction of the Germans. The company appreciated this typical gesture by its commander and followed him to a man."

They soon ran into very tough opposition from German paratroops but, disregarding the accurate Spandau fire and intense mortar and shell fire, put in three attacks before finally taking the strongpoint. Many of the Germans decided to run, and in the subsequent pursuit no quarter was given.

Returning in a tank, Symonds was seriously burned about the hands and face when it received a direct hit and at once 'brewed up'. With his usual thoroughness, however, he reorganised the remnants of his company before he was at last evacuated in great pain.

The citation for the Bar to his MC stated: "Major Symonds displayed superb gallantry throughout." Many of his comrades did not expect to see him again before the end of the war, but he returned to his company in time for the Rhine crossing in March and the rest of the battles in the campaign.

In 1947 Symonds was appointed second-in-command of the battalion and took command in 1951. He was appointed OBE two years later. After retiring from the Army, he became an agricultural valuer, auctioneer and land agent at Dorchester until his final retirement in 1980, and was a Fellow of the Royal Institution of Chartered Surveyors.

He farmed in partnership with family members, while hunting with the Cattistock for many years and riding into his eighties. Joe Symonds married, in 1940, Thelma Thornicroft. She predeceased him, as did a son. Their other son survived him.

PIPER BILL MILLIN

Piper Bill Millin (who died on August 17 2010, aged 88) was personal piper to Brigadier Lord Lovat on D-Day and piped the invasion forces on to the shores of France; unarmed apart from the ceremonial dagger in his stocking, he played unflinchingly as men fell all around him.

Millin began his seemingly suicidal serenade immediately upon jumping from the ramp of the landing craft into the icy water. As the Cameron tartan of his kilt floated to the surface he struck up with *Hieland Laddie*, continuing as the man behind him was hit, and sank into the sea.

Once ashore Millin did not run, but walked up and down the beach, blasting out a series of tunes. After *Hieland Laddie* Lovat, commander of 1st Special Service Brigade (1 SSB), had raised his voice above the crackle of gunfire and the crump of mortar to ask for another. Millin strode up and down the water's edge playing *The Road to the Isles*.

Bodies of the fallen were drifting to and fro in the surf. Soldiers were trying to dig in and, when they heard the pipes, many of them waved and cheered – although one came up to Millin and called him a 'mad bastard'.

His worst moments were when he was among the wounded. They wanted medical help and were shocked to see this figure strolling up and down playing the pipes. To feel so helpless, Millin said afterwards, was horrifying. For many other soldiers, however, the piper provided a unique boost to morale. "I shall never forget hearing the skirl of Bill Millin's pipes," said one, Tom Duncan, many years later. "It is hard to describe the impact it had. It gave us a great lift and increased our determination. As well as the pride we felt, it reminded us of home and why we were there fighting for our lives and those of our loved ones."

When the brigade moved off, Millin was with the group that attacked the rear of Ouistreham. After the capture of the town, he and Lovat headed towards

Bénouville, piping along the road. They were very exposed, and were shot at by snipers from across the canal. Millin stopped playing. Everyone threw themselves flat on the ground — apart from Lovat, who went down on one knee.

When one of the snipers scrambled down a tree and dived into a cornfield, Lovat stalked him and shot him. He then sent two men into the corn to look for him and bring back the corpse. "Right, Piper," he ordered, "start the pipes again."

At Bénouville, where they again came under fire, the CO of 6 Commando asked Millin to play them down the main street. He suggested that Millin should run, but the piper insisted on walking and, as he played *Blue Bonnets over the Border*, the Commandos followed. When they came to the crossing which later became known as Pegasus Bridge, troops on the other side signalled frantically that it was under sniper fire. Lovat ordered Millin to shoulder his bagpipes and play the Commandos over. "It seemed like a very long bridge," Millin said afterwards.

The pipes were damaged by shrapnel later that day, but remained playable. Millin was surprised not to have been shot, and he mentioned this to some Germans who had been taken prisoner. They said that they had not shot at him because they thought he had gone off his head.

William Millin, the son of a policeman, was born in Glasgow on July 14 1922. For a few years the family lived in Saskatchewan on the Canadian prairies, but returned to Scotland where Bill went to school in Glasgow. He joined the TA before the Second World War and played in the pipe band of 7th Battalion

Highland Light Infantry, then transferred to the Cameron Highlanders before volunteering to join the Commandos in 1941.

He met Lord Lovat while doing his Commando training at Achnacarry, north of Fort William. Lovat, hereditary chief of the Clan Fraser, offered him a job as his batman, but Millin turned this down and Lovat agreed instead to take him on as his personal piper.

The War Office had banned pipers from leading soldiers into battle after losses in the Great War had proved too great. "Ah, but that's the English War Office," Lovat told Millin. "You and I are both Scottish and that doesn't apply." On D-Day, Millin was the only piper.

When he boarded the landing craft bound for the Normandy beaches, he took his pipes out of their box and, standing in the bow, played *Road to the Isles* as they went out of the Solent. Someone relayed the music over the loud hailer and troops on other transports started cheering and throwing their hats in the air.

Like many others, Millin was so seasick on the rough crossing that the coast of France proved a welcome sight, despite the dangers that came with it. "I didn't care what was going on ashore. I just wanted to get off that bloody landing craft," he said.

He returned to England with 1 SSB in September 1944, but then accompanied 4 Commando to the Netherlands, and finished the war at Lübeck. After being demobilised the following year he took up the offer of a job on Lord Lovat's estate.

This proved too quiet for him, however, and he joined a touring theatre company with which he appeared playing his pipes on stage in London,

Stockton-on-Tees and Belfast. In the late 1950s he trained in Glasgow as a registered mental nurse and worked in three hospitals in the city.

In 1963 Millin moved to Devon, where he was employed at the Langdon Hospital, Dawlish, until he retired in 1988. In several of the Ten Tors hikes on Dartmoor organised by the Army he took part as the piper, and also visited America, where he lectured about his D-Day experiences. When a film was made of Cornelius Ryan's 1962 book *The Longest Day* Millin was played by Pipe Major Leslie de Laspee, the Queen Mother's official piper.

Millin played the lament at Lord Lovat's funeral in 1995, and donated his pipes to the National War Museum in Edinburgh. A life-size statue of him playing them was unveiled at Colleville-Montgomery, near where they landed on Sword Beach in 2014.

Bill Millin married, in 1954, Margaret Mary Dowdel. She predeceased him, and he was survived by their son.

SIGNALMAN ARTHUR TITHERINGTON

Signalman Arthur Titherington (who died on September 19 2010, aged 88) was the most vociferous campaigner for financial compensation and a full apology from the Japanese Emperor because of the cruelty that he and his fellow prisoners had suffered during the Second World War.

On returning home in 1945 after almost three years as a slave labourer in a copper mine on the island of Formosa (now Taiwan), Titherington found that few in post-war Britain knew or cared much about Far East captives. The government's outrage in 1944 on learning about their treatment was already giving way to a policy of restoring amicable relations with Japan.

And when the Anglo-Japanese peace treaty was signed in 1952, the prisoners received £76 10s in settlement, even though many continued to suffer from physical and mental scars as well as regular nightmares. A dogged Lancastrian, Titherington lost no opportunity to remind people that he had lost almost four years of his youth in captivity. "I do not forgive and I do not forget," he would repeat over the next fifty-eight years.

As the number of survivors declined and Japan's economic power, with its promise of lucrative markets, grew, the issue was expected to fade. But when the prisoners retired from their post-war civilian jobs in the 1980s they became increasingly frustrated both by the government's seeming indifference and by the public's assumption that only those who had been on the Burma railway had suffered.

Exasperated by what he saw of the mumblings and grumblings from other prisoners' lobby groups, Titherington started up his own Japanese Labour Camp Survivors' Association, whose members turned their backs on the Emperor Akihito in The Mall during a state visit in 1998.

On first meeting Tony Blair, he bluntly asked whether he was pursuing a policy of procrastination, like his predecessors. When the Blair government boasted of diplomatic success in winning an apology, which was followed by an article in *The Sun* by the

Japanese prime minister, Titherington pointed out that this was only a repetition of an apology made two years earlier. What was required, he insisted, was *shazai*, meaning: "I have committed a sin, for which I apologise."

Titherington then joined representatives of Australian and American prisoners in bringing a case before a Tokyo district court, where he wept in cross-examination during the four-hour hearing. When the judge ruled that there was no case to answer he walked out to the nearby Japanese Diet building, where he spat on the steps twice and said: "There is no justice in this country. They are lying bastards."

It was after another case was brought unsuccessfully in California in 2000 that Blair finally promised some 16,000 prisoners and their widows £10,000 each. Titherington accepted the money. But while most were at last satisfied, he still wanted a full apology from the Emperor. The campaign was not, he declared, a question of hatred or revenge but of justice.

The son of an iron foundry worker, Thomas Arthur Titherington was born at Darwen, Lancashire, on December 10 1921. The family moved to Birmingham, where he became an apprentice toolmaker before joining Royal Signals at 17 to become a despatch rider. On arriving in Singapore he was attached to 80th Anti-Tank Regiment, and found himself being shot at by British troops who mistook his crash helmet for that of a Japanese; he replaced it with an Australian bush hat.

As the British fell back, Titherington weaved his

way through the chaos, carrying his brigadier on the pillion of his Norton 16H, delivering messages and destroying abandoned vehicles. He scrounged food from empty shops and once slept on the billiard table in a golf club.

Eventually he was hurled into the air by an explosion and taken to Singapore General Hospital, where he recovered to work as an orderly. His last job after the surrender was to hide surgical equipment in the bandages of the walking wounded before being sent to Changi jail. At first, few Japanese were in evidence; there was plenty of food; and Titherington even took part in an England vs Australia cricket match.

On being shipped to Formosa, he and his fellow prisoners were told to learn six Japanese words a day and assured that they would be adequately fed for working diligently. But the three small daily portions of rice and pickled turnip proved totally inadequate for labouring in the Kinkaseki copper mine, where prisoners ended up wearing underwear and cardboard safety helmets under roofs that were in constant danger of collapsing.

Titherington loaded chunks of ore into bogeys in amounts that were steadily increased, then was made a driller with responsibility for laying the explosives. At the end of each day he had to climb 2,000 steps to his hut.

The guards beat the prisoners with their hands, rifles and bamboo poles for failing to salute, for singing and even for refusing to fall down under blows. Titherington took some satisfaction from hiding the occasional stick of gelignite in a bogey which might later explode elsewhere, and enjoyed referring to the guards as 'Frying Pan', 'Ghost' and 'The Beast'. When the war ended only about ninety of his fellow 523 fellow prisoners remained, and his weight had dropped to 5st 7lbs. Yet he managed three breakfasts on being taken aboard an American warship, and was fit enough to complete his military service.

Titherington married Iris Platt, with whom he had a daughter and brought up a stepson. Initially he joined the Oxfordshire Police at Witney, but he did not relish the discipline. He then became a local photographer. His strong competitive streak soon led him to take up golf and archery.

After becoming a councillor he was elected mayor of Witney three times, first as a Conservative and then as 'a bloody independent'. While willing to tread on toes he was able to reconcile different groups in order to plant trees in the market square, move the allotments and improve the street lighting. In 2001 he was named Midlander of the Year.

Yet although Arthur Titherington never wavered in his demand for the Emperor's personal apology, he had Japanese friends, drove a Japanese car and used a Japanese camera. When he met a Korean sex slave in Tokyo in 1995, he embraced her in tears, saying that she had suffered more than he had.

LIEUTENANT COLONEL DAVID ROSE

Lieutenant Colonel David Rose (who died on October 24 2010, aged 98) was a Black Watch officer awarded a DSO in British Somaliland and a Bar while commanding a battalion in the Korean War.

In 1940 British Somaliland was defended by a small force mainly composed of colonial troops, with 2nd Battalion the Black Watch (2 BW) held in reserve. Five Italian brigades, stiffened by Blackshirts and supported by aircraft, armour and artillery, forced the main British contingent to withdraw towards Berbera, having fiercely defended the only natural obstacle, a dry wadi known as the Tug Argan Gap.

On August 17 the battalion, equipped with a single anti-tank gun, was at Barkasan and acting as rearguard. After a long day's fighting, ammunition was running short and Rose, then a captain commanding the forward company, found himself at great risk of being cut off.

He decided to counter-attack and led his men down the hill in a fierce bayonet charge. After being wounded in the shoulder, he stuffed his arm into his belt to stop it flopping about and continued to lead the attack.

The Italian forces broke and fled, and many of their native levies were shot down by Blackshirts who had been waiting at their rear. The Highlanders pursued the enemy for a mile and left them so demoralised that they offered no further interference to the battalion's withdrawal under cover of darkness. Rose was awarded his first DSO, at that time an unusual award for a junior officer.

David MacNeil Campbell Rose, the son of Brigadier John Rose, was born at Alverstoke, Hampshire, on March 23 1912. Three of his brothers had distinguished careers in the Army in the Second World War. After Glenalmond and Sandhurst, David was commissioned into the Black Watch. Service in Scotland included a period spent on the Royal Guard at Balmoral. King George V was Colonel-in-Chief of the Black Watch and nearing the end of his reign. On one occasion, at the Ghillies' Ball, he discovered Rose and a fellow officer helping themselves to a bottle of champagne which had been specially left out for himself.

As a 'punishment' he ordered both young officers to dance with the Queen and then come shooting with him the next day. During the shoot, Rose's overenthusiastic dog retrieved a grouse from immediately behind the King's butt.

"My bird I think, Rose!" said the King. Not wishing to be deprived of one of his small bag, and aware that the King was very proud of being a superb shot, Rose replied, in some trepidation: "No, Sir, it must be one of mine. It's a runner!" After a snort, the gruff reply came back: "Proper little courtier, aren't you, Rose? All right. I suppose you can count it as one of yours!"

In 1938, 1 BW was deployed to Palestine. The troopship docked at Tangiers, allowing time for a run ashore. While visiting the souk, Rose was astonished to recognise his youngest brother dressed as an Arab and begging. The young man subsequently joined the Foreign Legion and was awarded the Croix de Guerre and Médaille Militaire.

After his exploits in British Somaliland, Rose attended staff college in Haifa. But soon after taking up his first staff appointment in Cairo, 2 BW urgently needed reinforcements following its attempt to break out from Tobruk, and he returned to the battalion as adjutant.

Rose was subsequently posted to Burma to command one of the two Black Watch columns in the second Chindit campaign. There he was wounded again in the shoulder, but managed to continue in command behind Japanese lines for some weeks before severe blood poisoning forced his evacuation and a long period of convalescence.

After a spell on a military mission in Cairo and a posting to Tripoli as brigade major, he was recalled from commanding the regimental depot in Perth to take command of 1 BW shortly before its departure for Korea in June 1952.

That autumn the battalion took over defence of 'The Hook', a prominent salient dominating the Samichon river valley. With the help of the Royal Engineers, deep tunnels were excavated in each company position to provide protection from bombardments and allow the soldiers to take cover if they were overrun. Rose was able to call for airburst shelling to be brought down on his own positions to break up enemy attacks before clearing the trenches by bayonet.

On November 18 and 19, 1 BW was subjected to repeated assaults from two Chinese battalions. On the first night, when they came under heavy bombardment, Rose was never out of touch with his forward platoons. The Hook was held and the

Chinese suffered large losses. In recognition of his outstanding leadership, Rose was awarded a Bar to his DSO.

In August 1953 he took the battalion to Kenya to help suppress the Mau Mau uprising. On returning to England, he went to the small arms school as chief instructor. He retired from the Army in 1958 and, settling in Perthshire, enjoyed shooting and fishing and creating a garden. David Rose married, in 1945, Lady Jean Ramsay, younger daughter of the Earl of Dalhousie. She predeceased him, and he was survived by their son and daughter.

SERGEANT 'TINY' BOYCE

Sergeant 'Tiny' Boyce (who died on November 21 2010, aged 95) was awarded an immediate Distinguished Conduct Medal for the daring rescue of two wounded men whom he dragged 300 yards to safety on top of a gate under fire.

In April 1945 Boyce was in command of a section of anti-tank guns in support of a troop of C Squadron of 53 Reconnaissance Regiment, which had been ordered to seize an important bridge at Kulverborstel, Germany. At a bend in the road the leading troop came under attack from Germans with a clear view.

As the armoured cars immediately deployed to the right, Boyce gave orders for his leading gun to engage the enemy with high explosive while he moved to another which had fallen silent because its

No 1 and loader had suffered severe leg wounds. He carried out a quick recce for a better position and ensured that replacements had it back in action.

Boyce then ran to the aid of the wounded men, applying dressings. Seeing that one had a shattered leg, he improvised a stretcher from a gate, his considerable strength enabling him to drag it, with the man aboard, for 300 yards until they reached safety. He then carried the gate back to the second wounded man, whom he also carried back under fire.

This remarkable feat undoubtedly saved the men's lives. Also, by effectively maintaining the section of guns, Boyce contributed largely towards the success of the troop operation which captured and held the bridge. He was awarded an immediate DCM, its ribbon being pinned on his chest by the relatively diminutive Field Marshal Montgomery.

Charles Bernard Boyce, one of four children, was born on May 15 1915 in Birmingham. He left school aged 14 and worked at a grocery store until called up in 1940 to do his basic training with the 2nd Monmouthshires. He made sergeant in only nine months, and his anti-tank company became part of 53rd Reconnaissance Regiment.

Boyce's war took him from Normandy to Hamburg, the 53rd seeing action in both mounted (fast-moving forward reconnaissance) and dismounted (heavy infantry support) roles. This included working with the Americans to trap the Germans at the Falaise Gap, where 8,000 enemy soldiers were taken prisoner. He helped to liberate Lille, while at the relief of Eindhoven, where Philips had a factory, the company's grateful employees presented Boyce and his comrades with a tiny wireless which enabled them to listen to the BBC.

The 53rd, always well forward, often had to deal with Germans making a last stand. Yet Boyce could never resist prefacing his recollections with criticism of supporting forces on his own side, recalling being on the receiving end of Allied rocket-firing aircraft and artillery — "as if the German 88s weren't enough". However, he always managed a smile, as if to say: "That's war." He was also involved in both the battles of Arnhem and the Bulge.

After being discharged in 1946, Boyce eventually joined the Prison Service, with which he became a senior officer. In 2002 he joined the Royal Hospital Chelsea to enjoy growing strawberries on his allotment and listening to the organ in chapel. 'Tiny' Boyce's wife Kath and a son predeceased him; he was survived by three daughters.

HAVILDAR LACHHIMAN GURUNG, VC

Havildar Lachhiman Gurung (who died on December 12 2010, aged 92) won the Victoria Cross while serving with the Gurkha Rifles in Burma in 1945; fifty years later he was part of the campaign led by the actress Joanna Lumley to allow former Gurkhas to settle in Britain.

At the end of April 1945, 89th Indian Brigade, 7th Division, was ordered to cross the Irrawaddy and destroy the enemy north of the Prome-Taungup road. By May 9 the Japanese, after a series of desperate attacks, had broken off contact and were withdrawing towards the Taungdaw valley. B and C Companies of 4th/8th Gurkha Rifles were positioned to block their route at the village of Taungdaw, on the west bank of the river.

When the Japanese arrived, the two Gurkha companies were surrounded and their lines of communication cut. On the night of May 12, Rifleman Gurung was manning the forward post of his platoon almost 100 yards ahead of the main company.

At 1.20 am, more than 200 Japanese attacked. The brunt of the assault fell on Gurung's post, which dominated a jungle track leading up to his platoon's position. Had the enemy been able to overrun it, they would have secured control over the whole of the field before them.

One grenade fell on the lip of Gurung's trench. He grabbed it and hurled it back at the enemy. Almost immediately another grenade came over. This one fell directly inside the trench. Again Gurung snatched it up and threw it back. A third grenade landed just in front of the trench. Gurung attempted to throw this back, but it exploded in his hand, blowing off his fingers, shattering his right arm and severely wounding him in the face, body and right leg. His two comrades were also badly wounded and lay helpless in the bottom of the trench.

The enemy, screaming and yelling, now formed up shoulder to shoulder and attempted to rush the position by sheer weight of numbers. Gurung, regardless of his wounds, loaded and fired his rifle with his left hand and kept up a steady rate of fire.

The attacks came in wave after wave, but the Japanese were beaten back with heavy losses. For four hours Gurung remained alone at his post, calmly waiting for each new onslaught, firing into his attackers at point blank range and determined not to yield an inch of ground. His comrades could hear him shouting: "Come and fight a Gurkha!"

Of the eighty-seven enemy dead found in the company's immediate locality the following morning, thirty-one lay in front of Gurung's section. The Japanese made repeated attempts to break through, but the 4th/8th held out until May 15, when they were relieved.

Gurung later said: "I had to fight because there was no other way. I felt I was going to die anyway, so I might as well die standing on my feet. All I knew was that I had to go on and hold them back. I am glad that helped the other soldiers in my platoon, but they would have all done the same thing."

Gurung was invested with the Victoria Cross by Lord Louis Mountbatten at the Red Fort in Delhi on December 19 1945. The citation declared: "This rifleman, by his magnificent example, so inspired his comrades to resist the enemy to the last that, although surrounded and cut off for three days and two nights, they held and smashed every attack. His outstanding gallantry and extreme devotion to duty, in the face of almost overwhelming odds, were the main factors in the defeat of the enemy." Partiman Gurung, Lachhiman's 74-year-old father, was carried for eleven days from his village in Nepal to witness his son being decorated.

Lachhiman Gurung was born on December 30 1917 at Dakhani village in the Tanhu district of Nepal. He enlisted in December 1940 and after completing basic training was recruited into 8th Gurkha Rifles. Standing just 4ft 11in tall, he was under the minimum height and would not have been accepted in peacetime.

After winning his VC, Gurung was evacuated to hospital, but lost his right hand and the use of his right eye. He continued to serve with the Gurkhas but transferred to the Indian Army after independence in 1947. He retired in the rank of havildar (the equivalent of sergeant) in the same year. Gurung married soon afterwards and had two sons and a daughter. Later, after the death of his wife, he had two sons from a second marriage.

He farmed a two-acre plot and owned several buffalo, oxen, goats and cows. In 1995 the VC and GC Association provided the Gurkha Welfare Trust with £2,000 donated by the Armourers and Brasiers' Livery Company, which was used to build a new house for Gurung and his family near the Gurkha Welfare Centre at Chitwan.

In August 1995 he was received at 10 Downing Street by the Prime Minister, John Major, who presented him with a cheque for £100,500 for the Gurkha Welfare Trust. In 2008 Gurung became closely involved in the campaign to allow Gurkhas to settle in Britain. The British government had refused entry to the 2,000 Gurkhas who had retired before July 1997, the date when their base was moved to the UK from Hong Kong.

Five claimants – including a Falklands veteran,

Lance-Corporal Gyanendra Rai; a Gulf War veteran, Birendra Man; and a Gurkha widow – launched a legal challenge, supported by Lachhiman Gurung and a fellow VC, Honorary Lieutenant Tul Bahadur Pun. Both men had been told that they would not be allowed to settle here because they had failed to "demonstrate strong ties" to the UK.

In the High Court in September 2008, however, Mr Justice Blake said that the policy should be reviewed, referring to the "Military Covenant undertaken by every British soldier by which, in return for their pledge to make the ultimate sacrifice, they are promised value and respect". He added: "Rewarding distinguished service by the grant of residence in the country for which the service was performed would be a vindication of this covenant." As the judge rose after his ruling, Gurkhas and their supporters shouted their battle cry, "*Ayo gorkhali*."

In May 2009 the government announced that all Gurkha veterans who retired before 1997 with at least four years' service would be allowed to settle in Britain. Even as this victory was secured, however, Gurung was appealing to the Queen and the Prime Minister for his 20-year-old granddaughter, Amrita, who had been facing deportation, to be allowed to stay in Britain to care for him.

"I have paid a great price for Britain," Gurung said, "but I do not complain as I love this country as much as I love my family. However, in my last days I ask Her Majesty the Queen to help by allowing my granddaughter to be with me and at my side." The Home Office relented, and granted her permission to stay.

In 2008 Gurung had settled at Hounslow, to which he was formally welcomed at a ceremony led by the mayor and the council; he was later made a Freeman of the Borough. He became honorary vice-president of the Chiswick branch of the Royal British Legion, and moved into the Chiswick War Memorial Homes.

One of Gurung's sons subsequently became an officer in the 8th Gurkha Rifles. His second wife, Manmaya, survived him with his five children.

CAPTAIN STEPHEN PERRY

Captain Stephen Perry (who died on January 15 2011, aged 90) kept a vivid battlefield diary of his experiences as an artillery officer over four months in Normandy, Belgium and the Netherlands during 1944.

On August 4 Perry – a troop commander serving with 86th (Hertfordshire Yeomanry) Field Regiment RA (86 HY) – was at Jurques, south-west of Villers-Bocage. The regiment was equipped with self-propelled guns (SPs), with 25-pounders mounted on a tank chassis.

Despite his CO's objections, the regiment's twenty-four SPs had been ordered to deploy on a forward slope overlooked by a long ridge 2,000 yards to their front. "The inevitable happened," he wrote.

"We were heavily shelled by 105mm artillery, but we managed to take cover in a sunken road. Then I took a dekko through my glasses and there was the flash! It was a tank – probably a Tiger – just below the skyline. I grabbed the first three chaps I could see and we jumped into an SP ... but [the Tiger] spotted us and a ding-dong battle began, round for round.

"After the 11th round, a cloud of smoke came up from the Tiger. Then we got in half a dozen rounds before he waddled off pouring smoke from his turret." Perry's courage in a critical situation was recognised by an MC.

Stephen Denys Perry was born on February 4 1920 at Bedford and educated at Tonbridge. He was commissioned into the Royal Artillery and posted to 86 HY. The regiment remained in England until D-Day. A staff officer told his CO that his superiors were expecting ninety per cent casualties.

On June 5 Perry embarked at Southampton. At 3 am he was awakened and packed his haversack – maps, protractors, water bottle, gas mask, gas cape and rations. He lamented the loss of his blue silk pyjamas, "which would have to be left behind for some merchant seaman, blast him!"

Just before 6 am, still seven miles from Gold Beach, the Landing Crafts (Mechanised) were lowered, and Perry realised for the first time how rough the sea was. Aircraft were roaring overhead to drop their bombs on the pillboxes and gun casemates but, to his relief, the Luftwaffe did not appear. Salvos from the destroyers sent up great sheets of flame in the half light as their shells hurtled towards the shore batteries.

Soon most of the invaders felt seasick and would rather risk the German bullets than any more buffeting by the waves. At 7 am, the twenty-four guns of the regiment opened up from their Landing

Craft (Artillery) and pounded the defences at Ver-sur-Mer and La Rivière. Shells from the Germans sent up huge spouts of water close to Perry.

An hour later their craft grounded on Gold Beach and the doors went down. The water was waist-high. Shells were falling, Spandaus were rattling from the seawall. To their right another landing craft exploded.

After the sappers had cut the barbed wire and taped routes through the minefields, Perry and his troop pushed on towards Creully, surviving encounters with snipers and a pair of 88mm guns. At 3 pm, after he had bolted down a chocolate bar and a biscuit, they encountered a German company concealed in a network of slit trenches. They attacked and took thirty prisoners.

At 5 pm three Sherman tanks were knocked out directly in front of the troop. The firing came from a wood 400 yards away, but no sooner had they chased off the enemy than salvo after salvo from the Royal Navy started falling among the Yeomanry. They called up the ship, but it was fifteen minutes before the shelling ceased; there were several casualties.

Just as it got dark, the men came up against a radar station surrounded by mines and barbed wire. Rockets from a six-barrelled *nebelwerfer* rained down on them from this strongpoint, but Perry bracketed the target in two rounds and his next six fell perfectly.

When they were five miles inland, the first German aircraft appeared, a Heinkel 111. "That," he wrote, "means a good pranging later on, so we had to dig deep." At 5 am an officer was brought in on a stretcher with a bullet through his chest. "A lesson learned," wrote Perry. "Don't ever swan around on a motorbike in the middle of the night when the battle is fluid."

On D plus 8, he was near Tilly-sur-Seulles supporting A Company, 6th Battalion Durham Light Infantry, in an attack on a fortified farmhouse. As he advanced on foot with the infantry across a wheat field, twelve Spandaus opened up.

The DLI took a number of casualties and Perry's wireless set was knocked out. He ran back to his carrier, thinking that every moment would be his last. Bullets from the Spandaus rattled against the side of the vehicle and then one came straight through the control box three inches behind his head.

As he returned to the infantry with a new set, he was fired on by a 75mm self-propelled gun. The nosecap of the HE shell hit the wing of the vehicle but failed to stop it. The DLI fixed bayonets, charged and took the building. As Perry went inside a bullet whistled through his battledress, grazing his shoulder blade.

86 HY took part in the push across the Seine and the advance into Belgium and Holland. On September 23, at Veghel, midway between Eindhoven and Nijmegen, Perry was severely wounded in the leg and returned home where he joined a firm of solicitors in Bournemouth. Stephen Perry married, in 1951, Kay Mitchell, who predeceased him.

OBERGEFREITER HENRY METELMANN

Obergefreiter Henry Metelmann (who died on July 24 2011, aged 88) fought ruthlessly on the Eastern Front as a dedicated Nazi; after the war he settled in England, where he joined the Communist Party and CND, and worked as a groundsman at Charterhouse School at Godalming, Surrey.

In 1991 he published a painfully honest memoir of his experience, *Through Hell for Hitler*, which formed the basis of a BBC *Timewatch* documentary in 2003. The book was not so much an act of atonement. "I can't say sorry," he told a *Sunday Telegraph* interviewer. "It wouldn't mean anything. After all this, it would just sound cheap." Rather, its account of how an ordinary individual can be sucked into a vortex of barbarity was intended as a warning from history.

An only child, Heinrich Friedrich Carl Metelmann was born on Christmas Day 1922 into a working-class family in Altona, an industrial town near Hamburg. His father, an unskilled railway worker, was a socialist, his mother a Christian.

When Heinrich was 11, his Christian youth group was subsumed into the Hitler Youth, of which he soon became an enthusiastic member. "It was smashing," he recalled. "For the first time in my life I felt someone. We were poor, my mother made my clothes, so I always felt a bit shabby; and suddenly I had a fine uniform. I'd never been on holiday; now they were taking us to camp by lakes and mountains."

He attended rallies, where he saw the Führer. "To us, he was the greatest human being in the world. People say he hypnotised us, but we hypnotised ourselves. Often we couldn't hear what he was saying: we all screamed anyway. We truly thought we were part of a crusade."

His father, who had fought in the First World War, told him that Hitler's talk of the glory of war was rubbish, and that Hitler was just a frontman for rich arms manufacturers. "Once he said it was just as well we had been brainwashed, that we would go mad if we knew what we were really fighting for. I wish now I could tell him: '*You* were right, I was the idiot.'"

Some children reported their parents' doubts to the Nazi authorities, with the result that they were arrested. Gradually Metelmann's father began to hold his tongue in front of his son. As soon as he was 18, he joined the Army and was sent as a tank driver with the 22nd Panzer Division to Crimea. He rose to the rank of *obergefreiter* (senior lance-corporal).

But as they advanced the 1,000 miles towards Stalingrad, Metelmann – who spoke a little Russian – got to know some of the people whose homes he occupied: "I fell in love with a Russian girl, although nothing ever came of it, and for the first time I began to doubt our racial superiority. How could I be better than her?"

His unit was nearly destroyed in the Russian pincer movement at Stalingrad in November 1942, and Metelmann only narrowly avoided capture. The reversal of the Wehrmacht's fortunes did not lead him to disobey orders. He recounted an episode when the tank he was driving approached a group of Russian prisoners carrying a wounded comrade.

As the Russians took fright and dropped the injured man in the road, Metelmann's officer ordered him to drive on – so he did. Once, his platoon mowed down some teenage girls they saw running for cover: "They were girls. It's inexcusable. But we were frightened."

Nine out of ten German soldiers who died in the war were killed in Russia – including half of Metelmann's own class at school. His lowest point came when one of his closest friends was wounded in the snow by fire from a Russian plane. "There was nothing we could do with him. So I held his head in one hand and with the other I took out my pistol."

Metelmann claimed to have survived through a mixture of luck and cowardice, both moral and physical. On one occasion Russian troops destroyed his vehicle, and in the chaos he went to fetch ammunition. He looked back to see Russian tanks rolling over his fellow soldiers. Instead of going back he ran away and hid in a shelter, ignoring the cries of the wounded. "I had no medical skills, I couldn't save them. When I came out they were covered by snow."

He was advancing on the outskirts of Stalingrad when the tracks of his tank became caught up in barbed wire; he climbed out to cut it free when there was a blast. He woke unhurt to see the tank upside down in flames, and never entered the city. Briefly captured he escaped to join the defence of a small town on the Rhine in the last stages of the war. When American forces entered the town he and six colleagues were hiding in a cellar.

After being taken prisoner, he was shipped to America, where his turning point came en route to a prison camp in Arizona. He picked up a magazine showing pictures of the piles of corpses and walking corpses at the newly liberated concentration camps.

Metelmann had swallowed Nazi propaganda that the camps were merely places where 'unsocial' elements were made to do a hard day's work. "At first I said to my mates: 'Look, just because we lost the war, they blame us for everything.'" But when he studied the pictures more closely he realised that they were not fabrications.

Later Metelmann was transferred to England, where he remained a POW until 1948, working as a farm labourer in Hampshire. By the time he returned to Germany, his parents were dead (his mother killed by Allied bombing). But it seemed that few of his fellow countrymen had learned the lessons of defeat: "The Germans were so bitter, saying, 'How can this rubbish defeat us?'"

After just four weeks he returned to the farm in Hampshire, where he was given his old job back and played with the local football team at Bentley in Hampshire. He was met with little prejudice. When there was an attempt to remove him from a bus the other passengers objected, and veterans of the First World War were glad to compare his experiences with theirs.

In 1952 Metelmann married Monika, the farmer's Swiss au pair with whom he had a son and a daughter. Later he took a job as a railway signalman and, on his retirement in 1987, Charterhouse offered him a job as groundsman on the golf course in the mornings and the chance to play in the afternoons. He donated a Metelmann Cup for which he would then compete every year.

While several of his old Army comrades committed suicide, he joined the Communist Party and CND and became a committed peace activist. In the 1960s he protested against the Vietnam War. Later he attended all the Stop the War marches against the invasion of Iraq and protested against the American bombing of Afghanistan.

After his wife died in 1980 Metelmann sat down to write his book. Some reviewers were repelled by his reluctance to admit any more than collective guilt for the crimes in which he had participated; but he explained that he was determined that people should understand the causes of the war and the processes of brainwashing to avoid making the same mistakes again.

Subsequently, a history master at Charterhouse asked Metelmann to give a talk to his pupils. More invitations followed from schools. At Eton, his audience included Princes William and Harry. "I got the best questions at that school, which rather surprised me," he recalled. "They seem to be completely on the mark when it comes to independent thinking, not as Establishment as I thought."

ENSIGN NANCY WAKE

Ensign Nancy Wake (who died on August 7 2011, aged 98) was 'White Mouse', one of the most celebrated and decorated secret agents of the Second World War.

A key figure in an escape ring in Vichy France and a leader of the Maquis against the German

Occupation, her exploits earned her the George Medal; the Croix de Guerre with palm (twice); the Croix de Guerre with star; the Médaille de la Résistance (a rare decoration for a foreigner); and the US Medal of Freedom with bronze palm.

When fighting broke out in 1939 she was the frivolous young fiancée of a wealthy Marseilles industrialist. But by the war's end in Europe she had become famed as a resourceful, dauntless Resistance leader, who topped the Gestapo's most-wanted list and had saved hundreds of Allied lives.

Nancy Grace Augusta Wake was born in Wellington, New Zealand, on August 30 1912, the youngest in a family of six. She grew up at Neutral Bay, Sydney. A good-looking girl with a streak of rebelliousness, she set out alone in December 1932 to explore Europe, via Vancouver and New York, living by freelance journalism.

From London she headed for Paris, where she sent reports to American press agencies. After Hitler's rise to power she witnessed in Vienna the Nazi brutality that she had heard of from German refugees. On seeing Jews being persecuted she "resolved there and then that if I ever had the chance I would do anything to make things more difficult for their rotten party".

In the summer of 1936 Nancy Wake met a 'charming, sexy and amusing' man in Juan-les-Pins named Henri Fiocca; though he had a reputation as a playboy they continued to see each other, and in 1939 he asked her to marry him. By the time France was overrun in 1940 they had married and, though initially squeamish, she began to drive an ambulance. Later, back in Marseilles with her husband, she embarked on an exhausting double life.

She had acquired perfect French, and a chance meeting in a bar led to her employment as a courier for Captain Ian Garrow, a Scot who had helped create an escape route for officers and airmen from Vichy France across the mountains into Spain. Fiocca contributed money freely to this enterprise.

She made frequent train journeys escorting escapers towards the Pyrenees; as a courier for a French Resistance group based in Toulon, she also provided the Fioccas' chalet at Nevache, in the Alps, as a safe house. When Garrow was captured and imprisoned in Meauzac concentration camp, she contrived his escape by bribing a guard.

In the autumn of 1942 the Germans occupied Vichy France, and the Gestapo became increasingly aware of the troublesome and elusive 'White Mouse'. Finally, when it seemed that the net was closing, Nancy Wake was advised by her husband to flee to England, where he hoped to join her.

In Toulouse, while she waited for the escape circuit to extricate her, she was arrested in a random round-up and accused (falsely) of blowing up a cinema. Bruised and weary after four days of interrogation, she was astonished when her group leader, Patrick O'Leary, appeared. O'Leary, who had succeeded Garrow in the role, was a Belgian Army doctor (real name Albert Guerisse) and his exploits would also become famous.

He told the French police chief that he was a friend of Pierre Laval, the Vichy premier, that Madame Fiocca was his (O'Leary's) mistress, and that the story she had told was a cover to deceive her husband.

The police chief felt he understood this intimate dilemma and set her free.

Nancy Wake made several attempts to reach Spain, but was thwarted each time by arrests that broke up the circuit. On her final attempt she had to leap from a train window and run for it with several companions, dodging bullets before escaping through a vineyard. She concluded that a German counter-agent had penetrated the circuit; and when O'Leary was arrested back in Toulouse, she knew she was right.

Eventually she found guides who buried her in the back of a coal truck with a New Zealander and two Americans, then led her by rocky Pyreneean tracks into Spain. She reached England in a convoy from Gibraltar in June 1943.

Within eight months Nancy Wake had become a fully trained agent of the Special Operations Executive, and had been commissioned into the First Aid Nursing Yeomanry. The official history of SOE in France records that her "irrepressible, infectious high spirits were a joy to everyone who worked with her". She and Violette Szabo once debagged an SOE instructor in London, hoisting his trousers up a flagpole.

Her training complete, she was parachuted into central France in April 1944, landing near Montluçon. As she came down her parachute became tangled in a tree. "I hope," said Henri Tardivat, the Resistance fighter who greeted her, "that all the trees in France bear such beautiful fruit this year."

Nancy Wake's role was as assistant to J H Farmer in running the circuit known as Freelance, part of

SOE's F Section, headed by Maurice Buckmaster in London. She threw herself into building up various Maquis groups into a formidable force 7,500-strong, controlling communications with London, allocating arms and equipment that were parachuted in, and holding the purse strings.

To coincide with the Normandy landings, the Auvergne Maquis launched a furious assault on factories and communications. A powerful German counter-attack, with aerial support, failed to stop them, but had the effect of cutting Nancy Wake's lines of communication with London when her wireless operator, Denis Rake, expecting capture, burned the code books.

To re-establish contact, essential before D-Day, she rode a bicycle from Auvergne to Châteauroux – 250 miles in 72 hours on a round trip through German-held territory. Rejected by one Resistance wireless operator because she had no password, by good fortune she found another, who informed London of the situation. "When I got off that damned bike I felt as if I had a fire between my legs. I couldn't stand up. I couldn't sit down, I couldn't walk. When I'm asked what I'm most proud of doing during the war, I say: 'The bike ride'."

For the remainder of the war Nancy Wake was involved in ambushing German convoys and destroying bridges and railway lines. When ten men in her camp refused to perform their water-carrying duties she persuaded them by emptying a bucket over each. She interrogated a woman spy and ordered her execution, but saved two girls she considered innocent.

She was also on a raid that destroyed the Gestapo's headquarters in Montluçon, leaving thirty-eight Germans dead. It was, she wrote later, "the most exciting sortie I ever made. I entered the building by the back door, raced up the stairs, opened the first door along the passage way, threw in my grenades and ran like hell."

On her 32nd birthday – shortly after the liberation of Paris – her Maquis comrades paraded in her honour at the chateau they had appropriated for their headquarters. "When we were fighting we were fighting," she said, "when we weren't we were having a jolly good time. I never was scared."

With victory came the bitter news that Henri Fiocca had been tortured and executed by the Germans. Nancy Wake was not only a widow, but also without means. She duly continued in intelligence, attached to the British embassies in Paris and Prague, where she developed a loathing of communism to rival her enduring hated of Nazis. Then, in 1949, she returned to Sydney. There she stood for the federal parliament in the Liberal cause against Labour's deputy leader, Dr HV Evatt; at the second attempt, in 1951, she got to within a few hundred votes of him.

Afterwards Nancy Wake returned to England, spending five happy years as an intelligence officer in the department of the Assistant Chief of Air Staff in Whitehall. In 1957, however, she married John Forward, an RAF officer, and resigned her post. Three years later they returned to Australia.

In the 1966 Australian elections she once again tried unsuccessfully to enter the federal parliament, running for the Sydney constituency of Kingsford

Smith. Her profile gradually lowered until 1985, when she published an autobiography, *The White Mouse*. She settled in Port Macquarie, on the north coast of New South Wales. After her husband died in 1997 she lived there for four further years until returning to England for good.

Initially she became a resident at the Stafford Hotel in St James's Place, off Piccadilly, which had been a British and American forces club during the war. Nancy Wake had ordered her first "bloody good drink" there in 1946, lured to the bar, like many former secret agents, by the hotel's then general manager, Louis Burdet, who had himself also worked for the Resistance in Marseilles.

In old age Nancy Wake was to be found on a leather stool in the hotel bar most mornings, nursing the first of the day's five or six gin and tonics. Though she celebrated her 90th birthday there, and the hotel's owners welcomed her, they were obliged to absorb most of the costs of her stay, helped occasionally by anonymous donors – thought to include the Prince of Wales.

The hotel said it was looking forward to planning her 100th birthday, but in 2003 Nancy Wake moved to the Star and Garter forces' retirement home just outside Richmond Park, where she remained until her death. Nancy Wake had no children. In 2013, her ashes were scattered near the village of Verneix in France, in a ceremony attended by the village's mayor and the Australian military attaché Brig Bill Sowry.

CAPTAIN PETER DORESA

Captain Peter Doresa (who died on February 1 2012, aged 87) was with 4th Battalion the Queen's Own Royal West Kent Regiment which arrived at Kohima, north-east India, to reinforce the garrison which was under increasing pressure from Japanese forces in April 1944.

As they approached the town, passing a deserted hospital and chaotically abandoned stores, their trucks were fired on and they made the rest of the way on foot. Two days later the Japanese closed in and, for almost two weeks, the battalion endured relentless bombardment by mortars and anti-tank guns by day; to this was added fire from snipers who strapped themselves into the tops of trees. By night, artillery concentrations were the precursor of charges of massed infantry screaming and blowing bugles.

Sometimes, the enemy's tactics were more subtle. The crack of a sniper's rifle at night was often designed to provoke a response and reveal the location of the defenders' trenches. Then the Japanese would mimic British voices with cries of "For God's sake let me through – the Japs are after me!"

Time and again, the enemy were found to be dug in too firmly to be dislodged by anything less than a full-scale attack which would threaten unaffordable casualties. Doresa, a platoon commander in D Company, was ordered to clear the enemy from some huts which were surrounded by an ammunition dump.

He went forward and bombed the position, setting the dump ablaze. Shells, mortar bombs, grenades and small arms ammunition exploded, sending shrapnel flying in all directions. The Japanese were driven into the open where they were shot by the remainder of the company. Doresa himself accounted for more than twelve and escaped with a minor wound.

Later in the battle, the Japanese infiltrated the regiment's positions under cover of darkness with their weapons wrapped in cloth to prevent any noise. Doresa waited until they were within a few yards of his trench before giving the order to fire. The whole platoon opened up with tracer and parachute flares forcing a withdrawal. Two of the battalion's companies inflicted about five times their total strength in casualties on the enemy.

After the battle, witnesses described the survivors as "sleepwalkers, haggard, hollow-eyed, bearded, their uniforms ragged and filthy, their faces caked with dried blood, some seemingly half-crazed with fatigue".

Doresa was awarded an immediate MC. Lance-Corporal John Harman, who served in the same company, was posthumously awarded a Victoria Cross for charging a Japanese trench that held five soldiers armed with automatic weapons.

Peter Constantine Doresa was born at Guildford, Surrey, on October 18 1924. He was nine when his mother died in a car accident. At Tonbridge he was frustrated when he was not selected to play for the 1st XI, so gave up cricket and became the best shot in the school.

He attended OCTU at Mons, Aldershot, and was then commissioned into the Royal West Kents. After the Battle of Kohima he was wounded again in the advance from Imphal, this time more seriously; he was evacuated to India, where he became an instructor.

After retiring from the Army, Doresa became a photographer, opening an office in Mayfair then moving to Leicestershire where he covered three-day events and agricultural shows before retiring to Hindhead, Surrey. Peter Doresa married, in 1947, Coral Millard. She predeceased him and he was survived by their two daughters.

LIEUTENANT COLONEL MICHAEL MANN

Lieutenant Colonel Michael Mann (who died on February 5 2012, aged 94) was awarded an MC in France for exemplary dash during the withdrawal to Dunkirk.

In May 1940, he and his small Royal Army Service Corps unit were working with the 1st Light Anti-Aircraft Battery about thirty miles south of Dunkirk. They were virtually surrounded by the Germans, and his CO at HQ told Mann that the heavy AA Battery being used to defend the nearby town of Hazebrouck was running short of ammunition. There had been a good supply of shells stored in a railway wagon, but a nervous stationmaster had shunted it, along with another containing fused mines, into the Forêt de Nieppe to the south, five miles inside German-held territory.

Mann took his Austin 7, a driver and a corporal

armed with a Bren gun to the goods yard. The stationmaster had fled, but there was a huge locomotive with steam up, a burly engine driver and a platelayer. Mann explained that he had to retrieve the wagon and they agreed to help.

The corporal climbed to the top of the heaped coal in the tender with his Bren gun, and they set off. After two miles they were strafed by an enemy fighter, and while they were not hit the blast blew the corporal from his perch into a bramble thicket.

Mann shouted that they would pick him up on the way back, and on they went. Three miles further down the track they saw the wagons. The one loaded with mines was ablaze and the track leading to it was bent.

"Thank God for the platelayer," said Mann afterwards – he straightened the rails in twenty minutes. Mann decoupled the burning wagon, collected the one with the shells as well as the corporal and returned to the station.

"There we found quite a committee waiting for us," Mann said in a letter to his sister. "How they knew, I never found out, for I never told anyone we were going." His Military Cross was gazetted in August 1940.

Michael Woodham Mann was born at Hurst Green, Sussex, on May 27 1917 and educated at Harrow, where he was captain of the shooting team. After Wadham College, Oxford, where he read Modern Languages and represented the university at pistol shooting, he was commissioned in 1939 into the RASC and went to France with the BEF.

A few days after the retrieval of the ammunition

wagon, Mann celebrated his 23rd birthday. He drove to Battery HQ to collect his men's breakfast and, seeing a bomb-damaged wine store in the town, helped himself to a bottle.

As he was enjoying a champagne breakfast, his lookout spotted two large German tanks. Mann signalled to his men to get down in their trenches and, through his glasses, observed the Germans breaking through a hedge about 600 yards away and slowly advancing.

He prayed that the tanks would not see his men or their lorries, but suddenly, to his right, a Bofors gun opened up. It had no effect on the tanks' armour. Seconds later, the Germans fired an answering shot, which blew the Bofors to bits and killed all but one of the crew.

The two tanks then turned their machine guns on Mann's lorries. He took up a Boys anti-tank rifle and, as he noted later, "had a go – one shot – a coconut. And what a coconut! I hit his track. It broke and, stripped, swerved through a right angle. It must have thrown the gunner off his seat. He shot his neighbour and, at point blank range, blew half its turret off and set it on fire."

Mann was determined not to leave the shells in his lorries for the Germans. He put petrol cans on top of them, emptied his pistol into them to hole them and soaked the ammunition boxes. "Can you oblige me with a match, corporal?" he asked the man at his side.

They ran as fast as they could, dodged two more German tanks and, piling on to gun tractors, set off northwards – bombed and strafed all the way. Mann's men dug pits under their vehicles and slept there. Mann himself went to a cemetery, chose the sturdiest vault, shot off the lock and slept on a shelf among the coffins.

During the evacuation from Dunkirk, Mann and his men were on the beach for four days without food or water. Eventually they got away by paddling a section of pontoon five miles off the coast, where they were picked up by an Isle of Man ferry. Mann subsequently commanded a motorboat company of the RASC, and then the Army Navigational Training School.

Demobilised in 1945 he worked in Perthshire as a land agent for a year before joining the staff of Felsted School, Essex, where he taught Modern Languages. He owned an eight-ton cutter and started the CCF naval section, also running the school's shooting for many years when it won many prizes in the Bisley Schools' competitions.

He was Master of the North Essex Foot Beagles from 1963 to 1974, and it was not unknown for him to wear hunting breeches under his academic gown. Mike Mann married, in 1945, Diana Stebbing, who predeceased him.

MAJOR JOE SCHOFIELD

Major Joe Schofield (who died on February 8 2012, aged 90) wore the SAS Badge and Wings for almost forty years, and had the distinction of being the only soldier to serve with all five of its regiments.

He joined 1st SAS in North Africa in 1941 as it was evolving from L Detachment, its earliest incarnation under its founder David Stirling. He was fortunate to survive his parachute training. The aircraft to be used were not equipped with static fixed lines, and Schofield said later that on his first jump the parachutes of the three men ahead of him 'roman-candled' and fell to their deaths: "I was Number Four in the stick." The air dispatcher just managed to grab him before he jumped.

He took part with the regiment in several raids on airfields and in the ambushing of convoys on the coastal road. After it was reorganised in 1943 as the Special Raiding Squadron (SRS) under Paddy Mayne, he saw action in the invasion of Sicily. Schofield was part of the force that scaled the cliffs at Cape Murro di Porco and knocked out a fortified farmhouse at the top. On the Italian mainland, he fought alongside the Commandos in the capture and then dogged defence of Termoli.

In Operation Haggard Schofield was dropped into France in August 1944, with a party from B Squadron 1st SAS and elements of the French and Belgian SAS. There they linked up with the Maquis around the Falaise pocket, harassing German units and signalling their positions to the RAF. The following winter he was involved in long-range reconnaissance patrols during the Battle of the Ardennes.

In April 1945, at Lorup, near Cloppenburg in Germany, Schofield was in the leading jeep, scouting ahead of a column, when he came under heavy machine-gun and rifle fire from two houses and a wood beside a country road. His commander was killed, and he was momentarily pinned by shrapnel through one leg to the bodywork of the vehicle. Dragging himself on to the bonnet to return fire, he was then hit in the other leg by a sniper. Bleeding profusely from his wounds, he and his driver were taking cover in a ditch when they were narrowly missed by two rockets from a *panzerfaust*.

Alerted by radio, Mayne went forward alone and cleared the houses with a Bren, shooting from the shoulder. With a volunteer manning the rear guns, he then drove his jeep up the road under fire, engaged the enemy troops in the wood, turned around, drove back down and then – while still under attack – returned a third time to rescue the wounded Schofield. He was recommended for the Victoria Cross but received instead his fourth DSO.

Albert Schofield was born at Stalybridge, Cheshire, on June 23 1921. His father worked for the railways delivering parcels in horse-drawn vans. He left school at 14 and was taken on by an engineering company. The owner had promised him work in the drawing office but then gave the job to his son. Offered alternative employment as a steel forger, Schofield walked out.

He enlisted in the Army Supplementary Reserve and, after a spell with the Cheshire Regiment, transferred to the Life Guards in 1938. His exemplary record with the Cheshires earned him promotion on transfer, but he found himself the smallest in the troop — his nickname 'Joe' originating from a popular cartoon character called 'Little Joe'. He was regularly given sentry duty around Whitehall, where tourists used to drop coins into his highly polished boots, providing useful beer money.

At the outbreak of war, Schofield was too young to go to France with the BEF and was put in charge of the horse lines in Windsor Great Park. He subsequently volunteered to join 8 Commando, and after rigorous training in Scotland formed part of a detachment that landed at Tobruk in 1941. On the night of July 17 it took part in an attack on a feature known as the Twin Pimples, a defensive strongpoint held by the Italians which dominated the Allied lines.

The defenders spotted the Commandos, but were firing on fixed lines so that the bullets passed over the heads of the attacking force as they crept towards them. Schofield said afterwards that they had gone in with fixed bayonets and that the fight was "short and bloody". Just when they thought that they had cleared the trenches, Schofield found the door of a concealed hatch. The Italians had constructed shelters underneath where more troops were hiding.

As he lifted up the door, a bayonet was thrust upwards which wounded him in the hand. Someone hurled a grenade into the shelter and he had to jump clear to avoid being killed in the explosion. After the order was given to withdraw, they set off across the desert.

Discovering that a great friend of his, Jackie Maynard, was missing, Schofield turned back and found him with an abdominal wound. Schofield carried him to base under continual fire, but Maynard died. He always regretted that he had not been able to stay with him.

Schofield was then selected for an undercover

mission in Turkey. The country was neutral, but there were fears that Axis forces might try to take over. Ostensibly supervising a team of engineers, his job was to lay explosive charges under strategically important bridges in Cappadocia. To his surprise, he discovered that the Germans had put in charges in the First World War which were still in place. His task became the simpler one of checking the explosives and adding to them or replacing them where necessary.

After being wounded in Germany, Schofield spent ten months in plaster. Following a spell as a parachute instructor at the Airborne Forces depot, in 1947 he was posted to 21 SAS as a permanent staff instructor. He served with D Squadron 22 SAS in Malaya from 1953 to 1955, served as regimental sergeant-major with 21 SAS then returned to Malaya for two more years before returning to England as RSM of 23 SAS.

In 1965 he was commissioned into 22 SAS as a captain, based at Hereford, and eventually became quartermaster. His tour of duty ended in 1971, but he extended his service until 1979 as a retired officer. Appointed MBE in 1969, he was an active member of the SAS Association and was tireless in organising visits to France to lay wreaths on the graves of members who had been killed (or in some instances, executed). In retirement he enjoyed gardening, fishing and family life. Joe Schofield married, in 1947, Sheelagh Ledwith, who survived him with their two sons and two daughters.

LIEUTENANT PHILIP MARTEL

Lieutenant Philip Martel (who died on February 23 2012, aged 97) won an MC in 1940 for his efforts to aid a farcical landing on occupied Guernsey ahead of an ill-fated raid by British Special Forces.

When the Germans invaded the Channel Islands on June 30, Winston Churchill declared in a minute to the War Cabinet that an attack on the invaders was an exploit that would suit the newly-formed Commandos. A force of 140 men was selected from 3 Commando, the first to be raised, and 11 Independent Company, made up of volunteers for special service. Operation Ambassador's objectives included the destruction of Guernsey's airfield, a machine-gun post and the German barracks at Telegraph Bay.

Martel, a second lieutenant in the Hampshire Regiment, and Desmond Mulholland of the Duke of Cornwall's Light Infantry were selected because they had both been in the Royal Guernsey Militia. They were ordered to land secretly ahead of the raiding parties and guide them to their targets, but were warned at their briefing they would be shot if caught.

Their equipment left much to be desired. They were unarmed but provided with torches which gave little light, Horlicks tablets and some chocolates, and arrived at Plymouth in sports jackets and flannel trousers.

There they joined a submarine and, shortly after midnight on July 10, rowed its dinghy to land near Le Jaonnet Bay. They were met by another agent,

Lieutenant Hubert Nicolle, who had landed a few days earlier to reconnoitre the German troop dispositions. He gave them a quick summary of his findings before returning to the submarine in the inflatable dinghy. Meanwhile, Martel and Mulholland climbed the cliff path into enemy territory.

Bad weather then led to a postponement for 48 hours, though there was no means of telling Martel and Mulholland who were on their own and on the run.

On the evening of July 14, the raiding force eventually embarked on two destroyers accompanied by six RAF air-sea rescue launches, but it encountered problems. Two of the launches carrying the Independent Company broke down and had to be left behind. Degaussing, to reduce the magnetic field, put the compasses 'out of true' and, as a result, the launch that Martel expected to meet at Le Jaonnet landed on Sark; the other ran into a rock.

The detachment from 3 Commando, under Lieutenant Colonel John Durnford-Slater, ignored their compasses and reached Telegraph Bay, close to the Jerbourg Peninsula. The tide was in and they got soaked landing among the rocks. Encumbered by their wet uniforms and equipment, they then had to climb several hundred steps to the cliff top. An aircraft, sent to deaden any noise that the raiders might make, circled overhead but this proved too much for the local dogs which set up a chorus of barking.

The Commandos surrounded the machine-gun post but, having jumped into the sandbagged circle, found themselves staring down the muzzles of each others' guns. There were no Germans present, and a search of the barracks proved equally fruitless.

On the way back to the beach a revolver went off by mistake and, at last, the Germans came to life and pursued them with tracer. The launches were 100 yards out but could come no closer because of the rocks. There was no alternative but to swim out to them – three of the party then confessed that they couldn't swim; they had to be left behind to become prisoners of war. Churchill was furious, describing the operation as a "silly fiasco".

Martel and Mulholland waited at Le Jaonnet for two nights, but their torch flashes in Morse code were mistaken for enemy signals and the submarine did not pick them up. They then lay low for three weeks and made two attempts to escape. First they stole a boat, but the sea was rough and they knew nothing about sailing; after giving themselves a bad fright, they returned to the shore.

Then they took a boat to Sark. There were German soldiers on board, and when they reached the island they discovered that all the fishing smacks were well guarded. After returning once more to Guernsey, they decided to give themselves up. Added to the continual strain of being on the run, there was the danger to their families and others who knew where they were.

They contacted the island's attorney general who drove them to the town arsenal where some uniforms of the Royal Guernsey Militia were altered into some semblance of British service dress before they were handed over to the German military authorities.

The two men were flown to France and interrogated separately. They were questioned closely about the Commando raid, but neither knew that there had been a landing, and their genuine bewilderment may have saved their lives.

Both were sent on to Germany, and Martel spent the next five years at camps at Tittmoning, Warburg and Eichstätt. While the POWs were being marched away from Eichstätt, they were strafed by Allied aircraft. The man walking beside Martel was killed and there were numerous other casualties. Martel was liberated from Moosburg in 1945 by American troops. His MC was gazetted the following year.

Philip Martel was born at Le Mont Durand, St Martins, Guernsey, on December 17 1914. He was educated at Elizabeth College, St Peter Port, and then moved between Geneva, Bristol and London learning watchmaking and optics.

After the war, he returned to Guernsey, where he inherited the family jewellery firm, which traded at St Peter Port as AP Roger, and retired after selling it in 1981. Philip Martel married, in 1948, Rosemary Robertson, who survived him with their two sons and a daughter.

MAJOR MICHAEL ROSS

Major Michael Ross (who died on March 20 2012, aged 94) spent more than a year on the run in wartime Italy, falling in love with – and eventually marrying – the daughter of a partisan who sheltered him.

His remarkable and romantic story began in the North African desert in January 1942 when he was serving with the Welch Regiment. Having been involved in the fierce struggle for Benghazi, 1 Welch was ordered to withdraw to the Egyptian frontier, and to split into individual companies and detachments, each to make its own way across hundreds of miles of desert.

Ross, in command of one unit, was ordered to use his three Bofors guns to delay any enemy armoured vehicles that might impede the column as it sought to withdraw. He and his men soon came under attack, and Ross decided that his eighteen-strong force should make for Regima, fifty miles to the north, to link up with British forces. When they got within sight of the town they realised that it had fallen to Rommel; they decided to split up, and Ross found himself on his own.

He made his way eastwards back to British lines, often receiving food and shelter from Senussi Arabs. Then, on the twelfth day, he was captured trying to cross a road. He was then shipped to Italy and incarcerated in a converted orphanage at Fontanellato, in the Parma region. Although Ross later described the accommodation as "five-star", he was determined to escape, and with a fellow officer of the Welch Regiment, Jimmy Day, hatched a plan.

The POWs had been invited by their captors to level out the surface of a fenced-in playing field located outside the main compound, to make it suitable for playing ball games. Their guards provided picks and shovels, and the prisoners dug a shallow trench, just large enough to accommodate Ross and Day, concealed by bed boards and a covering of soil. When their comrades were taken back to the compound at the end of the day, the two waited until nightfall then cut their way through the wire fence.

They set off north-west towards Switzerland, posing as German workers at the Fiat factory in Turin on a walking holiday, and after ten days were close to the Swiss border when they were challenged by a carabiniere and recaptured. On returning to Fontanellato they received thirty days' solitary confinement.

Following the fall of Mussolini and the Italian Armistice in September 1943, the prisoners were told by the Allies to remain in their camps and await the arrival of Allied forces – an instruction that ignored the possibility that the retreating Germans might take prisoners with them. The sympathetic Italian camp commandant ordered a wide gap to be cut in the perimeter fence to facilitate a quick evacuation, and when word came that German vehicles were approaching the camp he ordered the bugler to sound the alarm. Ross and many other POWs fled.

Ross teamed up with George Bell, a Highland Light Infantry officer who in civilian life had been a tea planter in Ceylon. Dismissing any notion of making for Switzerland (where they would have been indefinitely interned), they headed north-west with the intention of keeping to the mountains parallel to the coast, through Liguria and then into France.

After two months they were well into Liguria, where they encountered a small band of anti-fascists. Ross and Bell joined them, thus getting to know the head of the resistance group in the area, Beppe Porcheddu, a well-known engineer, architect, painter and illustrator. At great risk to himself and his family, Porcheddu sheltered Ross and Bell in his villa at the coastal town of Bordighera. He had a wife, 18 year-old twin daughters and a son, and was well aware of the danger in which he was placing his family.

As he folded into the daily life of the household, Ross fell in love with Porcheddu's daughter, Giovanna. Writing in his memoir, *From Liguria with Love* (1997), he noted: "I did not know whether my sentiments were reciprocated or not, although there were times when I thought I detected a mutual regard ... one could live only by the day and have hope for the morrow."

The danger of discovery was ever-present, for Porcheddu's connection with the partisans was suspected by the authorities. A secret room behind a wardrobe provided a refuge for Ross and Bell when fascists called at the villa.

Meanwhile, the two men were planning to complete their escape. An attempt to row to Corsica ended when their boat sank shortly after they left the beach, and by early 1945 they were still secreted at the villa. Then came news that Porcheddu was about to be arrested; the family fled and scattered.

Ross and Bell returned to the hills, where again they were sheltered by partisans. They also linked up with Captain Bentley, an SOE officer who had arrived on a mission to arrange the delivery of arms and supplies to the anti-fascists. A Royal Navy submarine was to bring these by rubber dinghies which, Bentley suggested, could take them back to the submarine and freedom.

Three night landings were attempted, but each time the beach was lit up by flares, and Ross, Bell and their partisan friends were lucky to escape. They later learned that the Germans had been tipped off by one of the partisans, a girl called Olga, who was executed with a shot to the back of the head.

The Allies had landed in the south of France in August 1944, and were occupying Monte Carlo, only fifteen miles from Bordighera. But an attempt to get through the German lines was a less attractive option than escaping by sea.

Ross and Bell kept on the move, never staying in the same place for more than one night – on one occasion the Germans ambushed and killed several partisans from whom the British pair had parted only hours earlier. They were now joined by two Americans, a Free French pilot who had been shot down and four Italians fleeing the fascists.

In March 1945 they managed to get a suitable boat and set out on a calm night from Vallecrosia, just west of Bordighera. But it capsized in a heavy swell, and Ross – hampered by the German greatcoat he was wearing – nearly drowned as he swam back to shore. For their second attempt, a few days later, the nine men used two boats. After rowing for seven hours, they entered the harbour at Monte Carlo just as dawn was breaking.

Following a slap-up breakfast at the Bristol Hotel, Ross and Bell were debriefed before returning to Britain. Ross was subsequently mentioned in despatches. After a period of leave he rejoined his regiment, shortly before the end of hostilities in Europe.

The following year he returned to Italy in a staff appointment and made his way to Bordighera for a joyful reunion with the Porcheddu family, all of whom had survived the war. He and Giovanna married later that year.

Michael Ross was born on April 10 1917, the son of an English master mariner and his Irish wife and brought up and educated at Penarth, south Wales. He trained as a teacher at Loughborough Training College where he excelled at athletics and rugby.

After the war, he was mentioned in despatches and remained in uniform working for the War Crimes Commission in Austria, then transferring to the Royal Army Education Corps to serve in Korea, Hong Kong and West Berlin. In the late 1960s he joined the Diplomatic Corps to serve as vice-consul in New York and Johannesburg before dividing his retirement between England and Bordighera, where he and Giovanna kept an apartment.

In *From Liguria with Love*, Ross paid tribute to Porcheddu, the partisans and the many ordinary Italians in the countryside who resisted fascism, aided escaping POWs and generally supported the Allied cause – often at great cost to themselves.

He was a man of great modesty, and few of his

friends were aware of his exploits until he published his book. One of his fellow POWs at Fontanellato had been Eric Newby, author of the popular *Love and War in the Appenines*, which described how he, too, had returned to Italy after the war to marry the daughter of a Slovenian who had risked his life for him. The two remained friends, and Newby generously acknowledged that Ross's book was by far the more exciting story. Michael Ross was survived by Giovanna, their daughter and two sons.

BRIGADIER TONY HUNTER-CHOAT

Brigadier Tony Hunter-Choat (who died on April 12 2012, aged 76) began his military career in the French Foreign Legion, with which he was decorated three times and took part in a coup to unseat Charles de Gaulle; he then joined the British Army to serve in the Indonesia confrontation and command 23 SAS and serve with Special Forces.

Born on January 12 1936 at Purley, south London, to a father who worked in insurance and a mother who was a schoolteacher, he was educated at Dulwich and then Kingston College of Art, where he trained as an architect. On holidays he hitchhiked around Europe, developing a taste for travel and an affinity for languages.

Deciding in 1957 that architecture was not for him, he resolved to indulge his thirst for adventure and made his way to Paris to enlist in the Foreign Legion. His mother pursued, keen to get her errant son back to his studies, but by the time she arrived he had signed up.

Hunter-Choat was sent for basic training to Algeria, then in the throes of an increasing anti-colonialist insurrection and volunteered to complete the extra training necessary to become a paratrooper. On October 15 he was duly posted to the 1st Battalion, Régiment Etranger de Parachutistes (1e REP), with which he would be involved in continuous operations for almost five years.

By the late 1950s the Algerian War of Independence had become a high-intensity conflict requiring the presence on the ground of 400,000 French and colonial troops to maintain a semblance of order.

Hunter-Choat and his comrades took part in hundreds of operations, and suffered and inflicted considerable casualties. In February 1958, as a young machine-gunner, he took part in the battle of Fedj Zezoua, in the woods east of Guelma, in the north-east of the country. Two armed units of the rebel Front de Libération Nationale (FLN) were dug in on a hillside.

The legionnaires began their attack at 7 am and met stiff resistance, but after being dropped by helicopter (balancing precariously on a cliffside) in the midst of the FLN positions, they overwhelmed the enemy. Hunter-Choat was awarded the first of three Crosses of Valour and the Médaille Militaire. Less than two weeks later he was wounded as the 1e REP pursued FLN groups through the wooded territory close to the border with Tunisia.

It was an odd fact of life in the Legion that one in four of his NCOs was German, and many had fought on the Russian Front. Hunter-Choat recalled that their homes were now behind the Iron Curtain and that, to such brothers-in-arms as Adolf, Rolf, Hans or Karl, the Legion had "become their country". Some were former SS troops who, he noted, were "superb soldiers and great trainers of men. They would expose themselves to danger in order to bring on the young soldiers."

After recovering from his wounds he was repeatedly involved in intense fighting against the FLN. But as the tide of war turned, and it became clear that Paris was preparing to negotiate Algeria's independence, he found himself fighting his own side.

The Algiers putsch, as it became known, was a coup launched by four retired French generals to oust de Gaulle and seize control first of Algeria, then of Paris. Hélie de Saint Marc, commander of the 1e REP, agreed to take part, and, on the night of April 21/22 1961, Hunter-Choat was part of the plotters' force which occupied key locations in Algiers.

A message was broadcast throughout Algeria declaring "The Army has seized control". The following day, however, de Gaulle appeared on television, wearing his 1940 uniform and calling for soldiers to back him.As his message was retransmitted through barracks, support for the coup collapsed. The 1e REP was disbanded; and as its men were marched out of camp they sang Edith Piaf's *Non, Je Ne Regrette Rien*.

Shortly afterwards Hunter-Choat's five-year term of service expired and he returned home where his father encouraged him to join the British Army. But his first application for a short service commission, in March 1962, was rejected by the War Office as he exceeded the age limit for a commission 'under any existing procedures'. By April a second letter, written by his father, elicited a more positive response: "It has been agreed that you may be accepted, as a special case, for consideration."

After passing out top of his course at Mons officer cadet school he was commissioned into the 7th Gurkha Rifles (Duke of Edinburgh's Own) and posted to Malaya. From there, in early 1963, he was sent to Brunei and on to Sarawak and Borneo, where he fought in the Indonesian Confrontation.

The scale and ferocity was considerably lower than in Algeria, but the climate and jungle environment made for hard soldiering. Jungle patrols often lasted several weeks and contact with the enemy, though infrequent, was frequently vicious. Hunter-Choat took part in cross-border raids into Indonesia (officially denied at the time) as well as coastal raids.

He was now keen to convert to a regular commission. On being told that he was too old for the infantry, he discovered that the Royal Artillery age limit was higher, and joined in early 1964. Upon transfer, he remained in Borneo, where he served as a forward observation officer until 1966, when he returned to Britain.

Hunter-Choat attended the staff college at Camberley in 1969-70, then served in 45 Regiment RA before becoming a battery commander and second-in-command of 3 Royal Horse Artillery in Hong Kong.

Between 1975 and 1977 he was on the directing staff of the junior division of the staff college at

Warminster and then, unusually for an officer without a British Special Forces background, was offered command of 23 SAS, a territorial unit. His accomplishments there were so highly regarded that he remained with Special Forces, in a variety of command and staff roles, for the rest of his Army career.

He commanded 23 SAS until 1983, though the sensitivity of his work during this period means that, to this day, few details of his service can be published. From 1983 to 1986 he was a senior staff officer at NATO headquarters and a Special Forces adviser to the Supreme Allied Commander Europe. His last post was as personal liaison between the Commander-in-Chief, BAOR, and his American equivalent. He was appointed OBE.

After retiring from the Army as a colonel he immediately became commander of the Sultan of Oman's Special Forces in the rank of brigadier. He was responsible for increasing numbers in the Sultan's Special Forces from under 1,000 to more than 2,000, and for improving their equipment and capability. In 1995 he was presented with the Omani Order of Achievement by Sultan Qaboos.

On leaving the Sultan's service in 1997, he helped verify the crumbling ceasefire in Kosovo and in 1998–99 became head of security for the Aga Khan. This involved helping to create a base for the Aga Khan at the celebrated racing town of Chantilly, France.

After the American-led invasion of Iraq in 2003, Hunter-Choat became head of security for the Program Management Office (PMO), which was involved in overseeing the distribution of billions of dollars of reconstruction funds to projects throughout the country. There he briefly became embroiled in controversy after the PMO awarded a contract worth $293 million to Aegis, a private security company headed by Tim Spicer.

According to *Vanity Fair*, Hunter-Choat and Spicer had known each other for years. DynCorp, a rival to Aegis, lodged a protest with the US Congress, but this was rejected, and there was no suggestion that Hunter-Choat had behaved improperly.

He was later responsible for the security plans for US Aid in Afghanistan, and became an accomplished lecturer on leadership and security issues.

Hunter-Choat was a Fellow of the Royal Society of Arts and a Freeman of the City of London. He was a former president and secretary general of the British branch of the Foreign Legion Association and a keen Freemason. Appointed an Officer of the Legion of Honour in 2001 he was promoted Commander in 2011.

Tony Hunter-Choat married in 1964 Maureen McCabe. The marriage was dissolved, and he married secondly, in 1982, Linda Wood who survived him with their son and two daughters as well as by two daughters of his first marriage.

MAJOR COLIN KENNARD

Major Colin Kennard (who died on April 13 2012, aged 92) won an immediate DSO at the Battle of the Bou in Tunisia, where a fellow Irish Guardsman was awarded a Victoria Cross in the same action.

On April 27 1943 1st Battalion Irish Guards, part of 24th Guards Brigade, was ordered to attack Points 212 and 214 on the Djebel Bou Aoukaz. These dominating features, forming a long bare ridge bounding the Medjez plain, were held in strength by the Germans, and their capture was vital to protect the left flank in 1st Division's advance on Tunis.

Already below strength, the battalion had spent the previous day in sweltering heat, crouching in shallow holes or squeezed behind rocks while the Germans seemed to loose off their 88mm guns like snipers' rifles at any sign of life.

Although originally intended to be a night attack, it began after several changes of plan at 3 pm. On the approach march through cornfields, the enemy opened up with guns and six-barrel mortars. "They threw everything but their cap badges at us," a guardsman said afterwards. The 'Micks' kept up their spirits with banter. "I'm not sure I would take my girlfriend out in this," one joked – but the battalion suffered heavy casualties.

After nightfall Kennard, a lieutenant in command of 3 Company, took Point 212 and held it with twenty-five men, the remnants of his company. The others lay in the cornfields or the olive groves, calling to the stretcher bearers, or silent, their resting place marked only by a rifle butt silhouetted in the glow of burning Arab huts.

Leading bayonet and tommy-gun charges, Kennard swept the enemy from the slopes and grenaded them down the hill, beating back five counter-attacks before he was relieved on May 1. In the citation, his CO stated: "More than any other single person, he was responsible for holding and retaining this vital position. He led the party which eliminated a pair of troublesome machine guns on a rise beyond hill 214. His unfailing energy, constant presence, cheerfulness, resolution and disregard for his own safety was an inspiration to the men of his company and to the whole force.

"Even when he was wounded and handed over command on the force commander's orders, he continued to visit his company, and could be seen limping and hopping from one rock to another encouraging the men and cursing the Germans.

"He somehow managed to get in the forefront of the last counter-attack, and when not hurling grenades was pointing out suitable targets to his riflemen. He won a sort of awed admiration from his men, who were continually asking how and where he was."

Some felt that Kennard deserved a VC like Lance-Corporal Patrick Kenneally who, armed with a Bren gun, had twice attacked a massed force of the enemy single-handed, and to break up their attack.

Colin David Kennard was born at Yeovil on October 6 1919 and educated at Radley and Christ's College, Cambridge, before joining 1st Battalion Irish Guards, where he was known as Rusty. In February 1945, he was fit again to rejoin 3rd Battalion in the advance through Holland and Germany, ending the war at Cuxhaven.

After being demobilised in 1946, he worked in the City for several years before moving to the West Country in the late 1950s, becoming involved in a number of local businesses. He played rugby for Wasps and London Irish. Later he enjoyed tennis, and was an avid follower of flat and National Hunt racing.

Colin Kennard married first (dissolved), in 1947, Rosemary Mackintosh. He married secondly, in 1987, Hilary Sandbach. He was survived by a son, who followed him into the Irish Guards, and a daughter of his first marriage and by two stepsons. His eldest grandson also followed his father and his grandfather into the Irish Guards and did an operational tour in Afghanistan in 2012.

COMPANY SERGEANT MAJOR NOEL ROSS

Company Sergeant Major Noel Ross (who died on April 25 2012, aged 91) won an exceptional Military Medal with 156 Parachute Battalion at Arnhem.

Then named Noel Rosenberg, with the rank of lance-corporal, he dropped on September 18 1944 as part of Brigadier 'Shan' Hackett's 4th Parachute Brigade, which was quickly given the task of securing the high ground north of the city to halt approaching German forces.

With wireless communications practically non-existent, Rosenberg volunteered to carry messages under fire, and as he moved about killed many of the enemy. "I didn't see them as men," he later said, "only as targets." During one charge a German suddenly ran at him so that their rifles clattered together before the point of his bayonet pierced Rosenberg's left hand. Rosenberg still managed to finish him off with his own bayonet and carry on.

With the battalion reduced to a third of its strength just thirty-six hours after landing, Rosenberg was regularly heard encouraging others. He was so dependable that he was promoted in the field to sergeant by his company commander Major Geoffrey Powell, who subsequently commanded what was left of the battalion.

Rosenberg was particularly conspicuous in the withdrawal to the 1st Airborne Division's defensive perimeter at Oosterbeek. When a wooded hollow had to be cleared Powell decided on a seemingly suicidal charge. Rosenberg directed devastating covering fire on the enemy, giving clearly shouted fire orders and simultaneously disposing of two enemy who suddenly emerged from behind a bush.

Joined by the remainder of 4 Brigade, but now surrounded, Hackett decided on a desperate second charge to reach the defensive perimeter, ordering Powell to select a man who would remain where he was to provide covering fire. Rosenberg was given a Bren, twelve magazines, six grenades and six phosphorous grenades for the task.

There was no relief in Oosterbeek, which was now the scene of a rearguard action against German armoured units and infantry. When Powell's position was targeted, a hole 'as big as a bed' was made in the roof of Rosenberg's hideaway.

But he carried on firing his Bren, inflicting many casualties. The Paras were now fighting from slit trenches and barricades, and Rosenberg continued to be a supportive presence despite six days' continuous action.

Powell and his men were ordered to withdraw to the Rhine for evacuation and Rosenberg was then detailed, with another man, to find a boat. This involved getting into the river and sinking to shoulder level to avoid a patrol. Powell eventually managed to get his men across, but because the boat was full, Rosenberg and his comrade had to hang on to the stern. After these actions Rosenberg was awarded an MM.

Noel Rosenberg was born in Lichfield on November 21 1920, one of five children. He joined the South Staffordshire Regiment in 1937, going to India and Palestine, then Libya. In 1941 he transferred to the Parachute Regiment. He served in Africa, Italy, France and Germany, and was mentioned in despatches. The post-war years saw him in Palestine, BAOR, Cyprus, the Canal Zone and the Arabian Peninsula.

In 1964 Ross (to which he had changed his surname following Arab suspicions) was posted to the Far East training centre in Singapore, where he was involved in the Borneo Confrontation. With only a small staff he handled 45,000 transient soldiers from fifteen nations, and was instrumental in helping the smooth dispatch of large numbers of troops from the Far East to Britain. He was awarded a BEM.

An unexpected treat for Ross on the 50th

anniversary of Arnhem was the presentation of a Jordanian flag to the Prince of Wales, Colonel-in-Chief of the Paras. A previous flag, given years before to commemorate joint exercises between the Paras and Glubb Pasha's Arab Legion, had become a good luck charm, but had been lost in the fighting at Arnhem.

Noel Ross left the Army in 1974, settling at Aldershot to work as an Army welfare housing officer until 1996. He was survived by his wife Barbara, whom he married in 1951, and their two sons.

MAJOR IAN SMITH

Major Ian Smith (who died on May 3 2012, aged 92) won two Military Crosses while serving with the Commandos, the Special Operations Executive and the Special Boat Squadron.

In April 1944 a bombing raid on coastal defences near Deauville was reported to have set off a series of flashes on the beach. Four reconnaissance operations, codenamed Tarbrush, were therefore mounted at short notice to examine mines and obstacles in the region – though not on the D-Day beaches themselves for fear of attracting attention to them.

The following month Smith was called to Combined Operations HQ for a top-level briefing, where he was ordered to find out whether explosive devices had been attached to the tops of stakes that the Germans had erected on the beaches. If they had, they might buckle the doors of the landing craft when detonated and the soldiers trapped inside would be sitting targets.

On the moonless night of May 16, Smith led a small detachment of 10 (Inter-Allied) Commando, which embarked from Dover in a motor torpedo boat. They left their engine-powered dory a mile offshore and landed by dinghy east of Calais. Armed with a Sten gun and accompanied by a sapper, Smith crawled up the beach. The smell of cigarette smoke alerted them to the presence of a sentry. Then they heard German spoken. The guard was being changed.

The sapper groped his way up one of the stakes and found an anti-tank Teller mine nailed to the top. Having decided not to remove it because the sentry would be sure to hear the noise, they returned to their dory, slid over the side and paddled until they were far enough from the beach to start the engine.

They transmitted their call sign by S phone, an early walkie-talkie, but received no answer from the MTB. A ship approached and, turning on its searchlight, scanned the sea. The Germans permitted no fishing at night, and Smith feared that it was one of their armed naval trawlers as they flattened themselves on the bottom of the dory. The vessel sailed past only a few yards away: "How it did not see us, I shall never know," said Smith.

Some minutes later it turned about and, directed by its radar or a signal from shore, loosed off some heavy gunfire in their direction. Just as it was getting very close there came a sudden ringing of bells and shouted orders; it seemed to have become stuck on a sand bank, and stopped.

Smith and his party eventually found the MTB, which had moved out to sea to avoid the trawler. He celebrated the success of the operation in a series of Dover hostelries where he became so inebriated that his batman had to take him home in a wheelbarrow. He was awarded a Bar to an earlier MC.

Ian Christopher Downs Smith was born at Keynsham, near Bristol, on April 22 1920 and educated at Wycliffe College. In 1939, as a Sandhurst cadet, he was one of a party taken to Aldershot to see an armoured division. Interspersed with a few tanks were soldiers holding up green flags. When asked what they were doing, they sprang to attention and replied: "I am a Mark II tank, sir."

Smith played rugby for Sandhurst, Harlequins and the Army. Shortly after being commissioned into the Royal Army Service Corps, he volunteered to join 2 Commando, precursor of the 1st Battalion Parachute Regiment. When training at Ringway, he and his comrades were reviewed by a disgruntled Churchill who was counting on many more volunteers.

In 1940 Smith moved to Lochailort in Scotland, where he was trained in unarmed combat, pistol shooting and explosives. A spell at Achnacarry as an instructor in fieldcraft was followed by a posting to 12 Commando. He then moved to Shetland to work with a Norwegian motor torpedo boat flotilla and was based at Sullom Voe.

On reconnaissance missions to spy on shipping in Norwegian territorial waters, they set off from Lerwick and hoisted the German naval ensign as they approached the coast. After creeping down a narrow channel in the cliff face, they docked, camouflaging the boat during the hours of daylight.

Smith was next ordered to the Isle of Wight to

become part of Fynn Force, based at Freshwater Bay. In September 1943 he was with a small unit landed between Dieppe and Le Havre to report on the enemy's coastal defences. Forbidden to use radio signals, they were provided with carrier pigeons to send back their information. But when they released one of the birds, it was promptly killed by a peregrine falcon; a second pigeon met the same fate.

In December that year Smith and a small reconnaissance group embarked in an MTB at Newhaven to land on the north coast of France near Criel-sur-Mer, where they had a difficult climb to the top of the cliff. He returned with valuable information on the German defences, but on the way back to the MTB they were almost cut off by a fast-moving enemy convoy, so that he needed all his navigating skills to elude it. He was awarded his first MC, the citation stating that he had led eight previous operations of a similar type.

Shortly before D-Day, Smith was recruited by SOE and flown to Bari in Italy where he was told that he was to be dropped into Yugoslavia to join Brigadier Fitzroy Maclean's mission and serve as British Liaison Officer with 5th Partisan Corps in Bosnia.

As he parachuted down, he heard a voice call out: "In a hurry, are you sir?" It was Corporal Nash, his signaller and bodyguard, whom he had overtaken because he was much heavier. Sharing a nomadic life in the mountains with the partisans, Smith was constantly on the move dodging enemy patrols as he arranged for supply drops of food and arms, called in air support when an attack was launched against the

Germans and helped to evacuate those who were badly wounded or were downed American airmen.

On the way back to Bari in a tank landing ship, Smith was enjoying a shot of navy rum with the boatswain when the steel walls of the cabin bent inwards as if they had received a blow from a gigantic hammer. A Liberty ship, loaded with thousands of tons of high explosives had blown up, causing devastation in the Italian port and great loss of life.

Smith was then attached to the Special Boat Squadron and commanded a small force in Crete. Living in a large cave and based in the east of the island, their task was to watch the remnants of the German and Italian occupiers and report back to their base.

A spell on the Greek mainland, followed by a raid on the Dalmatian island of Cres, brought Smith's active service to an end. When the war ended, he was promoted major, and after commanding an RASC unit at Bicester he went up to Jesus College, Cambridge, to learn Russian. Posted to Minden in western Germany, he interrogated deserters from the Soviet forces who were suspected of being agents posing as refugees.

In 1947 he joined the family textile business at Stockport, Cheshire, eventually moving with the firm to Wales. He managed a hotel for five years and, in the 1970s moved to Co Donegal, where he started a fish farm.

In August 1974 Smith was driving a car near Randalstown, Northern Ireland, when he was forced to stop by three armed masked men. They tied him up, put a bomb in his car and then ordered him to drive into town and park by an electrical shop. They told him that they would follow and shoot him if he did not do what they wanted, and that the bomb was timed to go off in twenty minutes. At the shop there were several members of the RUC, who told him not to stop but to drive out of town. He found a field, left the car and ran for his life. The bomb exploded on time.

Ian Smith remained in Northern Ireland, where his favourite recreation was watching rugby. He married, in 1944, Peggy Cropper. She predeceased him, and he was survived by their son. A daughter predeceased him.

LIEUTENANT JACK OSBORNE

Lieutenant Jack Osborne (who died on August 15 2012, aged 103) commanded Nigerian troops with "slashed cheeks and filed teeth" recruited from their country's jails to serve with the Chindits behind enemy lines in Burma.

During the Second Chindit Expedition of 1944, Osborne and his men were flown into a jungle airstrip and deployed in a strongpoint known as 'White City', which had been established by 77th Brigade under the command of Brigadier 'Mad Mike' Calvert at Mawlu, 800 miles north of Rangoon.

Soon after their arrival a Japanese force "appeared from nowhere" and launched a full-scale assault. Osborne watched as artillery devastated a hill to his left; the bombardment was so intense that the troops there were all but wiped out.

Then his position was singled out for the same treatment. As shells exploded around them, Calvert bellowed: "Osborne, are you scared?" The young soldier replied that he most certainly was. "Good!" came the resounding reply.

After the bombardment, a Japanese tank emerged from the forest, apparently leading the assault. But the vehicle broke down and ground to a halt. Osborne watched in astonishment as one of the crew calmly emerged to carry out repairs. "We were so amazed we forgot to shoot him," he later recalled.

The infantry attack on White City soon began, and was pressed home so effectively that Japanese troops threatened to overrun the position until the gallant Nigerian ex-convicts saved the day by launching a bayonet charge. Osborne was struck by the fighting qualities of his soldiers and would later recall their courage with pride. "They did learn and they did learn quickly," he said. "And they scared the enemy."

Walter John Osborne – always known as Jack – was born in Smethwick, near Birmingham, on July 22 1909. Before the war he graduated in History from Birmingham University and worked as a college lecturer. He was commissioned into the King's Shropshire Light Infantry in 1941 before joining the Royal West African Frontier Force in Nigeria.

Here, recruitment for the war effort took place in unusual ways. Britain governed northern Nigeria indirectly through local rulers, and these potentates were asked to supply volunteers. The Sultan of Kano obliged by emptying his jails. Osborne found himself commanding an assortment of ex-convicts from the arid regions of northern Nigeria, with a few hailing from the French colonies of the Sahara.

They were a "mixed bunch" who "got on well together" and soon became highly effective soldiers. His men were Hausa-speakers, so Osborne – a gifted linguist – mastered their language. At the age of 32 he was at least a decade older than most of his troops, who privately called him 'Grandad'.

Osborne's unit, part of the 81st Division, began the long sea voyage to India, en route to Burma. On board, however, he was alarmed when some of his men inexplicably curled up and died. Questioning revealed that they believed the explanation to be witchcraft: the dead men were the supposed victims of someone in their home village who had cursed them. The ship stopped off in Durban where any soldiers who thought they had been cursed were taken ashore for treatment. "What medication against witchcraft there is, I don't know," Osborne later said. "But they were all right afterwards."

Osborne was demobilised in 1946 and returned home with two souvenirs from his war service; a samurai sword, which he would use to chop nettles in Hertfordshire, and his Army beret with a bullet-hole right through it.

In civilian life, he was an instructor at Newland Park teacher training college in Chalfont St Giles until retiring in 1974. Having mastered Latin and Greek before the war and Hausa during it, he would later teach himself Russian, French, Spanish, Portuguese and Italian. In his nineties, he enjoyed visiting Exeter University to help students translate medieval Latin texts. Jack Osborne's wife, Sylvia, predeceased him. He was survived by two sons.

CAPTAIN DOM ALBERIC STACPOOLE

Captain Dom Alberic Stacpoole (who died September 30 2012, aged 81) won a Military Cross in the Korean War, then joined Ampleforth Abbey where he stood out among his brethren as an enthusiastic name-dropper and prolific letter writer to *The Daily Telegraph*.

When 1st Battalion Duke of Wellington's Regiment arrived at the crescent-shaped ridge, known as the Hook, north of the Imjin river in May 1953, it was clear that the enemy was preparing for a major assault. Second Lieutenant John Stacpoole and his forty men mounted standing patrols and made occasional forays into enemy lines to take captives, but then were switched to laying a forest of protective wire.

This involved digging trenches, preparing bunkers, laying booby traps and laying dannert wire from dawn to dusk and in bright moonlight. Although the enemy were only a few hundred yards away their mortar fire every fifteen minutes was so regular that the Dukes were able to take shelter until it was over.

The weather was so cold that they had to keep sliding the moveable parts of their weapons and to shift their bodies to prevent them freezing to the ground. Space heaters burning petrol provided some warmth, though these had a habit of going up in flames when difficult work was being undertaken. Each man also received a large bottle of Japanese beer every day. While some officers enjoyed firing their pistols at the rats, Stacpoole read *Anna Karenina* under a Tilley lamp late into the night.

Over three weeks his patrol created a web of wiring with duckboards connecting the trenches that recalled the Western Front in the First World War. When the Chinese launched their final attack they became deeply entangled as the allies' defensive fire poured on them; leaving many boots on the field with legs inside. But as the battle reached its climax Stacpoole was wounded by shrapnel, and three days later he drank a toast in hospital to the Queen's coronation, with Coca Cola.

The citation for his MC declared that his gallant service had ensured that the wire held. But he was always conscious that the Dukes' achievement at the Hook had been largely overlooked by history because it coincided with the conquest of Mount Everest by Sir Edmund Hillary and Sherpa Tenzing Norgay.

Humphrey Adam John Stacpoole was born into a military family in Belfast on April 19 1931 and educated at Ampleforth. His father served in the Royal Irish and the West Yorks regiments. One uncle led the Royal Ulster Rifles' gliders at D-Day. Another won an MC and Bar with the Special Boat Service and later became the last Lord of Appeal in Northern Ireland to sentence a man to death. John's boyhood memories included the chaos in Belfast after an air raid in 1941 and later travelling alone through London during a doodlebug raid.

After coming home after Korea to a year at Aldershot, Stacpoole became adjutant of the 2nd Parachute Regiment in Cyprus, where he once hunted down some EOKA terrorists hiding beneath the burning hearth of a cottage. He used to attend the Orthodox liturgy on Sundays, though the Cypriots drew the line at the soldiers receiving Communion.

When the Suez crisis broke out he landed at Port Said and was sent on a long march, hugging walls and arcades under periodic firing until finally halted at midnight. Britain's post-war weakness was clear.

On returning home he sent a highly combative paper on the campaign to the Foreign Office, where it landed on the desk of a recently arrived Ampleforth contemporary who hastily passed it on.

Stacpoole next served as ADC to Major General Ken Exham in West Africa during the run-up to independence. On resigning his commission he contemplated seeking a political career or joining the missionary White Fathers, then opted for monastic life. But this did not dampen his interest in the Army. The day he set off for the Ampleforth novitiate to take the name Alberic in religion, Stacpoole collected the latest *Royal United Services Journal*, which contained an article he had written on the Russian penetration of West Africa.

While accepting that monastic life was "not quite the same" as that of the Army, he admitted he would have liked to have been part of the Falklands campaign, and that he missed the career pattern of military life. Going up to St Benet's Hall, Oxford, he dictated his papers to obtain a First in History after falling off a bicycle and breaking an arm. He continued to write on subjects ranging from St Bede to the rebellious Downside historian Dom David Knowles and the women in St Luke's Gospel. He also edited *The Noble City of York* (1972) and *Vatican II by Those Who Were There* (1986).

A Fellow of the Royal Historical Society, he proved a competent editor of the *Ampleforth Journal* though some old boys felt that he made it too academic. Never one to take a hint, he would persevere in offering advice to his brethren – who did not always appreciate finding his elegantly written notes on pink, blue or green paper in their pigeonholes.

Stacpoole's military background did not make him an ideal housemaster, and he was blunt in running a parish, where his sermons could contain a surprising number of references to the Royal Family. He was perhaps happiest as senior tutor back at St Benet's, where he built up the military history section and surprised some undergraduates by asking to which clubs their fathers belonged. He was disappointed not to be made Master.

Stacpoole was a devoted secretary of the Ecumenical Society of Our Lady and a frequent attender at reunions on the battlefield of Monte Cassino, though his demand for the Germans to be allowed to march with the Allies regularly stirred controversy.

His regular letters to *The Daily Telegraph* would range from the better claims of Kieran of Clocmacnois to be the patron saint of Ireland rather than the shadowy half-historic Patrick, to a defence of Eric Gill's stations of the cross at Westminster Cathedral after revelations about the sculptor's sexual behaviour, and his own claim to have celebrated the first Catholic Mass at Knole Park in Kent since Archbishop Warham in 1522.

Alberic Stacpoole did not always win his abbot's approval, but nobody could fail to recognise the underlying sincerity which went with his genial, deadpan manner.

COLONEL CLIVE FAIRWEATHER

Colonel Clive Fairweather (who died on October 13 2012, aged 68) was second-in-command of the SAS when it overcame Arab terrorists who had seized the Iranian embassy in London for six days.

On April 30 1980 Fairweather was at Hereford preparing to send a team to Yorkshire for a training exercise when he learned from an unofficial source that a terrorist incident was taking place in South Kensington. It was quickly decided to despatch them to London instead.

By the time a call came from the Cabinet Office, ordering B Squadron to move, the soldiers were already reconnoitring the embassy. With them was the regiment's commanding officer, Lieutenant Colonel Michael Rose. Fairweather's assurance to Whitehall that he was in charge of the base was met with some disbelief because he spoke in a strong Scots accent. He was told to fetch a 'proper officer'.

It soon emerged that the embassy had been seized by a heavily-armed group of separatists who had taken hostage twenty-six people inside to force the release of prisoners jailed for demanding independence for an Arab-speaking region of southern Iran. Fairweather's primary task during the siege was to co-ordinate the logistics that would enable the SAS to respond to developments. Information had to be gathered about the layout of the building and its construction.

Three separate teams then had to be kept in readiness – one on standby to assault, one resting and another rehearsing an attack. Snipers also had to be infiltrated into Hyde Park, across the road from the embassy. In addition Fairweather had to arrange for aircraft to change their flight paths into Heathrow so that the noise of their engines would cover the preparations being made to storm the building.

Then, at short notice, he was also required to organise an operation against the IRA in Belfast. Faced with severe demands on his available manpower, he had to make frantic efforts to recall troopers scattered across the world. The Belfast operation ended in tragedy when the officer leading it was shot dead.

The assault on the embassy, three days later, might have suffered a similar fate had the terrorists been watching television when it began. Cameramen had managed to get to the rear of the building and broadcast the initial stages of the attack.

Fairweather – never afraid to speak his mind – afterwards publicly disagreed with the official policy towards the media during the siege, arguing that, instead of operating in an atmosphere of mutual suspicion, it would have been more sensible to have worked with them to ensure that the SAS's plans were not jeopardised.

As it was, the assault was judged a success. Two groups of soldiers abseiled from the embassy's roof to a second floor balcony then entered a window to kill five terrorists and apprehend another while nineteen hostages were released, though one other died. The dramatic resolution of the siege brought the regiment out of the shadows and significantly enhanced its standing at a time when proposals had been made to disband it. Margaret Thatcher visited members afterwards to thank them.

Clive Bruce Fairweather, the only child of a policeman, was born in Edinburgh on May 21 1944 and was educated at George Heriot's School, which he was said to have left early for the good of both the other pupils and the staff. At Sandhurst he proved just as unruly.

He attended his commissioning Ball under close arrest following an incident involving a fellow cadet and a thunderflash. Many years later, when he returned to give the Special Forces lecture to senior term cadets, he arranged for an SAS team to burst into the hall at the end of his speech. Firing blanks and flinging flashbangs, they dragged him off to a waiting helicopter. The authorities were far from amused by this stunt, which was typical of Fairweather's maverick sense of fun and willingness to cock a snook at those he thought took themselves too seriously.

In 1964 he joined 1st Battalion King's Own Scottish Borderers (KOSB). After seeing active service in Sarawak, followed by a spell in Germany, he was recruited by 22 SAS. Promoted captain, he commanded a troop on operational tours in Sharjah, Northern Ireland, Iran, Oman, Dhofar and Jordan.

Fairweather also served as an adviser to the Sultan of Brunei's Special Forces and to those of Iran. He was subsequently posted to Belfast as adjutant of 1 KOSB, and was fortunate to escape serious injury when a booby trap exploded in his office at Fort Monagh, killing a sergeant and wounding two other soldiers.

In 1974 he was posted back to the SAS to command

D Squadron. After attending staff college, he went two years later to HQ Northern Ireland as GS02 Intelligence. Fairweather instilled into his men the importance of operating within the law and, in the face of considerable opposition, insisted that Army Legal Service lawyers were present at the briefing of soldiers deploying into hazardous situations.

During this tour he had to deal with the consequences of the abduction and murder of Captain Robert Nairac, GC, who had posed as a member of the IRA. Like many in the SAS, Fairweather had become concerned at the lack of supervision of Nairac's activities. After retiring from the Army, Fairweather was censured by the Director of Special Forces for speaking to an author who was writing a book about the affair.

As second-in-command of 22 SAS during the Falklands conflict, Fairweather had to cope with the repatriation of the bodies of twenty members killed in a helicopter crash. Following promotion to lieutenant colonel, he moved to HQ SAS, where he directed operations to help the mujahideen in Afghanistan during the Soviet occupation.

In 1985 he took charge of the Scottish Infantry Depot, Glencorse, before being given command of 1 KOSB in Berlin. The battalion was in the middle of a serious disciplinary crisis, and among his most pressing tasks was the stamping out of a much-publicised culture of bullying during initiation ceremonies.

He restored order, and there is little doubt that his leadership saved the unit from being disbanded. The battalion was also involved in the demolition of

Spandau prison, where Rudolf Hess had been held until his death. The rubble was buried in a quarry so that it could not be used as a shrine by neo-Nazis.

He was appointed OBE in 1990, while commanding officer of Edinburgh Garrison. He ended his Army career as colonel of the Scottish Division, where he played an important role in implementing the amalgamations within the Scottish Infantry brought about by the Options for Change programme.

In 1994 he was appointed chief inspector of prisons for Scotland. His robust common sense and determined advocacy led to a range of improvements in the treatment of offenders, many of whom were subjected to overcrowding. He appreciated that, if they could be rehabilitated, they would be less likely to prove a burden on the public purse in future.

He also agitated for better conditions for those held on remand, in an effort to reduce the high suicide rate. This led to clashes with ministers over moves to privatise prisons and reduce spending on them; in 2002 his appointment was not extended. After a case for constructive dismissal was settled, he was advanced to CBE.

For the next seven years Fairweather acted as one of the principal fundraisers for Combat Stress, helping to highlight the plight of servicemen who needed support long after their military service ended. His other interests included exploring the lines of the former railways in the Borders. An excellent game shot, he was also a keen glider pilot, fell runner and pianist. Fairweather died of a brain tumour. He married, in 1980 (later dissolved), Ann Dexter. She survived him with a son and two daughters

PRIVATE JOHN JORDAN

Private John Jordan (who died on October 20 2012, aged 87) won an immediate Military Medal in Normandy in 1944 while serving with Essex Regiment's 2nd Battalion, known as 'the Pompadours'.

The award followed operations in the Bas Brenil Wood, part of Field Marshal Montgomery's plan to destroy the German armies in the Falaise Gap. Essex Regiment, having landed on D-Day near Hamel on the French coast, had fought its way inland at some cost, and on August 12 1944 was advancing in difficult bocage country. This included having to negotiate a ravine, which was slow, hazardous work.

In earlier attacks that day a forward patrol, outnumbered and outgunned, had been forced to withdraw by fires caused by enemy smoke bombs (*nebelwerfern*). At 4 pm, C Company was attacked and, in a sharp engagement, the company commander, Captain Peter Chell, was killed in close-quarter fighting while defending his HQ. Jordan's platoon position was also attacked, with Jordan himself engaging the enemy with a Sten gun which was shot out of his hand.

Jordan took a wound in the right arm, and, seeing his position being overrun, lay down in his trench as if dead. He then picked himself up and followed the enemy to where two of them were engaging Allied troops with a Spandau.

Armed with only a previously captured German pistol, he approached them from the rear so as to take them by surprise and killed them. Jordan was subsequently surrounded and taken prisoner – but not before he had jettisoned the pistol which, being

German, could have cost him his life had it been discovered.

Minutes later the area came under fire from three British regiments firing 25-pounders and 4.2in mortars, causing many enemy casualties and enabling Jordan to escape in the confusion. He subsequently reached Battalion HQ at Courmeron with valuable information. The citation for his MM praised his great courage and initiative under most difficult conditions.

Having recovered from his wound, Jordan rejoined the Pompadours in the Netherlands for the hard-fought final phase of the war. He went on to serve in Africa, where he was part of the Guard of Honour for the tour in 1946–47 of King George VI.

In Africa he was able to indulge his love of animals. While serving in Rhodesia he adopted an orphaned cheetah who was so well trained that he allowed it to sleep at the foot of his camp bed.

John Humfrey Jordan was born on August 18 1925 at Rimpton, Somerset, and educated at Stowe. After leaving the Army in 1950 he went to live in the Dordogne, where for some years he supplemented his private income by subsistence farming. One year he lost his automatic steel Rolex watch while ploughing a field – only to rediscover it in the mud when he ploughed the same field a year later (the watch still works to this day). He later worked as a translator, salesman and draughtsman, eventually returning to Britain.

John Jordan married, in 1952, Marie-Ange Germain, with whom he had two sons and two daughters. After they divorced he married, in 1977, Anne Manger; she died in 1997, and he was survived by his first wife and their four children.

PRIVATE ISAAC FADOYEBO

Private Isaac Fadoyebo (who died on November 9 2012, aged 86) survived for nine months behind enemy lines in Burma after being critically wounded in a Japanese ambush and left for dead.

A Nigerian medical orderly serving with the Royal West African Frontier Force, Fadoyebo was rescued by a Burmese villager who risked execution at the hands of the Japanese to conceal the injured soldier in his home.

After returning to Nigeria, he composed a full and clear account of his experiences, which was eventually lodged in the Imperial War Museum. This gripping sixty-page work is the most outstanding of a handful of written records in English left by the 100,000 Africans who fought for Britain in the Burma campaign.

Fadoyebo's brush with death came at about 8 am on March 2 1944, as his unit was breakfasting in the Arakan's Kaladan valley, when the Japanese were about to spring a devastating ambush.

When the assault began, the firing was so intense that Fadoyebo had no chance to take cover. As his comrades were cut down around him, a bullet struck his right leg, shattering the femur, while another penetrated his stomach. With his battledress soaked in blood, he lay helpless among the corpses as Japanese soldiers approached to strip the dead of their weapons and ammunition. Fadoyebo remembered them killing Captain Richard Brown of the RAMC who was trying to treat his wounds and thought they probably did not finish him off because they believed he was about to die anyway.

But he clung to life, heartened when it became clear that there was another survivor – a soldier from Sierra Leone called David Kagbo, who was also wounded. The two men encouraged and supported one another; years later Fadoyebo would refer to this man as "my comrade in adversity".

Then, out of the rainforest, came some Burmese villagers. They were Rohingya Muslims who supported the British against the Japanese. They dressed the Africans' wounds with traditional herbs and brought them food and water. Later, when Fadoyebo and his companion were capable of being moved, they moved them to a nearby village.

One villager, known as Shuyiman, took the immense risk of concealing the African soldiers in his home alongside his family. "The chances were they were going to be executed, perhaps along with us," Fadoyebo wrote.

For protection he took the Muslim name Suleiman after being shown by Kagbo, who had been brought up a Muslim then sent to mission school, how to pretend to be a follower of the Prophet. The two friends kept up their spirits singing *Abide with Me* in Yoruba every evening at dusk, just as Fadoyebo's father did at home.

Japanese patrols occasionally carried out searches,

but the fugitives were never found. In December 1944 British soldiers liberated the area and took them to hospital to complete their recovery before being repatriated to their respective homelands.

Isaac Folayan Fadoyebo was born on December 5 1925 at the village of Emure-Ile, south-western Nigeria. In 1941, he left his Anglican primary school at Owo at 16 and, irritated that his father would not pay for him to continue his education, volunteered to join the British Army in a fit of what he later described as "youthful exuberance". He then embarked on the six-week voyage from Lagos to Bombay, via the Cape, in late 1943.

After his war service, Fadoyebo returned to Nigeria and settled in Lagos, where he became a civil servant in the Ministry of Labour, visiting both Britain and the United States.

In 2012, Barnaby Phillips, a British journalist with Al Jazeera International, who had seen his manuscript at the Imperial War Museum, learned in Burma that Shuyiman was dead but his daughter and grandchildren were traceable. He then visited Fadoyebo in Nigeria, who recalled how his village had thrown sand at him on his return to see if he was a ghost, and his mother had fainted on his arrival. The ex-soldier was unconcerned that he had never received a medal but was delighted to be given documentary evidence of his service.

Fadoyebo's family persuaded him he was not strong enough to make the journey to Burma. But Phillips's documentary (which later became the book *Another Man's War*) showed him delivering a letter of thanks from the Nigerian, hailing Shuyiman as "the man whom God sent to save my life". Isaac Fadoyebo's wife, Folasade Florence, predeceased him, and he was survived by six daughters.

CAPTAIN JOHN MALING

Captain John Maling (who died on December 16 2012, aged 92) won an MC on a patrol in North Africa from which his comrades were astonished to see him survive.

Maling landed at Bougie, Algeria, in November 1942 with the 6th Battalion the Queen's Own Royal West Kent Regiment (6 QORWKR), part of 78 Division, which was among the leading troops in the dash for Tunis. The Germans reacted quickly, and within a week had a strong infantry force supported by tanks in and around Tunis, as well as complete air superiority.

On November 17, after a twenty-mile march during which they were continuously strafed by bombers, he and his platoon arrived at the village of Djebel Abiod at 4 am with orders to defend the strategically important road junction at all costs. Tired and hungry, they were in a forward position and knew that their lives depended on the speed at which they could dig in and camouflage their slit trenches. That afternoon, a motorcyclist from a reconnaissance unit arrived saying: "The bleeders are coming."

Eighteen German Mark IV tanks followed by lorry loads of infantry rumbled down the road heading for

Djebel Abiod, unaware of the presence of Maling's platoon, or of the Allied anti-tank gunners in support. The gunners opened fire with solid shot at point-blank range, disabling half the Mark IVs, and three lorry loads of infantry stopped fifty yards from his position and started to debus.

Maling, who had held his fire until the leading tanks had driven over his slit trenches, then gave the order to shoot. His men, armed with three Bren guns and about twenty rifles, were well trained and could not miss. The platoon killed forty to fifty of the enemy (who turned out to be elite German paratroops) for the loss of only one man.

At dusk, the Germans withdrew their surviving tanks. As it grew dark, Maling realised that he had to move, but did not dare go back to the battalion, fearing that they would be so jumpy that they would shoot him and his men in the belief that they were Germans.

He therefore went into enemy territory and carried out a big encircling movement to return to his lines at dawn. Just before his unit arrived, a German fighter plane flew low over them – but they 'froze', and managed to escape detection.

When Maling reported to Battalion HQ, officers were amazed to see him with platoon intact. A party had been sent out during the night and reported that the position had been abandoned. His colonel was convinced that they had all been captured. Maling received an MC.

John Allan Maling was born in London on February 13 1920 and was educated at Uppingham before joining up at the outbreak of war. On his first night in barracks, he was appalled to discover that none of the soldiers wore pyjamas and resolved to gain a commission as soon as possible. After the action at Djebel Abiod, Maling took part in the capture of Tunis, the invasion of Sicily and then the long slog up the length of Italy, finishing the war in Austria.

When the war ended he trained at St Thomas's Hospital, and then served as a general practitioner in Royal Tunbridge Wells, retiring in 1980 to enjoy fishing, gardening and reading military history.

John Maling married, in 1952, Judy Haines, who survived him with a son and a daughter. Another son predeceased him.

SERGEANT DON BURLEY

Sergeant Don Burley (who died on February 16 2013, aged 94) was awarded an exceptional Distinguished Conduct Medal after finding himself commanding a troop of Queen's Bay tanks which had been sent to confront a powerful German counter-attack on the Gothic Line at Coriano Ridge in September 1944.

The regiment had lost all but three of their tanks and suffered ninety-eight casualties in a matter of minutes when they were sent against a screen of German anti-tank guns. As they advanced to the ridge across open ground, the two leading squadrons came over the crest to face a hail of fire. Burley's tank was the only one in his squadron to reach the top of the hill. His troop leader's and corporals' tanks had been knocked out, leaving him to take charge.

Realising that the ground over which he would have to attack was almost entirely covered by enemy anti-tank guns, he dismounted and set off to find a covered approach up the hill to the enemy position. He carried out his reconnaissance under constant and accurate fire and, on his return, reported to an infantry company commander and suggested a plan of attack.

The plan was agreed on, and Burley led infantry into the enemy position, using his guns so effectively that they arrived there with few casualties. The Germans were forced to withdraw and, under cover of the tank fire, the casualties from the earlier engagement were evacuated.

Later the enemy counter-attacked again. Burley beat them back, inflicting heavy losses; but was badly wounded on foot as he reconnoitred an alternative fire position for his tank. He managed to return to it and, despite being in great pain and suffering from loss of blood, continued to fight on until the enemy had again been dispersed.

Burley's citation concluded: "This NCO, throughout, showed resource, initiative, powers of planning, and skill in execution which would be considered outstanding in a commander of much higher rank. In addition, he showed great personal courage in continuing to command his tank when so severely wounded. The fighting spirit of Sergeant Burley undoubtedly inspired all who cooperated with him in this action."

Donald Lloyd Burley was born at Aylesbury, Buckinghamshire, on January 29 1919. He was educated in Canada, where his family had moved shortly after the First World War but returned to England in 1935. At 16 he joined the Queen's Bays, accompanying the regiment to France in 1940. The following year saw him in North Africa, joining in all the regimental campaigns in the desert.

Burley recovered from the Coriano action in time to take part in the advance from the Montone river to beyond the Lamone. His troop played a notable part in supporting infantry in holding the bridgehead against determined counter-attacks. He was mentioned in despatches.

After his discharge from the Army in 1946, he did various jobs before joining Central Mining (later Charter Consolidated) in the City. He retired in 1979 after thirty years' service, and from 1948 to 1952 served with the City of London Yeomanry (the Rough Riders). Don Burley married, in 1940, Margaret Brockett, who survived him with their two sons.

MAJOR PROFESSOR TOBY GRAHAM

Major Professor Toby Graham (who died on March 8 2013, aged 92) was the co-author of a classic work on artillery in the two world wars, which he wrote in Canada with Brigadier Shelford Bidwell, who was in England.

They first met in the bar at Sandhurst after a lively seminar discussing whether massed artillery had caused a deadlock on the Western Front, and were commissioned to produce a book by a publisher who was standing beside them. The necessity of exchanging chapters by post was a complication. But as retired gunners with sceptical minds and a keen delight in argument they never fell out, meeting when Graham was in England on vacation from the University of New Brunswick, where he was director of military history.

Fire-Power (1982) described the evolution in military thinking from the early 20th century when Douglas Haig's tactical vision was said to embrace ground seen through the ears of a horse. Tracing developments in training, machine guns, wireless and air power, they showed how skilfully directed artillery was not just an extra wheel on the war machine but a vital element when used in cooperation with other arms during the First World War; however, gunnery officers' lingering love for horses afterwards meant that much needed to be relearned in the Second.

The authors followed this highly original work with *Tug of War* (1986), a lively narrative of the Italian campaign from 1943 to 1945 which contained vivid biographical sketches of the commanders and drew on Graham's personal examination of the terrain at Monte Cassino. But whether they were right in claiming that Italy was not an expensive sideshow is still disputed.

Their last joint effort was *Coalitions, Politicians and Generals* (1993), in which Graham did the bulk of the writing and Bidwell drew on his experience as deputy director of the Royal United Services Institute to do the editing. The canvas was too broad to be definitive, but they offered a stimulating commentary on the British, French and German staff systems and compared the political pressure applied by Lloyd George on Haig and by General George Marshall on Eisenhower.

Dominick Stuart Graham was born into a naval and military family on July 24 1920. Always known as Toby because as a baby his family thought that he looked like the dog in *Punch and Judy*, he went to Bradfield and then the Royal Military Academy Woolwich.

In 1940 he was sent to Narvik to command an anti-aircraft battery. It rarely hit the Heinkel bombers attacking the harbour, but he rowed out to collect a harvest of stunned fish for his men when ships had been sunk, and was wounded while rescuing a gun detachment on an airfield during an air raid.

Graham next commanded a battery at Dover during the Battle of Britain, which he remembered BBC journalists reporting as if it was a Cup Final. Eighteen months later he was on patrol outside Tobruk in North Africa when his observation car was hit; he plodded through the desert for two days before being captured.

His attempt to escape through a sewer from Chieti POW camp, in the Abruzzi province of Italy, was foiled by fire. Soon he was transferred to Fontanellato from which he got out for a day only to be caught at a railway station. On being freed at the Italian armistice in September 1943 he set out to link up with the expected Allied armies.

In *Escapes and Evasions of an Obstinate Bastard* (2000), Graham described how he wore peasants' clothes and a scarecrow's hat while walking for six weeks around and over steep mountains, lodging in barns and shepherds' huts while being fed by Italian sympathisers. He was fired at several times by Germans scouring the woods for food and escapers, before finally being escorted with a party of seventeen by a drunken guide to a village near Ortona. There a Canadian patrol found him being shaved in a barber's chair.

On February 16 1945 Graham was commanding a battery with the Guards Armoured Division in north-west Europe when he went forward to replace a wounded forward observation officer shortly before an enemy counter-attack. As the German pounding increased Graham received a shell splinter in his arm, but continued to direct defensive fire on his wireless, only reporting his injury after the first attack was repulsed. When a relief officer failed to reach him, he refused to be evacuated for four hours.

The citation for his MC declared that Graham's disregard for his safety, and his calm while giving concise orders under heavy fire, enabled more enemy counter-attacks to be repelled and a successful thrust to be made by the 5th Coldstream.

After the war he became an instructor at Sandhurst, a staff officer in Germany with 6th Armoured Division and commanded the first British missile battery. He was also a member of the British cross-country ski team at the Winter Olympics at Cortina in 1956. Then, fed up with peacetime soldiering, he emigrated to New Brunswick, where he started a cross-country ski club, fished for salmon on the Miramichi river and shot partridge in the woods.

Graham's first job was as a maths teacher at St John High School. But his keen military interest led him to obtain a degree in History at the University of New Brunswick and then earn a PhD at London University before joining the staff at UNB, where he would brutally put down the comments of those who had never peered through the sights of a 77mm artillery piece.

After a small book on Monte Cassino in 1970, he wrote *The Price of Command* (1993), a disappointing life of Guy Simonds, a protégé of Montgomery who was Canada's most distinguished general. It won few friends in Canada, for blaming Simonds's politically minded superior, Harry Crerar, for not halting the Dieppe Raid and for the uneasy way it dealt with Simonds's strained personal life.

When Graham's first marriage to Valerie Greig, with whom he had two daughters, broke up he resigned his academic post and was 17,000ft up K2 in the Himalayas the day he was appointed professor emeritus.

Coming home he married his childhood sweetheart Mary Hawson and settled in Yorkshire to work on her family estate and gardens. When she died he took a container ship to visit his daughter in New Zealand, and met the only other passenger, Ursula Behringer; they married in 2002.

Every year Graham came down to London for the annual lunch of the San Martino Trust, which brings twenty young Italians to Britain in thanks for the wartime aid given to Allied escapers. When he was no longer able to make the journey he alarmed friends by vanishing from his Co Durham care home until found lunching at the Army and Navy Club in London.

WARRANT OFFICER JIM FRASER

Warrant Officer Jim Fraser (who died on March 21 2013, aged 92) won a Military Medal in North Africa and, as General Montgomery's personal tank driver, was responsible for his adoption of the beret that became associated with him.

Serving with 8th Battalion Royal Tank Regiment (8RTR) in November 1941, Fraser took part in the battle of Sidi Rezegh; part of 'Crusader', the operation to raise the siege of Tobruk. On November 23, during an attack on an airfield, he saw a German 75mm gun coming straight towards him through clouds of smoke as he rounded a corner.

As he hauled on the steering sticks of his Valentine tank, the gun opened up with armour-piercing shells. The first caught the tank a glancing blow on the side. The next one went straight through the back of the tank into the engine but failed to explode.

With fighting going on all around them, the crew could not bail out of the crippled vehicle and were forced to spend the night inside. Fraser emerged at daybreak to a scene of burning tanks and dead bodies. His commander, standing on the turret with his binoculars, was then hit, and much of his knee was sliced off. A tourniquet was applied, but it was a makeshift job, and Fraser set off across the desert to find help.

He was lucky to find a dugout manned by British soldiers, some of whom he led back to his tank. The injured officer was taken off by field ambulance. The citation for Fraser's MM said that he had undertaken the rescue under heavy shell fire – despite strict orders not to do so because there was no way of knowing who was in possession of the ground that he would have to cross.

James Marshall Ralston Fraser was born in Glasgow on September 17 1920. His family moved to Colchester when he was 12, and he attended the Blue Coat School until he was 14. In 1937 he enlisted in the Royal Armoured Corps, and was posted to the Royal Tank Corps.

Fraser was wounded three times during the war, and had just rejoined the regiment (as it had become) after a spell in hospital when Montgomery took command of the Eighth Army. Monty had a specially modified command tank, and Fraser was selected to be his driver.

On the first occasion that he drove Monty, the general was wearing a large Australian bush hat. The wind blew it off, and Fraser – who had to stop the tank while it was being retrieved – shoved his own beret up into the turret and muttered to the ADC: "Tell the General to wear this and maybe we will get there a bit quicker." Montgomery wore Fraser's beret – which is now in the Bovington Tank Museum – until he acquired one of his own which had both a general's badge and a Royal Tank Corps badge.

On his rounds of inspection in the desert, Monty would often tell Fraser to stop the tank (affectionately known as 'Monty's Charger') so he could talk to the soldiers. They were astonished that an officer of such exalted rank would take the trouble to do so, and thus the Monty legend grew. Fraser served in India and Korea before retiring from the Army in 1959 as a warrant officer Class II.

He became a postman, served on the executive committee of the Union of Post Office Workers and subsequently held the office of national chairman. He was also a Labour borough councillor for Colchester, an Essex county councillor and a magistrate. As a young man, he played rugby and football for the Combined Services. In 1956 he was awarded the BEM.

After finally retiring, he made regular tours to commemorate the anniversaries of the battles fought in Egypt and Libya. Jim Fraser married, in 1944, Margaret Agnes Storey who predeceased him. He was survived by their son and two daughters.

GENERAL SIR MICHAEL GOW

General Sir Michael Gow (who died on March 26 2013, aged 88) was an exceptionally long-serving Scots Guards officer and a Commander-in-Chief British BAOR from 1980 to 1983. In addition he was a perceptive and witty author of several books notable for dealing with the lighter side of Army life.

In 1980 Gow was posted to Rheindahlen in Germany as Commander-in-Chief British Army of the Rhine and Commander Northag, the Northern

Army Group of NATO. Six feet four inches tall, he was keen on exercise. He used to say that if he kicked a BAOR football it whizzed off the toe of his boot – but a NATO ball sank into the ground and he was lucky if it moved at all.

On one occasion his NATO HQ was located in barracks occupied by a battalion of Footguards. He overheard his sergeant-major asking the RSM to make sure that the guardsmen did not laugh at the NATO soldiers because they looked well below standard in comparison. This was at a time when Dutch soldiers were allowed to grow their hair so long that they had difficulty putting their hats on.

James Michael Gow was born in Sheffield on June 3 1924. He did not come from a military family; his forebears were artists, musicians and academics. His father died when Michael was a child, and he was brought up in the household of his maternal grandfather.

After education at Winchester he enlisted in the Scots Guards in 1942. There were two young men ahead of him when he went to the recruiting office in New Scotland Yard; the first was a peer, the second an earl. "Don't tell me," said the sergeant when his turn came, "you must be Jesus Christ."

On his first morning at the Guards Depot, Caterham, the recruit standing at the next basin tried to commit suicide with a cut-throat razor. Another abiding memory was being told by the drill sergeant that he looked like a bag of manure tied up with pink string.

Gow attended a wartime Royal Armoured Corps OCTU at Sandhurst. Physical fitness was much prized, and he had his nose broken three times in the boxing ring. After being commissioned into the Scots Guards in July 1944 (when he was reminded by the regimental adjutant never to travel on public transport or carry a parcel in town) he landed in Normandy with the 3rd (Tank) Battalion. He was wounded in Belgium in October and evacuated to England, rejoining the battalion in April 1945 to take over the duties of quartermaster and serve with the Control Commission in Berlin.

In 1946 he took his future wife to the Guards Boat Club Ball at Maidenhead with the intention of softening her up for a proposal of marriage. He had planned everything with great care and took her to a punt which he had placed by the jetty in advance.

As he cast off, he failed to detect a number of his brother officers hidden in the shrubbery who had removed the bung. The punt rapidly filled to the gunwales, and it was only with great difficulty that they regained the bank. Gow's intended, who had been a Leading Wren at the end of the war, spent the rest of the ball crouched over a brazier in a cloud of steam, drying off.

The Gows married so young that they had to wait several years before the Army acknowledged their marital status. It was difficult to make ends meet, and they seriously considered moonlighting by hiring themselves out as a cook and butler; Gow even got to the point of visiting Moss Bros to reserve a yellow and black striped waistcoat and a swallowtail coat with large gold buttons.

In 1949 he went to Malaya as a company commander with 2nd Battalion Scots Guards on anti-terrorist operations during the Emergency. A spell as equerry to the Duke of Gloucester was followed by staff college and then appointments first as brigade major and subsequently regimental adjutant before returning to the staff college as an instructor. Gow commanded 2nd Battalion Scots Guards in Kenya in 1964 shortly after a mutiny by soldiers of the former King's African Rifles. After a move to HQ London District as GSO1, he commanded 4th Guards Brigade.

In 1970 he attended the Imperial Defence College, then went to HQ BAOR as Brigadier General Staff (Intelligence). He was GOC 4th Division BAOR for two years before becoming Director Army Training. Impatient with Whitehall bureaucracy, and never happy to be tied to a desk, he spent most of the working week looking at training at home or overseas. In 1979 he was appointed GOC Scotland and Governor of Edinburgh Castle.

After his tour as Commander-in-Chief BAOR, his final appointment was as Commandant Royal College of Defence Studies. When he retired in 1986 he was, with the exception of two very early predecessors, the longest-serving member of the Scots Guards since the regiment was raised in 1642.

Gow was ADC General to the Queen from 1981 to 1984. He was Colonel Commandant Intelligence Corps from 1973 to 1986 and of the Scottish Division in 1979-80. He was Brigadier Queen's Bodyguard for Scotland, Royal Company of Archers, and president of the Royal British Legion for Scotland from 1986.

Appointed KCB in 1979 and GCB in 1983, he believed that soldiering should be fun. But while he had an easy-going style, he accepted nothing less than the highest standards. He was not entirely impressed by the modern world, saying that the Major government's cuts would make him hesitate to take up a military career. During the Gulf War he wrote a letter to *The Telegraph* criticising military men pontificating on television which was signed 'Sir Michael Gow (General, definitely rtd)'.

His books were *Trooping the Colour: a History of the Sovereign's Birthday Parade by the Household Troops* (1989); *Jottings in a General's Notebook* (1989); and *General Reflections* (1991). Michael Gow married, in 1946, Jane Emily Scott, with whom he had a son and four daughters.

MAJOR GENERAL JACK DYE

Major General Jack Dye (who died on June 10 2013, aged 93) commanded the South Arabian Federation's Regular Army from 1966 to 1968, the most difficult period of its existence.

The federation was composed of seventeen states in what would become South Yemen, and Dye had the daunting task of carrying out policy decisions against the background of the impending British withdrawal from Aden, tribal rivalries within the Army and virtually no support from the weak federal government to whose ministers he was responsible.

Despite being subjected to pressures from many quarters, he never lost sight of the importance of keeping his force intact as the single stabilising factor in the fluid and volatile state of affairs in South

Arabia. His men were dangerously susceptible to the propaganda of the extremists but, with an adroit mixture of firmness and tact, he managed to achieve a balance between the opposing factions within the Army.

None the less, on the morning of June 20 1967, elements of the Army mutinied. They burned down their barracks and broke into the armoury. It is a measure of Dye's success that the rest of his force remained loyal and played a vital role in helping to restore order.

The welding of the Army into an effective force was achieved at considerable personal risk. Deprived of the support from above and below which a commander could normally expect, Dye lived a lonely and at times dangerous existence. He was appointed CBE at the end of his tour.

Jack Bertie Dye was born at Great Yarmouth, Norfolk, on December 13 1919 and educated locally. He joined the Royal Norfolk Regiment and took part in the D-Day landings in June 1944. On March 1 1945 he was in command of a company which led a battalion night infiltration near Kapellen, a few miles west of the Rhine.

The objective was a fortified house and their route took them through a dense forest. The position of the Germans was not known and the operation had to be performed without alerting the enemy. Dye spotted them, however, and guided the whole battalion through without incident – apart from the silent grabbing of a prisoner.

Taking one of his platoons up to the house, he achieved complete surprise, captured five prisoners and sent them quietly to the rear. With another platoon, he attacked a group of the enemy in the garden and took more prisoners. When he and his men came under heavy artillery fire, he swiftly organised his defences and, two hours later, drove off a determined counter-attack.

Later that day he led his men through the forest again, repelling more attacks on the way, and established an outpost on the far side. His inspired leadership over a period of three days and nights with scarcely any sleep was recognised by the award of an immediate MC.

In the 1950s Dye served in regimental and staff appointments in Egypt, Hong Kong, Cyprus and Germany and was an instructor at the School of Infantry at Warminster. From 1962 to 1965 he commanded the 1st East Anglian Regiment and, subsequently, the 1st Battalion the Royal Anglian Regiment. He took the battalion to Aden in 1964 and, under his direction, it quickly mastered its role on internal security operations in the Radfan and the border areas.

He was GOC Eastern District from 1969 to 1971 and Colonel Commandant of the Queen's Division from 1970 to 1974. After leaving the Army, Dye was a governor of Framlingham College for thirty-eight years and for almost twenty years chaired the finance and general purposes committee.

From 1976 to 1982 he was Colonel of the Royal Anglian Regiment then Vice Lord-Lieutenant of Suffolk, where he farmed strawberries and asparagus. Until the end of his life he ran two shoots and enjoyed fly fishing in Scotland. He was also an accomplished picture framer. Jack Dye married, in 1942 Jean Prall, who survived him with their two daughters.

COLONEL JULIAN FANE

Colonel Julian Fane (who died on August 11 2013, aged 92) won two Military Crosses and the Croix de Guerre in the Second World War, then had a successful career in the City.

In April 1940, he was serving with 2nd Battalion Gloucestershire Regiment (2GR) in Belgium. The following month he was one of the few survivors of a desperate rearguard action to delay the German advance so that the bulk of the British Army could escape from Dunkirk.

The battalion was ordered to hold the strategically important hilltop town of Cassel, north-west of Lille, to the last round and the last man. They were surrounded by the enemy and fought off several assaults under aerial bombardment, artillery fire and tank attacks before receiving on May 28 a message to make a break for it and head for Dunkirk.

At the head of a small group, Fane slipped away in the darkness. He was wounded in the arm by a mortar bomb as they scrambled through hedges and over ditches while guided by the flashes of guns on the coast and the light from burning farm houses. At 3 am they hid in a barn to sleep. During the day, the Germans arrived and the farmer climbed up a ladder and whispered to them to stay concealed under the straw. The next night, Fane and his men crept past an enemy bicycle patrol which was fast asleep under a hedge beside a towpath.

On June 2, after covering more than twenty miles of enemy-held country, he was standing in the doorway of a small terrace house close to the beach when a bomb fell nearby. The house collapsed and he was blown into the street. His party reached Dunkirk in time to be evacuated back to England, and Fane received his first MC for his part in the fighting withdrawal.

Julian Patrick Fane was born in London on February 17 1921 and educated at Stowe. With the outbreak of war imminent, he completed the short course at Sandhurst before being commissioned into the Gloucestershire Regiment.

On his return to England after evacuation from Dunkirk, he joined GHQ Liaison Regiment, known as Phantom, the forward reconnaissance unit that provided up-to-the-minute battlefield information to be transmitted to senior commanders. He served with them on the Dieppe raid, in North Africa and in Sicily. In Tunisia, following the capture of Bizerte in May 1943, he was awarded the Croix de Guerre.

He then rejoined 2GR until the end of the war. On January 20 1945, his company was ordered to clear both sides of a street about 100 yards in length in the village of Zetten, near Nijmegen, the Netherlands. The Germans had barricaded themselves in the houses and were well supplied with automatic weapons and bazookas.

Calling for artillery fire on the houses was not practical, and in fierce, close-quarter fighting, casualties quickly mounted. The attack was faltering when Fane rallied his men. Blazing away with his Sten gun, he led them in a determined assault which resulted in the street being cleared of opposition. His bravery and outstanding leadership were recognised by a Bar to his MC.

After the war he transferred to 12th Lancers and served in Palestine and Malaya. Then, in 1951, he joined the embassy in Cairo as the military attaché. A fluent French speaker, he subsequently served as liaison between the British and French during the Suez Crisis.

When 12th Lancers merged with the 9th, Fane was seconded to the Life Guards and served as a senior major until he assumed command in 1962, taking the regiment to Germany and to Cyprus. He was appointed GSO 1 London District before being seconded to the US Command and General Staff College at Fort Leavenworth, Kansas.

Leaving the Army in 1968 he joined the merchant bank Samuel Montagu, as director of personnel. At a time when the City was generally poor at managing its staff, he made an immediate impact. Messengers and doormen looked smarter, telephones were answered more quickly and junior managers learned how to manage. Within a year, he was made a director.

When Midland Bank bought Samuel Montagu, he joined Orion Bank as a main board director from which he retired in 1984 and settled in a Berkshire village. He was a good shot and enjoyed his fishing.

Julian Fane married first, in 1949, Lady Ann Mary Lowther, who predeceased him. He married secondly, in 1959, Diana Ewart Hill, who survived him with a son and a daughter of his first marriage and a son and a daughter of his second.

MAJOR GEOFFREY COCKSEDGE

Major Geoffrey Cocksedge (who died on January 16 2014, aged 93) was awarded an MC in Italy on the night of December 8 1943, when as a lieutenant with 2nd Battalion Royal Inniskilling Fusiliers (2 RIF), he was ordered to take a fighting patrol across the Sangro river, near Castèl, on a reconnaissance mission.

The river was in spate and regarded as unfordable. The far bank was reported to be mined and booby-trapped, and his orders were to find out if the Germans were holding positions there and, if so, in what strength.

Showing the greatest determination, he succeeded in getting his men across but was engaged by one machine-gun post and then by another. He left his support section to deal with these and led his patrol another five hundred yards. This tactic forced two more machine-gun posts to disclose their position. Cocksedge might have considered that he had accomplished his task, but in a bid to obtain prisoners he worked into a position from which he could assault one of the posts.

After an exchange of grenades, his patrol charged, driving the enemy away while leaving their weapons behind. By this time, the Germans were moving a strong party towards the river in a bid to cut him off.

Cocksedge skilfully withdrew, driving off the encircling enemy and getting his patrol, which included a wounded man, back across the river. The citation for his immediate MC paid tribute to the determination, coolness and courage with which he had obtained very important information despite being heavily outnumbered.

Geoffrey William Horace Cocksedge was born on September 6 1920 at Ballygrooby, Co Antrim, and educated at Bedford School. He was commissioned into the Royal Inniskilling Fusiliers in 1940 and posted to its 2nd Battalion.

Cocksedge took part in the invasion of Sicily and then the Italian campaign. A few weeks after the action in which he won his MC, he led his patrol in a bayonet charge on a village near Cásoli on the Sangro, capturing prisoners and gleaning much valuable material. He was severely wounded before the end of the war and, after recovering, was stationed near Villach, Austria, where his battalion was on garrison duties.

From November 1950 until the following March he was in Korea on attachment to 1st Battalion Royal Ulster Rifles. He was wounded once again, and on his way to hospital his train was bombed. An injured American fell from the top bunk and broke three of his ribs. While in hospital, an officer came into his ward, failed to see him and announced that he had "copped it". Cocksedge wanted to laugh but found it too painful.

After convalescing in Japan, he was posted to Hong Kong and then rejoined 2RIF in Cyprus during the EOKA Emergency. He subsequently served with 1RIF in Berlin, where part of the battalion's duties involved guarding Rudolf Hess in Spandau Prison.

Cocksedge returned to England in 1958 and, after a spell in Omagh as training major to the TA, retired from the Army in 1961. Settling in Bedfordshire, he took up poultry farming and enjoyed fly fishing. He loved gardening and, when it was too dark to see unaided, he wore a miner's lamp attached to his head. Geoffrey Cocksedge married, in 1945, Joy Chiles, who survives him with their two sons and two daughters.

MAJOR GENERAL DARE WILSON

Major General Dare Wilson (who died on August 15 2014, aged 95) had an adventurous military career which included commanding 22 SAS, winning a Military Cross, making a world record-breaking free fall parachute jump and hurtling down the Cresta Run on a toboggan in old age.

Born at Burnopfield, Co Durham, on August 3 1919, Ronald Dare Wilson was educated at Shrewsbury before going up to St John's College, Cambridge, to read Economics. The outbreak of war interrupted his studies and, after enlisting in Royal Northumberland Fusiliers (RNF) he was posted to 8th Battalion with command of a scout car platoon.

In April 1940 he arrived in France to experience the blitzkrieg and the evacuation from Dunkirk. A spell as an instructor at 3rd Division Battle School was followed by attendance at Middle East Staff College, Haifa, and then a staff appointment with Eighth Army in the Italian Campaign. Between September 1944 and the end of the war in north-west Europe, Wilson commanded a squadron of 3 British Reconnaissance Regiment.

He had three narrow escapes. The half-track in which he was travelling was blown up by a mine, causing many casualties; a salvo of *nebelwerfer* rockets landed so close to him that the blast propelled him many yards and knocked him out; a high velocity shell then struck his armoured car seconds after he had left it to reconnoitre, killing all his crew.

On the night of January 27 1945 Wilson crossed the Maas river, west of Nijmegen, Holland, in command of a fighting patrol. The river was 250 yards wide and fast-flowing, and two sappers were in charge of the boat. In the snowbound landscape, caps, weapons and magazines were bound with strips of white linen and the men rubbed their faces and gloves with white flour and sprinkled it over their hair.

The raiding party's objective was to reach the main road, near Afferden, about a mile away, lay an ambush and take a prisoner. The patrol reached a house close to the road where they stopped and listened. Two German sentries accosted them and had to be killed. Surprise had been lost, so they made their way back to the river.

Wilson ordered one section to recross the river and led the other along the bank. They had gone about 600 yards when two enemy soldiers in snowsuits approached. Wilson and his men scrambled into cover to open fire at close range, wounding one and taking the other.

They then had great difficulty carrying the wounded man, who was heavily built. Twenty minutes passed and they had covered only 200 yards when they saw a ten-strong enemy patrol approaching.

Wilson deployed his men to open fire at close range with Stens and light machine guns.

After an hour's battle, in which three of the enemy were killed and two wounded, the remainder withdrew. Wilson's men had suffered no casualties. He led them back across the river, taking the wounded prisoners with him to earn an MC for his skill, courage and brilliant leadership.

In October 1945 he was posted to Palestine to command a squadron of 6th Airborne Armoured Reconnaissance Regiment, then returned home three years later to be commissioned to write *Cordon and Search,* a well-received history of 6th Airborne in Palestine from 1945 to 1948.

Wilson commanded a company of 1st Battalion Parachute Regiment in Germany and took a team to Bisley which became the runner-up in the Army Championship. In October 1950 he was secretary to the Joint Intelligence Committee at the Cabinet Office. The following year he joined 1 RNF in Korea. On arrival in September, he commanded a company and saw fierce fighting.

After a three-year posting as an instructor at the staff college Camberley, Wilson commanded the RNF Depot at Fenham Barracks, Newcastle, training recruits. He was a member of the successful Army winter sports team competing at St Moritz and captained the English Regiments Team at Bisley in the Methuen Cup, which they won in a field of thirty teams from all three services.

In March 1960, Wilson assumed command of 22 SAS at Hereford. A team of free fall parachutists from 10th US Special Forces Group arrived soon afterwards and, at a cocktail party, persuaded Wilson to do a free fall jump with them. He did so, and the Americans' so-called Halo (High Altitude Low Opening) technique was subsequently introduced by the SAS in clandestine operations.

Wilson established a link with Handley Page involving the use of its Dart-Herald aircraft which could carry eight parachutists up to a height of more than 30,000ft, and the SAS decided to attempt a free fall jump from the maximum height the plane could achieve. The temperature at that altitude would be minus-fifty degrees centigrade, and an adequate supply of oxygen would be needed.

In January 1962 he led the attempt, in which they exited the plane at 34,350ft, free falling for almost six miles. They reached speeds of 230mph before setting the world record for a team free fall. Tragically, one of the team was found dead with both of his parachutes unopened.

In 1961 the SAS Free Fall Team had secured the first six places in the British National Parachute Championships and was selected to represent Great Britain in the 6th World Championships. In the 7th World Parachute Championships in 1964, they again represented Great Britain, with Wilson as team leader.

A year at the Canadian National Defence College was followed by a posting to 1 (British) Corps, BAOR, as Colonel General Staff (Operations and Intelligence). After a move to Aden as Chief Administrative Officer Land Forces at HQ Middle East Command, he was appointed Director Land/Air Warfare.

Appointed CBE in 1968 he retired from the Army in 1971, returning to Cambridge to finish his degree in Land Economy and to stay on to do research for two years. There he met Sarah Stallard, whom he married in 1973 – he was the oldest mature student, she the youngest in the group.

Settling at a farm near Dulverton, he became Exmoor's National Park Officer and, once it was established as a going concern, became a consultant to the European Federation of National Parks.

Wilson was a dedicated fisherman and shooting man – a 12-bore shotgun accompanied him throughout the war. Charming and self-effacing, he never lost his appetite for adventure. In his autobiography, *Tempting the Fates* (2006), he wrote: "It was a great experience at the age of 80 going down the Cresta Run, lying on my stomach doing 90 miles an hour with my chin four inches from the ice." Dare Wilson's wife survived him with their two sons.

MAJOR HARRY PORTER

Major Harry Porter (who died on August 20 2014, aged 89) was awarded a military MBE during peacekeeping and mine clearing operations in Palestine for attempting to prevent hostile Israelis and Arabs clashing as British forces prepared to withdraw for the United Nations to supervise the partition of Arab and Jewish territories in 1948.

A 22-year-old lieutenant with the 60th Rifles (KRRC), he was deployed with his company to an isolated fort, suggestive of *Beau Geste*, at the Arab port of Ashdod to prevent clashes between the two sides. *The Annals of the King's Royal Rifle Corps* records: "If there was one regimental character associated with the last days of the British Mandate in Palestine it would be Captain HRM Porter. In March and April 1948, he interposed on three major occasions in firefights between Arabs and Jews at great personal risk, and by bluff, diplomacy and force of character he restored the situation."

His old friend Field Marshal Lord Bramall, who later became Chief of the Defence Staff, was once Porter's slightly despairing instructor. He recalled: "To be honest, Harry wasn't good at the bullshit aspect of training – he was a bit dishevelled in his dress and when on parade he tended to fidget and look around him a lot. But he made up for those defects with qualities of leadership, fearlessness and gallantry."

On one occasion Porter arranged the evacuation of many badly wounded Jews from the battlefield, and on another threatened both sides with a PIAT anti-tank weapon and a non-existent back-up force. Believing his story about the imminent arrival of fighters, the two sides duly dispersed.

During a particularly bloody battle at Bureir, on April 21 1948, he was shot in the leg by a Jewish fighter who, recognising him, arranged for him to be treated on the battlefield with morphine. Porter had attempted to broker a peace deal between the leaders of the two communities, but on the day of the battle he and his sergeant returned to their 'half track' to find on the mudguard of the vehicle the severed head of the leader of the Jewish settlement with whom they had been negotiating the day before.

One of Porter's vital contributions to the Palestine mission was his knowledge of the Schuh-mine 42, or German glasmine, which was extremely difficult to detect with conventional equipment because it was made from glass and wood. He wrote of one night when a stream of vehicles came from the Julis Jewish settlement, and mines were laid around Arab villages. "Early the next day we set off to see whether I could deal with the mines. Luckily they were Schuh mines and I was able to show the Arabs precisely how to neutralise them." During the war Porter had learnt how to disable the mine, but unfortunately, equipped with this knowledge, the Palestinians re-laid the mines around Jewish settlements.

When Porter was awarded a military MBE, he received a letter from King George VI apologising for not presenting it personally because of sensitivities following the booby-trapping of the bodies of two Army intelligence corps sergeants by the Jewish underground group Irgun.

Henry Robert Mansell Porter was born in Birlingham, Worcestershire, on August 11 1925, to Colonel Henry Porter, DSO, who served on the Western Front in the 60th for most of the First World War, and Enid, who was to become the first woman to run health and education services in the county.

After Wellington, he joined the 60th as a rifleman and was commissioned in 1944. Following victory in Europe, Porter's regiment began training for 'suicidal' glider landings, which would have formed part of the Allied invasion of Japan.

In 1960 he cut short his Army career to run the estate that had been in the family since the 18th century and was burdened by heavy death duties caused by his father's premature death. Subsequently he went into industry, buying and expanding an automotive parts manufacturer, then setting up a gas detector business.

During the 1960s he was closely involved in constituency politics, chairing the Conservative Association during Sir Gerald Nabarro's time as MP. He and Nabarro rowed about Britain's membership of the EEC, which Porter supported (though he was far less enthusiastic about today's European Union). At dinner once with Edward Heath, Porter erupted after the prime minister said that he had asked the Queen to do away with the socially divisive rituals of Royal Ascot.

Keenly aware of what he regarded as his family's obligations, Porter combined a portfolio of local duties involving the church, Royal British Legion, alms houses, youth club and cricket club (whose beautiful ground he owned) with passions for steeplechasing and sailing.

He had several horses in training and owned a Redwing, which he raced at Cowes and Bembridge Sailing Club, where he did an innovative stint as commodore. In his last years he was a familiar figure at National Hunt fixtures, moving at breakneck speed about the course on his battered red mobility scooter.

In 1951 Porter married Anne Seymour, the daughter of Beauchamp Seymour, who, like Porter's father, was a veteran of both the Boer War and Western

Front. She survived him with their two sons, one of whom is the journalist and author Henry Porter.

REGIMENTAL SERGEANT MAJOR TOMMY COLLETT

Regimental Sergeant Major Tommy Collett (who died on September 4 2014, aged 94) was awarded a Military Medal in the Korean War when 1st Battalion Argyll & Sutherland Highlanders crossed the Nakdong river, south-west of Taegu, under heavy shell fire.

Their objective was the town of Sonju, eight miles away, but first they had to capture Point 282, a dominant feature which the North Koreans were using to direct harassing fire at any units trying to cross the river. Shortly before 5 am on September 23 1951 two companies attacked.

The hill was taken after a sharp engagement. But this had a false crest since it was overlooked by Point 388, which was in enemy hands, and the Argylls dug in feverishly in expectation of the counter-attack, which started with shelling and mortaring. Casualties were mounting and the North Koreans were forming up.

But the Argylls reckoned that shrewdly directed American artillery could be counted on to break up any attack. At this critical moment the American officer in command was inexplicably ordered to return to his HQ. Vigorous protests, all the way up to the general, were unavailing. Supporting artillery fire for the infantrymen crouching in their foxholes was lost.

The order was given that the position be held to the last man and the last round. The most pressing problem was getting the wounded off the steep 900ft hill. Collett superintended the evacuation, constantly moving about in the open under heavy fire.

The North Koreans were getting ever closer and the Argylls losing more and more men. Soldiers fit for fighting had to be employed as stretcher-bearers. The round trip took an hour and Collett told his comrades that he was timing them with a stopwatch. "No stopping for a fag at the bottom of the hill! Got it?" They got it. Incurring the CSM's wrath was feared every bit as much as a bullet.

Considerable enemy infiltration had already taken place when an infantryman reported that his weapon was out of action. Collett handed the man his own rifle and continued his work unarmed. At that moment, his company area was napalm-bombed and then strafed with machine-gun fire. An Allied air strike had hit the position by mistake, setting the hilltop ablaze.

The survivors fell back but Collett rallied them, retook the lost ground and then organised a fighting withdrawal. One wounded man that he carried to safety exclaimed, "I never thought I would have my arms around your neck, sergeant-major." "It will cost you a pint, one day," his rescuer retorted – and, subsequently, it did. Collett was among the last to leave the position. His courage and inspiring leadership were recognised by the award of a Military Medal.

Thomas James Richard Collett was born in

Camberwell, south London, on December 3 1919 and educated locally. In September 1935, he enlisted in the Loyal Regiment and was posted to 1st Battalion. In 1940, he took part in the BEF's evacuation from Dunkirk and, after transferring to the Argylls, served in Palestine and Hong Kong before embarking for Korea. Home postings in Scotland were followed by a spell in British Guiana.

Final postings to Berlin and Bury St Edmunds, Suffolk were followed by a final appointment with the Glasgow University OTC. On retiring from the Army in 1962 he became a publican, enjoying golf and bowls. Tommy Collett married, in 1945, Eva Iley. They were survived by their son.

CAPTAIN JOHN HODGES

Captain John Hodges (who died on September 23 2014, aged 93) was a cavalry officer awarded an MC for knocking out enemy guns on mountain road in Italy.

On June 17 1944, he was commanding one of the forward troops of 3rd King's Own Hussars (3 KOH) in the advance on Città della Pieve, north of Orvieto. The approach to the town curved around the side of a hill. On one side was a steep drop, on the other an unclimbable bank and, above them, an orchard was teeming with German paratroopers.

Hodges's three tanks nosed carefully around the corner and past an enemy 88mm anti-tank gun with its crew lying dead beside it. Between him and the nearest houses, there was a stretch of 500 yards completely devoid of cover.

Suddenly, two anti-tank guns opened up from 400 yards away. The leading tank of Hodges's troop sergeant was hit and slewed across the road, its rear end see-sawing over the edge of the precipice and blocking the way forward. The tank behind was also hit and immobilised, its 75mm gun silent because the gunner was lying huddled on the floor of the turret, impervious to threats or inducements.

Hodges's tank returned fire until a high-velocity shell passed within an inch of his head with the noise of an express train. He yelled "Bail out!" down the intercom – but his crew, unaware just how precarious their situation was, chose to stay put.

Hodges jumped out and, using hand signals, directed his driver to reverse around the corner. He then remembered that, concealed inside his sergeant's tank, was a precious bottle of Canadian whiskey; so he moved forward and mounted it. There was already a round 'up the spout'. He aimed by kicking the barrel with his feet and fired in the general direction of the town.

The citation for his MC recorded that he had knocked out three enemy guns and had enabled the infantry to get into the town without suffering casualties. More important to him, however, was the successful recovery of the treasured whiskey.

John Henderson Hodges was born at Abergavenny on July 31 1921 and educated at Monmouth School, where he was good at sport and won a prize for playing the piano. In the spring of 1940 he was studying Phonetics at the Sorbonne and at the British Institute when the sound of approaching

German artillery could be heard. Climbing over the railings at the Gare St Lazare he boarded the last train leaving Paris and eventually arrived at St Malo to find a vessel bound for Southampton.

After basic training at Warminster, Wiltshire, in August 1942 he was commissioned from Sandhurst into East Riding Yeomanry. In January 1943, after three months at sea, he arrived at the Royal Armoured Corps base camp near Cairo where he transferred to 3KOH, which had suffered heavy losses at Alamein.

The following month, while Hodges was travelling by night from Aleppo to Beirut, a saboteur ran two trains into each other. There were few survivors. Hodges regained consciousness after the crash to hear a nurse admonishing some passengers in the corridor. "Keep quiet," she warned, "there's a man dying in there." "Who is that?" he asked himself, "I am the only one here, and no one has told me."

After a long convalescence, he recovered and rejoined 3KOH in autumn 1943 near Pardes Hannah, Palestine. One day he arrived back at the camp to find no trace of his tent and the whole area blackened and smoking. A careless soldier from a nearby unit had dropped a lighted match, setting the grass ablaze and driving the flames towards an ammunition dump. Seventeen thousand shells and 700,000 rounds of small arms ammunition had been blown sky high, along with all his personal possessions and those of 350 soldiers. There was only one fatality.

In March the following year Hodges formed part of the advance party that left Alexandria for Taranto, Italy, and moved up to the Allied front line south of Monte Cassino before fighting its way northwards to winter quarters near Pesaro.

In January 1945 the regiment returned to Syria and Palestine, where it was equipped with Staghound armoured cars for internal security patrols. Based at Sarafand, near Tel Aviv, one of Hodges's duties, using a road which ran alongside the railway line, was to escort the night train as far as Gaza.

They were not allowed to use guns and drove at high speed with their sirens wailing. One stormy night during a riot in Tel Aviv in November 1945, the driver did not spot concrete blocks that terrorists had used to barricade the road, and they drove straight into them. Hodges suffered severe injuries to his feet and spent the last eight months of his Army service in hospital.

After being demobilised with a small disability pension in autumn 1946, he went up to Christ's College, Cambridge to read Modern Languages, then taught French and Spanish at King Edward's School, Birmingham, where he was a housemaster and played leading roles in the Combined Cadet Force.

For several years before retiring in 1981, he was an extremely successful Second Master, combining reliability and calm with authoritative leadership tempered with a sense of fun. He and his wife sang for many years with the Birmingham Bach Choir and then the City of Birmingham Choir. But he also coped uncomplainingly with her bipolar illness, which meant that his career ambitions had to be sacrificed.

They spent almost thirty-five years at Sicklinghall, in Yorkshire, where he took pleasure in his vegetable garden, while playing the church organ, and enjoying bridge with the nuns who lived opposite. John Hodges married, in 1947, Norah Stratford. She predeceased him, and he was survived by their son.

MAJOR TONY HIBBERT

Major Tony Hibbert (who died on October 12 2014, aged 96) called himself the 'Maverick Major' – with good reason. He played a spirited role in the botched operation to capture the Arnhem Bridge over the Rhine; and as the war ended, took over the German port of Kiel four hours before the Russians were to arrive.

As brigade major of 1st Parachute Brigade, he landed outside Arnhem in September 1944 without challenge, but noticed both a lack of despatch and the periodic disappearance of the operation's senior officers by the time he joined Lieutenant Colonel John Frost's 2nd Battalion on the north end of the bridge. On establishing his headquarters in the attic of a nearby office block, he was unable to make wireless contact with a promised relief force. He felt that a vital opportunity was lost when he pointed out that a road to the bridge was still open and was informed that 3rd Battalion had been halted for the night.

As the situation deteriorated, Hibbert was kept busy by the faulty communications, while sniping and keeping an hourly diary. Finally he saw a large enemy gun arrive and extracted his party just before it blew his entire building to pieces. After three days pummelling, 100 able-bodied and walking wounded were left with about five rounds of ammunition each. There was no water to extinguish fires, and little food or medicine.

Taking over command when Frost was wounded, Hibbert agreed to a truce for the evacuation of the wounded, then organised a withdrawal in small sections to link up with the still expected XXX Corps. But the sound of his men crunching through the glass-strewn streets alerted the Germans, and he was caught hiding in a coal shed. After being marched to a church hall, he tried to escape up a chimney and then by pulling up floorboards before being put onto a lorry taking captives to Germany.

An SS guard became so infuriated by the way the prisoners made V-signs to any Dutch the lorry passed that he halted it several times, threatening to kill them. On the third stop, Hibbert slipped over the side and zigzagged through some gardens to hide under a pile of logs. The guard panicked and shot dead six others in the back of the lorry; for Hibbert it was a burden he would carry to his grave.

He was followed by a member of the Dutch Resistance, who whistled *It's a Long Way to Tipperary* whenever Germans were nearby, but Hibbert was so dishevelled that a farmer refused him shelter, unsure whether he was German or British. The next morning he proved his bona fides to another farmer by drawing a Union Flag alongside a German flag with a line through the swastika.

Some 200 survivors of the battle were sheltered in and around the town. Disguised as a Dutchman in flashy green plus-fours and white socks, Hibbert formed a brigade headquarters above a butcher's shop where, with two senior officers, he arranged for weapons and new uniforms to be dropped while they planned a mass escape.

After five weeks the evaders and escapers were driven in Dutch lorries to the river, on one occasion politely standing aside to let another German patrol on bicycles pass by, ringing their bells.

But after the successful crossing, aided by Easy Company of the American 101st Airborne, Hibbert was sitting on the bonnet of an overcrowded Jeep when it hit another vehicle in the dark. He was sent somersaulting onto the road and broke a leg.

Five months later he was discharged from hospital, still in plaster, to command a unit of the 650-strong T-Force (Target Force) that was to prevent the Russians from taking Kiel and Denmark in defiance of the Yalta agreement. However, the instructions from T-Force headquarters directly contradicted his orders from British HQ and required him to cross the 'ceasefire line' drawn up at the surrender of German forces at Lüneburg Heath.

Arriving at Kiel four hours ahead of the Russians, Hibbert hobbled up the steps of the German naval headquarters, saluted its commander captain, who was armed with a sub-machine gun, and invited him to surrender on what he (dubiously) claimed were the direct orders of General Eisenhower.

In the wake of the surrender, Hibbert was promptly arrested for disobeying orders – on the orders of Captain Brian Urquhart (who had been sent home for warning that the Germans were waiting in the trees at Arnhem). He left Hibbert in custody, with a bottle of champagne. On the last day of the war Hibbert's corps commander arrived, and accused him for behaving like a "bloody commando" instead of a responsible staff officer. He then released him saying he would have done the same thing, and recommended him for despatches.

James Anthony Hibbert was born on December 6 1917, the son of a Royal Flying Corps pilot with a Military Cross and two Bars as well as a DFC. He left Marlborough at 16 and went to Germany to work in a vineyard in preparation for joining the family wine business. But having been lodged with a *gauleiter* and his two Nazi sons, he joined the Royal Artillery on his return home.

At the start of his war Hibbert was under arrest for crashing a car carrying rum rations, and later enjoyed the symmetry of being under arrest on both the day the war started for him and on the day it ended. He was first posted with the Expeditionary Force to France. There he commanded a half-battery defending the northern perimeter of Dunkirk for four days before destroying his guns when the ammunition ran out; he was mentioned in despatches.

Back in England, Hibbert volunteered for 2 (Parachute) Commando, with which he did a night jump from a balloon in full mess dress and spurs, only to be reprimanded for appearing late for dinner in torn trousers. After becoming a staff officer in North Africa he was involved in sixteen aborted operations before Market Garden, the Rhine operation which took place after only a week's planning.

Hibbert left the Army in 1948 with a Military Cross awarded for his service at Arnhem. Over the next two decades he worked his way up to managing director of a family firm supplying provisions to liners at Southampton; during this period he helped to invent the International Moth class of dinghy and founded the Salterns Sailing Club for children at Lymington, Hampshire.

In 1949 he married Eira Bradshaw; they had a son and three daughters, with whom they brought up his brother's son and daughter; he also had another daughter. In their later years the Hibberts bought Trebah, a dilapidated house overlooking the Helford estuary in Cornwall. On touring their grounds they discovered twenty-metre high rhododendrons, huge Australian tree ferns and hundreds of rare trees. The couple set about clearing twenty-six acres to reveal and revive a once celebrated Victorian subtropical garden.

They planned to spend the first three years of their retirement on the project, but it took a quarter of a century. The gardens opened to the public in 1987 and now rank alongside the Lost Gardens of Heligan and the Eden Project as one of Cornwall's biggest horticultural attractions. "If it were not for this garden I would have died of gin and boredom years ago," Hibbert said in 2011. "It is a real Cornish garden. The hand of man is invisible. A great garden, one with heart, takes its cues from nature itself."

Eventually he created the Trebah Garden Trust to secure its future. In 2006 he was appointed MBE for his contributions to tourism and sailing. Hibbert managed a website dedicated to the Dutch Arnhem Fellowship and regularly returned to the city, where he stayed with two Dutch ladies called Nink and Dink, whose father had brought him a bicycle while he was in hiding. He also returned to Kiel, where in

2010 the city's Great Seal was bestowed on him in honour of his bravery during the closing days of the war. Tony Hibbert's wife died in 2009, and he was survived by his son and four daughters.

CAPTAIN JOHN MACDONALD-BUCHANAN

Captain John Macdonald-Buchanan (who died on October 14 2014, aged 86) rescued vital code books under fire but was later unhorsed at the Horse of the Year Show.

On March 2 1945 he was commanding a troop of Churchill tanks with 3rd Battalion Scots Guards in an attack on Winnekendonk, north-west of Duisburg, Germany. It was his first battle as a troop leader.

The light was failing as he left the start line, but the moment his troop emerged from the woods they came under attack from armour-piercing shot and high explosive shells from the front and both flanks. Two of his tanks were knocked out. One was hit five times.

Despite heavy mortaring and shellfire, the tanks and infantry managed to force their way into the town. It was now quite dark but, by the light of burning buildings, fierce hand-to-hand fighting took place between the infantry and a crack unit of German paratroopers.

The remainder of Macdonald-Buchanan's troop was under constant attack from bazookas and grenades, but they managed to support the infantry until they had reached the far end of the town. His tank then fell into a bomb crater and had to be abandoned.

He and his crew jumped out, scrambled on to the back of another tank and fought off a series of determined attacks in the narrow streets lit by blazing buildings. To his dismay, Macdonald-Buchanan discovered that he had left a code book that could prove of great value to the enemy in the abandoned tank.

Taking just one guardsman, he made his way back to the crater. They had to fight their way there and back before returning with the precious codes. The citation for his immediate MC stated that the infantry could not speak too highly of his coolness, courage and the support that he had given them.

John Macdonald-Buchanan, the son of Major Sir Reginald Macdonald, was born in London on March 15 1925. His mother, Catherine, was the only surviving child of James Buchanan, Lord Woolavington, the founder of Buchanan's Black & White whiskey. She and Sir Reginald joined their surnames the day before they married.

John was brought up at Cottesbrooke Hall, Northamptonshire, which his mother purchased in 1936 when Lavington Park, the family home in West Sussex, was sold. He was educated at Eton before attending Sandhurst, from which he was commissioned into the Scots Guards. During the war he served with William Whitelaw and Robert Runcie (later Home Secretary and Archbishop of Canterbury respectively), both of whom also won MCs.

Macdonald-Buchanan was in Malaya for two years during the Emergency before returning to regimental duties at Pirbright, Chelsea and Wellington barracks.

Shortly after the end of the war his polo pony,

Matilda, was selected to appear at the Horse of the Year Show at Olympia and to bring the whole week to a spectacular conclusion. On the Monday night, Macdonald-Buchanan, resplendent in his uniform, galloped through the curtains and into the spotlight of the darkened arena, waving his polo stick while the band played *Waltzing Matilda*.

Two laps of the arena were followed by two figures of eight. At the end of the second verse, he reined in at the far end of the arena before hurtling towards the bandstand, pulling up in a single stride amid a cloud of dust to thunderous applause.

This went without a hitch that night; and for the next four nights, while Macdonald-Buchanan was on regimental duties, his groom took his place. On the Saturday night, Macdonald-Buchanan arrived late, changed in the taxi and swung himself into the saddle. The groom tried to warn him that over the previous four nights Matilda had become increasingly impatient during the preliminary manoeuvres, and was interested only in the final dash of the grand finale. The band was already striking up. "Nonsense! Nonsense!" cried the captain. "Tell me tomorrow."

Macdonald-Buchanan burst through the curtains, and it was all that he could do to hang on as Matilda pelted round the arena, going faster and faster while the conductor strove to keep up. There was no chance to rein in; but as soon as Matilda heard the second verse she whipped around, took off straight for the bandstand, stopped in one stride and catapulted her rider into the band, just below the royal box. Disentangling himself from the trumpets and violins, Macdonald-Buchanan got up in time to hear his groom remark: "Horse of the Year! Ass of the Year, if you ask me!"

Retiring from the Army in 1952, he hunted with the Pytchley, Beaufort and Heythrop, and steeplechased under National Hunt rules. The renowned Lavington Stud was founded by his grandfather and, as an owner and breeder, he had many successes with horses on the flat. Worthy of special mention is 'Sans Frontieres', winner of the Irish St Leger in 2010.

A friend said of Macdonald-Buchanan: "He was magnificent looking, ramrod straight, quick thinking and sometimes pretty curt. He was nearly always right, and when he said something very offensive it was always with that marvellous smile and a flick of the moustache – and he got away with it!"

On one occasion, he had a horse running at Baden-Baden. The top brass of the German Jockey Club, very Prussian-looking and marvellously kitted out, turned up to meet him and his companions. There was much clicking of heels and bowing.

The first man sprang to attention and said, "My pleasure!" The arm that was thrust out had a hook on the end of it. The second man had a patch over one eye. The next had a wooden leg. Turning to his friends, Macdonald-Buchanan, said, "D'you know, I had no idea we did so well!"

He was a member of the Horserace Betting Levy Board from 1973 to 1976 and senior steward of the Jockey Club from 1979 to 1982, a period when the appointment was by no means a sinecure. His acts of kindness were legion, and his family, friends, employees and the soldiers who served under him were devoted to him.

He was a governor of Christ's Hospital School, Sussex, a committee member of Victim Support in Northampton and a founder member of the Northampton Five Charities Association. At various times he was Vice-Lord Lieutenant, High Sheriff and Deputy Lieutenant of Northamptonshire.

John Macdonald-Buchanan married first (dissolved) in 1950, Lady Rose Fane, a daughter of the 14th Earl of Westmorland. He married secondly, in 1969, Mrs Jill Trelawnay, daughter of Major General Cecil Fairbanks, who survived him with a son and two daughters of his first marriage and two daughters of his second.

COLONEL SIR TOMMY MACPHERSON OF BIALLID

Colonel Sir Tommy Macpherson of Biallid (who died on November 6 2014, aged 94) was awarded three Military Crosses and three Croix de Guerres during a wartime career which called to mind the adventures of John Buchan's hero, Richard Hannay.

Born Ronald Thomas Stewart Macpherson in Edinburgh on October 4 1920, the fifth son of a high court judge in India, he was struck down with osteomyelitis as a boy, and spent several months in bed reading a novel by Sapper, Dornford Yates, A E W Mason or Buchan every two days.

On recovering he shaved eight seconds off the school record for the mile at Fettes, and won the top Classics scholarship to Trinity College, Oxford. But instead of taking this up on the outbreak of war he was commissioned into the Queen's Own Cameron Highlanders, TA, and asked to raise a platoon in his village.

Volunteering for the Commandos he embarked for Suez in 1941 with 11th (Scottish) Commando and arrived in the desert inexplicably accompanied by sandbags destined for the Eighth Army. Macpherson's first operation was against the Vichy French on the Litani river in Palestine. But although he fulfilled his instructions to capture a bridge under strong attack, the overall plan was postponed for a day so that the surprise was lost, with resulting heavy casualties.

Posted to Cyprus, as the only officer with a working knowledge of Greek, he was appointed military governor of the north-east of the island, then ordered to carry out a beach reconnaissance for a planned raid on Rommel's HQ in Cyrenaica (now Libya). With three comrades he was landed by submarine near Apollonia. When the submarine failed to return to the arranged rendezvous after two days, they started to walk to Tobruk.

They had no food, water, maps or adequate footwear, and he was dressed only in PT shorts. After splitting up, two were captured. Macpherson and another comrade reached the outskirts of Derna, where they sabotaged a telephone exchange: an unwise decision which led to them being picked up by an Italian patrol.

During their interrogation, an Italian officer brought in an unloaded automatic and asked to be shown how it worked. Macpherson obligingly loaded it with a spare magazine he was still carrying, then held up their captors. But he suddenly developed a severe attack of cramp, was disarmed and placed in solitary confinement. Three days later he was caught trying to get away on a motorbike, and transferred to the Gavi fortress, near Genoa.

After the Italian armistice in September 1943, the Germans shot many of the guards, and imprisoned others as they took over the camp. When the POWs were loaded on to a train bound for Austria Macpherson made another escape, and was caught quickly; one guard was so annoyed that he emptied his rifle in single shots between his prisoner's feet as he marched him to the station. There he was put against a wall to be shot as a warning to others until an officer countermanded the order.

Undaunted, Macpherson was transferred to a transit camp, where he and a New Zealander exchanged clothes with two Frenchmen, mingled with a party of agricultural workers and got away.

Recaptured again by Austrian Alpine troops the pair were sent to a Gestapo camp on the Polish-Lithuanian border then taken to another ranks' camp, from which they slipped away under two perimeter fences. This time contact with the Polish Resistance led to them being put onto a Swedish vessel carrying iron ore.

When customs officials boarded Macpherson and two comrades climbed down into the hold and tunnelled a hiding place in the iron ore. On reaching the limit of territorial waters, German soldiers with dogs came aboard. The hatches were lifted and the dogs sent down, but the dust proved too much for them and they had to be brought out.

As soon as the ship reached international waters, Macpherson and his comrades gave themselves up to the Swedes, who took them to Stockholm. Two years after being captured in Egypt Macpherson arrived in Scotland to be awarded an MC for his part in the Litani river raid and his successful escape.

Within days he was recruited for one of the first three-man eccentrically named 'Jedburgh' teams to be parachuted into occupied Europe just before D-Day. Together with a French officer and a radio operator he was dropped into the borders of the Lot and Cantal departments to lead Maquis groups, who, on first seeing his kilt, assumed he was the French officer's wife.

Several days after their arrival, the 'Jeds' led an operation against the Das Reich Panzer division. They demolished a bridge, which delayed the Germans for several hours, then defended another for six days against enemy attacks. Mounting a raid on the road and railway from Montauban to Brive they eliminated all rail traffic between Cahors and Souillac.

Macpherson set about organising ambushes on enemy convoys and, as the Allied armies advanced from the south, coordinating large-scale operations. At Le Lioran, 300 Germans and 100 Milice (Vichy French militia) were trapped in a tunnel. When they attempted to escape, he went into the tunnel at great personal risk, and blew up the railway track, thus sealing in 400 enemy.

By now traitors infiltrating the Maquis were making frequent attempts to trap him, putting a 300,000 Franc price on his head while French civilians were growing exasperated at his success in blowing up bridges and electricity pylons which would soon be needed when the Germans were driven out. Even his superiors were becoming exasperated with him. When told to expect the arrival of ten American OSS officers, he replied that he would prefer ten more containers of explosives, which led to the reply: "Do not be insubordinate."

After being awarded a Bar to his MC he was next sent to seek vulnerable rail targets in north-east Italy. The Germans nearly captured him when Slovenes carved a huge arrow in the snow to indicate his hiding place. Friends immediately brushed it away.

When the war ended in Europe, Macpherson received a second Bar to his MC for his behind-the-lines operations, particularly in the marshalling yards at Udine. But he was told to remain for several months to patrol the border with Italy which the Communists in Yugoslavia were threatening.

When he complained that, in Yugoslavia, anyone commanding more than thirty men called himself general, General McCreery's chief of staff advised him to put up red tabs and call himself a brigadier general. After that, there were no more problems with rank, though he was uneasy about his role in foiling a plot to incorporate the Friuli-Venezia region of Italy into communist Yugoslavia.

Some years later when Macpherson was holidaying on the Italian side of the border, he was summoned to meet Marshal Tito at his summer residence: "Ah, Macpherson," said the Marshal. "I have been looking forward to this meeting. We tried so hard to kill you."

On being demobilised in September 1945 still aged only 24, Macpherson went to Trinity, where he took a First in Philosophy, Politics and Economics. He represented the university at rugby, hockey and athletics (once beating Roger Bannister, who was to break the four-minute mile) and was also a Scottish student international at athletics. He also joined the Duchess of Kent's household for a spell as a tutor to the young Prince Edward (later Duke of Kent), then entered the timber company William Mallinson & Sons as personal assistant to the chairman.

After marrying, in 1953, Jean Butler-Wilson, who was to survive him with their two sons and a daughter, he helped to increase Mallinson's profits as he went on to enjoy an Establishment career, becoming a director of Brooke Bond, Scottish Mutual Assurance and the National Coal Board as well as the Prices and Incomes Board for two years. He was also chairman of the Association of British Chambers of Commerce (1986–1988) and of Eurochambres from 1992 to 1994.

But Macpherson did not lose touch with the Army. He commanded 1st Battalion London Scottish TA from 1961 to 1964, became Deputy Commander HQ 56 Infantry Brigade TA and Colonel of London District before retiring in 1968 with a CBE (Military).

Knighted in 1992, he joined the Royal Company of Archers and was made a Chevalier de la Légion d'Honneur. He was personally awarded the Star of Bethlehem and a papal knighthood by the Pope. Among many charitable activities, he was particularly proud of being chieftain of the Newtonmore Highland Games and vice-president of the local shinty club.

By the time he reached his eighties Tommy Macpherson was increasingly conscious that his military career had been forgotten along with much else about the war. So he settled down to complete his memoir *Behind Enemy Lines* (published in 2010) in the realisation that he was now one of the most highly decorated surviving Commandos from the Second World War.

SERGEANT JOE DUNNE

Sergeant Joe Dunne (who died on Remembrance Day, 2014, aged 100) was awarded an immediate Distinguished Conduct Medal with 1st Battalion Irish Guards for his spirited leadership after the amphibious landings at Anzio during January 1944.

The idea was to draw the Germans down from the Gustav Line so the Allies could advance on Rome. But when there was no opposition, 24th Guards Brigade were ordered inland to recce the village of Carroceto which, unknown to them, had been reinforced by the Germans.

On January 26 Dunne, commanding 13 Platoon of 3 Company, was holding the left flank of the battalion's position when the Germans counter-attacked, over-running one platoon and knocking out two anti-tank guns and one medium machine gun. His position became exposed to highly explosive small arms fire from enemy tanks. But he immediately reorganised his platoon's position so that they were able to beat off two determined attacks.

During the night attack of January 29/30, he was again seen leading his men with the highest skill and determination. When they were held up by fire from a fixed-line machine gun, he dashed forward and single-handedly destroyed the enemy post, killing two enemy.

Next day Dunne's company and another from the American 894th Tank Destroyer Battalion carried out an offensive sweep to clear the enemy's machine guns and snipers from a ridge on the left flank of the area. Acknowledged as more capable of preparing his platoon for battle than any officer, he led his men with such courage that it suffered no loss and destroyed three posts. He was said to have gone through enemy positions "like a dose of salts – driving Krauts out in all directions."

During the morning of January 31, he located a German sniper's nest, where he killed five of the six occupants. The remaining sniper continued to be a nuisance, having taken refuge from 13 Platoon's pursuit in the shrub area beyond Vallelata Farm. Later in the day, Dunne completed the job by routing him out of a culvert and despatching him.

But on the night of February 3/4, 3 Company was overrun by a German battalion. Dunne was captured, escaped, was then recaptured to end his war in Stalag 7a, a POW camp at Moosburg, Bavaria. In his detailed account of the incident, he failed to mention he had been wounded earlier in the evening when fighting his way back to his own lines.

Dunne's skill, determination, marksmanship and courage were of the highest order, his CO wrote, and merited the award of an immediate DCM by his fellow Irish Guardsman, General Alexander.

Joseph Dunne was born at Killurin, Co Wexford, on June 8 1914. He first worked as a forester then decided, with two friends, to join the New York Police. But they were advised first to spend some time in the British Army. Dunne duly enlisted in the

Irish Guards in 1936, and had his first taste of action in Palestine when Arabs destroyed a Jeep carrying mail, killing a soldier. Alexandria offered a happier memory, when he was ordered to collect a young officer misbehaving in a casino and returned to barracks with his charge and half a case of beer from the grateful proprietors.

After war broke out Dunne was sent to Norway aboard the Polish troopship ship *Chobry* which was attacked by Heinkels, killing the CO and several senior officers before the 'Micks' abandoned it with exemplary discipline as it rapidly started to sink. He then fought in the battle of the Bou in Tunisia in which a planned night operation was changed several times before, seriously under strength, the battalion advanced in the afternoon sunlight up a hill on which they were badly mauled.

When peace returned in 1945 Dunne settled in London where he became the quietly spoken barman with a knowing smile and a keen interest in racing at the Junior and then the Senior Carlton clubs. He served every Tory prime minister from Churchill onwards, though when Mrs Thatcher first visited he had to turn her away from his then exclusively male sanctuary.

In 1947 he married Bridie Monaghan, who bore him five young children before her early death. There were repeated attempts to split up the family. When the youngest daughter was old enough to be beyond the supervision of the local social services department Dunne burnt her file in front of a social worker on his doorstep.

After retiring to Killurin he was presented with a

replacement set of medals plus the recently created Arctic Star at a regimental dinner in Dublin, where he was the sole survivor present of those who had served in the Arctic Circle. On his 100th birthday Joe Dunne received a personal letter of congratulations from Prince Harry, honorary colonel of the 'Micks'.

BOMBARDIER JACK CHALKER

Bombardier Jack Chalker (who died on November 15 2014, aged 96) produced sketches and watercolours which are a vital record of the brutal conditions endured by Allied soldiers in Japanese prison camps when there was almost no photographic record during the Second World War.

They depict prisoners clad only in shorts working on the Burma-Siam 'death railway' sixteen hours a day while sustained by an inadequate diet and under constant threat of beatings that seemed to leave the human spirit shining dimly through skeletal frames.

Yet although more than 12,000 Allied prisoners perished during the construction, along with at least 90,000 Asian labourers, Chalker was bemused that the Japanese had a strong sense of beauty while being capable of such cruelty.

The 258-mile railway line between Bangkok in Thailand to Rangoon in Burma during 1943 was intended to provide a supply route for Japanese forces. Chalker, who had been captured in Singapore, was employed on a stretch of the line at Kanchanaburi, west of Thailand, where torture, malnutrition, illness and execution were daily perils. "If you weren't working hard enough they would make you stand and hold a stone above your head," he recalled. "You picked it up, which was better than collapsing because then they kicked you all over the place."

His sketch of a sick, beleaguered man holding a boulder aloft is one of more than 100 pictures he made between 1942 and 1945. After the surrender, Chalker hid a few watercolour paints and pencils in a secret compartment of his haversack. He stole paper from his captors and used the pre-printed postcards that prisoners were given to send home.

The result is a gallery of horrors: emaciated prisoners at the dysentery latrines; cholera tents; a man being held down as his hands were hammered for stealing food. One picture illustrates a spoon used to scoop away dead flesh which had been cleaned by maggots. Another shows the Australian surgeon Colonel 'Weary' Dunlop carrying out an amputation.

It was thanks to Dunlop's patronage, under cover of giving him nursing tasks, that Chalker not only sketched people, places and landscapes but systematically recorded medical and surgical procedures in a tiny diary.

He stashed his work in hut roofs, bamboo poles which he buried, and even in a prisoner's artificial limb. Only once did he get caught. "A guard found me hiding some stuff and I got beaten up," Chalker recalled. "The guard tore one drawing up in front of me, but when I came back later I found the pieces under a rice sack. All the others had been destroyed, but this one had survived. It is a symbol of the whole thing."

Jack Bridger Chalker was born on October 10 1918

in London, the son of a stationmaster appointed MBE for dispersing troops during the First World War. He won a scholarship to the Royal College of Art where his studies were interrupted by the outbreak of war.

Joining the Royal Field Artillery he manned a Norfolk belfry watching for enemy aircraft before being sent in 1942 to Singapore, where he was captured. He was in Changi Gaol and two labour camps before being sent to a railway camp on the Konyu river in Thailand after a five-day train journey.

Learning of Chalker's artistic talent the camp commandant made him paint watercolour postcards to send back to his family in Japan. "I was ordered to produce twenty paintings a day under threat of being beaten up and incarcerated unless they were forthcoming, and this I did for a few wearisome weeks," he said. In contrast to the human devastation, there are also pictures which show the beauty of the local plant life and sensitively portray his fellow inmates.

The art helped him to retain a semblance of humanity. "I was glad to have something to do," he remembered, "and it was such a privilege to be with so many interesting, wonderful people." He met his fellow artist Ronald Searle, already working on his humanised cat pictures, at a concert party. "There was one man, who was absolutely skeletal, a senior lecturer in mathematics at university, and he really loved mathematics. He talked quietly about maths and what a lovely subject it was, and he made me feel that calculus must be wonderful. And then he suddenly died one afternoon."

On Chalker's release in 1945 he was sent to the

Australian medical headquarters in Bangkok to assist in completing official records. But while comfortably lodged, he saw Japanese soldiers being carried off by the lorryload and Thais fighting Chinese in the streets so that he had to carry a Sten gun to extricate himself from skirmishes.

No great lover of the British officer class, he would have liked to follow Dunlop to Australia. Instead he was returned to England, where he resumed his studies and graduated from the Royal College of Art. For more than a decade after his repatriation he could not sleep properly, or look at his drawings and paintings.

In 1950, after teaching History of Art at Cheltenham Ladies' College he became principal of Falmouth College of Art and, in 1957, principal of West of England College of Art, where he remained until his retirement in the mid-1980s. He was elected a fellow of the Medical Artists Association of Great Britain and, in retirement, made anatomical models for the medical firm Limbs and Things, and was said to be 'famous for his bowel'.

But after almost forty years packed away in trunk, interest in Chalker's prison camp pictures was rekindled when Dunlop asked to include some in his published war diaries. In 2007 Chalker brought out his own illustrated memoir, *Burma Railway: Images of War*.

He was now sought out by the Japanese media as part of the healing process. A BBC Four documentary, *Building Burma's Death Railway: Moving Half the Mountain*, drew heavily on his stark images; and some of his sketches appeared in the 2013 film of Eric

Lomax's *The Railway Man*.

Reluctantly, he auctioned about 100 works at Bonhams in London. "I feel in a way guilty about doing this, but it will help us out," he said. Bidding was fierce and many works were later donated by a buyer to the Australian War Memorial. They included *Two Working Men*, the pen, brush and ink work on paper which seventy years ago had been ripped up by a Japanese guard.

Jack Chalker married, first, during the war, Anne Maude Nixon; the marriage was later dissolved. He married, secondly, in the 1950s, Jill, which was also dissolved. Thirdly he married Helene (née Merrett-Stock), who survived him with a son of his first marriage and a son and daughter of his second marriage.

CAPTAIN SIR JOHN GORMAN

Captain Sir John Gorman (who died on November 26 2014, aged 91) was a Northern Ireland Catholic with an unflinching sense of service, which he first demonstrated by winning the Irish Guards' first Military Cross in the Normandy campaign.

The son of a Royal Irish Constabulary officer who won an MC during the First World War and went north to join the RUC after the division of the island in 1922, John Reginald Gorman was born on February 1 1923 at Mullaghmore House, Co Tyrone. He was educated by Loretto nuns at Omagh then at the Imperial Service College in Windsor. After war broke out, he was sent to Portrora Royal School, Enniskillen.

Commissioned into the Irish Guards despite the lack of a private income, Gorman was known in the regiment as 'Blockhead' for his single-minded determination in tackling any task. He first experienced action as a tank commander during Operation Goodwood on July 18 1944.

Leading his troop over a bridge into a bog, near Cagny, he was pulled out to confront the first of the powerful German Tiger Royal tanks to be seen on the Western Front. Having discussed with his crew what they would do in such an eventuality, Gorman's gunner fired a high explosive round into the German's turret from 50 yards while his driver rammed their Sherman into its rear side as the Tiger's 20ft field gun slowly turned towards them.

Both crews bailed out. Gorman led his men to safety behind a hedge then raced 400 yards to leap into a lone Firefly tank, where a sergeant had been decapitated and two other crew members were in shock. But the vehicle was still workable. After removing the body and wiping the blood from the gunsights, he fired it to disable the Tiger and his own tank, which were locked together, before driving behind three more Tigers to score two hits. He then carried three burning men from another Sherman to an aid post.

Settling down under his tank that night he was joined by a Belgian spaniel which was to remain with him for several months. The next morning he was informed of his immediate MC.

Outside Brussels the regiment was surrounded by a sea of happiness in the belief that the war had ended, and an elderly woman gave Gorman a copy of *Some*

Experiences of an Irish RM, which had been left at her parents' house in 1914. But the war was not over yet.

Gorman attended the briefing for the impending Arnhem operation at which Lieutenant-General Sir Brian Horrocks, commander of XXX Corps, announced that "the honour of leading this great dash, which may end the war, will be given to the Irish Guards." There was a muttered rumble.

Gorman remembered saying "Oh my God." But it was probably the forthright Lieutenant Colonel Joe Vandeleur saying "Not us again, surely?" that prompted Horrocks to ask: "What did you say, Vandeleur?" "I said how honoured we all feel, sir," said Vandeleur, evoking the reply "Yes, that's what I thought you said." The truth of this exchange was set in celluloid in the film *A Bridge Too Far*, with Michael Caine as Vandeleur and Edward Fox as Horrocks.

Gorman was caught in a bottleneck, where many tanks around him were destroyed by deadly fire on the road to Arnhem. When the hostilities ended he was deeply uneasy at having torn a strip off an Irish Guardsman for his dirty tank, only for Guardsman Eddie Chapman to be awarded the last VC of the war for retrieving his comrades from a desperate situation at the cost of his own life.

On coming out in 1946 Gorman joined the RUC as a district inspector at Ballymoney, where one of his more unusual cases involved receiving a declaration from a girl dying after an abortion operation. He found himself investigating the release of poisonous flax water into the Bushy river, chasing thieves who illegally supplied plovers' eggs to London restaurants and ensuring that pubs closed on time to satisfy Presbyterian sensibilities.

There was also some bubbling IRA activity, which led him to undertake secret missions to the South, carrying rod or gun, to liaise with MI6 contacts. A double agent led him to a bomb factory under Armagh's Catholic cathedral, which led to the arrest of three armed gunmen in the confessionals. Then, as the determined opposition of President de Valera and the co-operation with the Garda Sichona seemed to be eliminating the terrorism, Gorman was asked to take charge of security for BOAC.

His first priority was the politically motivated strikes and gold smuggling by cabin staff and the strains of a period of enormous growth. His ability to arrange a long Royal tour in the Indian sub-continent led to him being asked to become the airline's personnel director though the increasing demand for redundancies and a pilots' strike to obtain pay scales matching those of American airlines added to the jealousy and hostility he experienced.

By the late 1960s Gorman was being groomed as a possible chief executive in Canada, where he resisted demands that the airline transferred from Montreal to Toronto because of strong anti-English feeling. On being moved to Delhi, he was reminded of the troubles in his homeland when Cardinal O'Fiaich, Archbishop of Armagh, compared Maze prisoners with the poor of Calcutta. His sharp letter of protest was turned down by *The Times* but published in the *Belfast Newsletter*.

After a change at the top of BOAC blocked Gorman's path to the top, he returned home to become deputy chairman and chief executive of the Northern Ireland Housing Executive. He had some success in cleaning up corruption and selling off council houses, much to the approval of the Thatcher government. When he next became head of the sagging Northern Ireland Institute of Directors he successfully invited Charlie Haughey to address a meeting, not as Taisoeach but president of the European Union.

As a supporter of the RUC and the restoration of the provincial government at Stormont, Gorman had been closely involved with David Trimble. This led to his entry into the political fray when Westminster appointed him interim chairman of the Forum for Political Dialogue to move on from the Anglo-Irish Agreement. He was likened to Captain Mainwaring in *Dad's Army*, and certainly cut an unusual figure as an Establishment member and lone Catholic in the Unionist camp. As Ian Paisley attacked a passing remark that could have been interpreted as suggesting some approval of Gerry Adams, Gorman was flooded with points of order from all sides, which he did not understand.

But he stuck to his guns and, after two years was elected an Ulster Unionist member for North Down though the poor showing of Trimble's supporters meant he only became Deputy Speaker, instead of Speaker, of the assembly until it was suspended in 2002. One of the more striking scenes on the province's television screens showed him urging (in grand military manner) an astonished Gerry Adams and Martin McGuinness to blow up their arms in one big bang.

John Gorman was appointed MBE in 1959, CVO in 1961 and CBE in 1974. He served as High Sheriff of Belfast in 1977-88 and was knighted in 1998. In 1948 he married Heather Caruth. She survived him with their two daughters and two sons, one of whom, Johnny, won the Irish Guards' first George Medal when he rescued a man from a building during a landslide in Hong Kong in 1973.

MAJOR HUGH POND

Major Hugh Pond (who died on December 19 2014, aged 91) took part in the D-Day assault on the strategically important Merville battery on the coastline of Normandy.

The battery was manned by a strong garrison and protected by anti-aircraft and machine guns, minefields, an anti-tank ditch and barbed wire obstacles. It was equipped with four 100mm guns, in thick steel-reinforced concrete casemates, capable of laying down a devastating fire on Sword Beach where British 3rd Infantry Division was to land.

9th Parachute Battalion, part of 3rd Parachute Brigade commanded by Lieutenant Colonel Terence Otway, was given the task of destroying the battery before the seaborne invasion began at dawn on June 6. The strategy was to crash-land an assault force of three gliders inside the defences while the main force was parachuted in to attack from the rear.

Bangalore torpedoes were to be used to blast a path through the coils of barbed wire. Taping parties were tasked with lifting the mines and marking corridors through the fields. If the attack, set for 0430 hours, had not succeeded by 0550, the light cruiser

Arethusa had orders to bombard the battery. The brigade commander called it a "Grade 'A' stinker of a job", and Major General Richard Gale, addressing the battalion before the operation said: "Only a fool would go where we are going."

Aircrews, many of them inexperienced, faced gusting winds and low cloud. The difficulties of navigation were exacerbated by dust and smoke from Allied bombing and incoming tracer fire. Several gliders carrying vital weapons, ammunition, marker flares and star shells were lost in the Channel.

Within minutes of arriving over the dropping zone, the main force ran into anti-aircraft fire and began to take evasive action. As a result, instead of being dropped in a concentrated area, most of the battalion was scattered over fifty square miles of Normandy. Many, weighed down by 100lb of equipment, drowned in marshes or submerged irrigation ditches.

The glider carrying the leader of Pond's small force landed east of the battery. The second glider broke a tow rope and did not leave England. No sooner had the glider carrying Pond cast off from the tug aircraft it was hit.

Pond was appalled to see one of his men on fire; but as they were coming in at a speed approaching 100 knots and heading straight for a minefield, he could do nothing to help him. The pilot, Staff Sergeant Dickie Kerr, lifted the glider over the casemates and the heads of the main assault force waiting to attack and made for a small orchard about 500 yards away.

The force of the landing smashed open the blazing tail section, catapulted the pilot through the Perspex cockpit and cracked three of Pond's ribs. When a company of German infantry came up the lane, Otway's men were in danger of being attacked in the rear just as they were entering the minefield; but Pond set up an ambush and, after a sharp fire-fight, drove them off. He was awarded an MC.

Hubert Charles Pond (always known as Hugh) was born on February 22 1923 at Twickenham, Middlesex, and educated at Thames Valley Grammar School. He was commissioned into the Royal Tank Regiment, but a motorcycle injury prevented him from joining his comrades in the Middle East. Bored with hanging around the Royal Armoured Corps depot in Dorset, he volunteered for the Parachute Regiment and was posted to 9 Para as a platoon commander.

The training was tough. After a forced march of fifty miles in full kit, Pond collapsed from dehydration five miles from the end. He had forgotten to take his salt tablets. His furious CO made him do the whole route again by himself the following week.

On D-Day, without the right explosives, the 'spiking' of the Merville battery guns was rudimentary, but the enemy gunners had been dealt with, and it proved effective. The crew of *Arethusa* learned that the operation had succeeded just minutes before it was due to bombard the battery.

On D-Day plus one, the rest of what remained of 9 Para were ordered to move to Chateau St Côme, south of the village of Bréville. Pond lost his way in the dark and took his men through the village and past 200 Germans who were asleep on either side of the road.

They dug in near the chateau at the Bois du Mont

and resisted a series of determined counter-attacks. Pond narrowly escaped being hit by an artillery shell but the blast filled the air with dust. He sneezed violently and split the ribs that he had cracked during the crash-landing. Unable to move he was evacuated to England despite his protests.

Pond returned to Normandy after his recovery to take part in the forced crossing of the Rhine. When peace returned he was granted a short service commission with the Middlesex Regiment and served with 9 Para in Palestine.

Invalided back to Britain after a parachute accident he again recovered, and served with the Commonwealth Division in Korea where he was mentioned in despatches. In 1953 Pond was posted to Berlin as public relations officer.

He subsequently joined the *Daily Express* as military correspondent and, in 1961, moved to the Tupperware Company, eventually becoming president for Europe, Africa and the Middle East. From 1985 he was based at the company's international headquarters at Orlando, Florida, and worked in South America and South-East Asia.

On retiring he lived in Surrey, but continued to travel widely. He was a wildlife enthusiast and numbered photography and cookery among his many interests. He published *Freely I Served* (1960), a ghosted autobiography of the Polish General Stanislaw Sosabowski; *Salerno* (1961); *Sicily* (1962); and *British Agent* (1966), the ghosted story of a spy.

After two earlier marriages, Hugh Pond married, in 1960, Mila Ackerley (née Neyrone), who survived him with a stepson. Their daughter died in a parachute accident in 1989.

MAJOR RONALD BROMLEY

Major Ronald Bromley (who died on December 30 2014, aged 96) was awarded a Military Cross for leading microphone parties into enemy minefields in Holland to check the ground and place two groups with sound-ranging equipment near the banks of the Maas near Breda.

On the night of November 6 1944, his troop of 9th Survey Regiment RA found themselves under heavy shelling in front of their own infantry but were quickly deployed in the most effective positions.

On the border between Belgium and Holland, a brother officer found a dilapidated, battle-scarred Jeep with four dead Polish soldiers lying beside it. After burying them he brought the Jeep back to the regiment repaired and painted with the regimental insignia.

A few days later, however, a furious Dutch liaison officer with the Polish Division arrived to claim his property. He instigated a high-level inquiry, which resulted in Bromley being escorted into the presence of Lieutenant-General John Crocker, commander of I Corps, to receive a 'severe reprimand'.

Some weeks afterwards, Bromley was due to appear before Crocker again. The brigade major, who was no friend, made no attempt to conceal his glee. "You won't get off so lightly this time," he chuckled. "You are for the high jump!"

To the chagrin of the brigade major, Bromley

emerged from his meeting with an MC ribbon. The citation for the award stated that his total disregard of risks to himself had ensured that the best counter-battery measures were taken to prevent casualties to British troops.

Ronald Arthur Bromley was born on June 13 1918 into a farming family in Kent. He was educated at Dover County School and taken on as a pupil by the surveyor of Canterbury city council.

After war broke out in 1939, he was called up and selected for officer training at Larkhill before being commissioned into the 1st Sound Ranging Battery, Dover. Its main task was to locate the static guns firing in the Pas de Calais. This was achieved by triangulation on to the Town Hall, Calais, Napoleon's column, near Boulogne-sur-Mer, and the lighthouse at Cap Gris Nez.

After being posted to 9SR in 1941, Bromley was sent to different sites in England and Scotland to train for sound location of artillery and for amphibious landings in preparation for D-Day. In Normandy, he set up sound ranging equipment to pinpoint the positions of the enemy guns and, in August 1944, when Calais was being attacked, he had the job of flash spotting and sound ranging for his regiment. The commander of artillery in the German garrison later admitted that they refrained from taking countermeasures because the Allied guns were so powerful that they dared not risk retaliation.

Bromley saw further action in Belgium, Holland and Germany before being demobilised and returning to local government. He retired in 1979 as the engineer and surveyor of Elmbridge council.

A keen cricketer and rugby player, he was a dedicated Rotarian and worked closely with many local charities. He played a notable part in the restoration of Painshill Park, near Cobham, and showed several generations of schoolchildren how the water wheel worked.

Ronald Bromley married, in 1953, Lena Bartlett. She predeceased him, and he is survived by their two sons.

BRIGADIER THE 8TH DUKE OF WELLINGTON

Brigadier the 8th Duke of Wellington (who died on New Year's Eve 2014, aged 99) led a level-headed and responsible life in the shadow of his great ancestor, the victor of Waterloo.

He earned a Military Cross in the Second World War, spoke up for the Army and rural communities in the House of Lords, and served as a Hampshire county councillor as well as president, trustee, governor and member of a wide variety of bodies.

Well aware of the social changes that followed the Second World War Wellington once remarked, tongue in cheek, at a meeting of the Zoological Society that perhaps dukes should be made a protected species. He remained as determined as any owner of a suburban semi to protect his property, and took steps to secure his family's interests in Britain, Spain and Belgium against threats posed by politicians; he was not afraid to be seen backing causes in which he had a personal stake.

Above all, he kept a judicious eye on both the 1st Duke's reputation and the battlefield of Waterloo, becoming exercised by the commercialisation of the site, where he felt that the predominant number of imperial eagles and other items bearing the initial 'N' in the gift shop implied that Napoleon had won.

After seeing the 'inglorious flag' of the European Union flying over the site in 1995, he wrote to *The Daily Telegraph* to protest against the 'unnatural' celebrations of the battle's 180th anniversary. "We British have a feeling and respect for the past, something that not all nations understand or share," he explained; in addition he noted that Napoleon's headquarters, which had once housed a small museum, was now a discotheque.

Shortly before the letters column's deadline, he rang to add another line below 'Duke of Wellington' at the bottom of the text: 'Prince of Waterloo'.

Arthur Valerian Wellesley was born in Rome on July 2 1915, the centenary year of his great-great-grandfather's victory over the French. His father was Lord Gerald Wellesley, the third son of the 4th Duke, an author, diplomat and Surveyor of the King's Pictures who later qualified as an architect and succeeded as the 7th Duke in 1943.

Val's mother was Dottie Ashton, a wealthy industrialist's daughter and poet who married her husband in 1914 and published one volume of letters from the poet W. B. Yeats and another of her letters written to him after his death. The boy became bored at having to listen to Yeats reciting *Inisfree*. But his idyllic childhood was destroyed at the age of seven when his parents' marriage broke up because of his mother's uncontrolled drinking and friendship with the sapphic writer Vita Sackville-West.

At Eton (where she never visited him) he was a member of the shooting VIII. While serving in the CCF, he fainted during a parade at Windsor, and when Queen Mary asked afterwards what had been wrong he said he thought he had measles – drawing the comment from George V (who believed such diseases should be experienced in childhood): "And high time, too."

Although Val wanted to go straight into the Army, his father sent him to read History and Languages at New College, Oxford, where he was a member of the Bullingdon Club; at the same time he enjoyed London society, dancing with suitable girls at grand balls and less suitable ones in subterranean nightclubs.

As a result he failed his finals and was sent to a London crammer, run by an attractive widow, and then to France to learn French. He was commissioned into Royal Horse Guards, which taught him sword, lance and revolver drill, tent pegging and other cavalry exercises. Before embarking for Palestine in 1940, he paid an Indian at Liverpool docks to tattoo his regiment's emblem on his left arm.

After being posted to Tulkarm with 1st Household Cavalry, Wellesley made patrols through Arab villages, but was upset after a few months to be ordered to shoot fourteen black horses, which had taken part in George VI's coronation, when the regiment was mechanised.

He was then part of a column which advanced 500 miles into Iraq, where he found himself hunting, and being hunted by the canny nationalist leader Fawzi al-Kawukji who, in league with the Vichy French in Syria, was harrying British supply lines.

On one patrol Wellesley found himself crawling at night through the ruins of the ancient city of Palmyra, outside which he found a French officer's scarlet cloak; it would remain on the ducal bed for many years until the Duchess threw it out as moth-eaten. On another he was turned back by enemy armoured cars outside El Beida.

"Apart from the above incidents," the citation for his MC declared, "this officer's conduct throughout the operations in Syria was exceptionally gallant and he was a magnificent example to all ranks of his squadron."

While in Cairo he enjoyed the friendship of a Druze princess, who once hid him in her bedroom while she remonstrated with an enraged admirer. He took part in the battle of Alamein before being injured when a 'brew-up' of tea exploded. It was in late 1943 that he learned that his cousin Henry the 6th Duke, his elder by three years, had been killed with the Commandos at Salerno. Wellesley's father succeeded as the 7th Duke, and Val took the courtesy title, Marquess of Douro.

On being posted to the staff in Jerusalem he met Diana McConnel, who worked in the office of her father, Major General Douglas McConnel, the GOC. Shortly before their marriage in January 1943 a bomb was discovered outside the Anglican cathedral; it had been due to go off on their wedding day. Nine weeks later Douro was sent to Italy where, in the course of the difficult advance, he was given a duck, which instead of eating he kept with a pointer in his armoured car. His men called it 'The Dog and the Duck'.

In Germany after the war, he considered leaving the Army until King George VI asked him to stay on, saying: "I like to have people I know in the Household Cavalry." Douro stood guard for twenty-two periods at the King's lying-in-state.

His next significant post was as commanding officer of the Blues in Cyprus, where he always slept with a pistol under his pillow. He then commanded the Royal Armoured Corps in Germany before a final appointment as military attaché in Madrid. This meant he was in the unusual position of being a diplomat in a country where he was heir to a title (Duke of Ciudad Rodrigo) and to 2,500 acres which had been conferred on the 1st Duke.

On retiring from the Army in 1968 in the rank of brigadier, Douro turned his attention to the family estates. These were in an unsatisfactory state since his father had handed over the running of the main holdings to the government in the hope of preserving them. As a result these became a 'parliamentary estate', vested in the Prime Minister, the Speaker of the Commons and the Chancellor of the Exchequer, an arrangement with great disadvantages which was dissolved in 1972.

After succeeding as the 8th Duke in the same year, he sold off 1,135 acres at Silchester and 230 at Wellington, Somerset (whence the family originated) in order to meet death duties. In the following years he sold paintings, drawings and a 120-piece Sèvres dessert service made for the Empress Josephine. When it was learned that the buyer of the Sèvres was the French government there was a storm of protest in Britain, and an export licence was delayed before it eventually went to the Victoria and Albert Museum for £450,000. The Iron Duke's papers were despatched to Southampton University as part of an agreement with the Treasury.

A plan to modernise the Wellington estates included opening to the public Stratfield Saye, the 17th century house with 7,500 acres between Reading and Basingstoke which had been given by the nation to the 1st Duke, and the creation of a 700-acre country park. In the course of forty years, it was estimated that he planted more than one million trees.

The democratic age sometimes posed a threat to the Wellington properties abroad. In Spain, 500 farm workers staged a sit-in on the ducal hunting estate near Granada. In Belgium during the 1970s and 1980s, two retired senators (one a descendant of a Napoleonic general) called the Duke's right to an income of £20,000 a year from the 2,600 acres next to the battlefield of Waterloo, a "feudal and medieval annuity". However the Duke found that some 103 tenants on the land were not keen on the proposed plan for urban and industrial development.

For all the privileges there were plenty of duties as well as disadvantages and irritations, such as the persistent press interest in his daughter Jane's friendship with the Prince of Wales in the early 1970s; and he could be sure that, wherever he was in the world, nobody would miss the opportunity to serve him Beef Wellington.

Speaking in Parliament, until the peers declined

to put their names forward for election to the Lords after the Blair government's reforms, he was particularly critical of the wanton cutting of the Army in the light of the fall of Soviet communism. Drawing on his experience as a tank officer in Italy, he warned in another letter to *The Daily Telegraph* that most women were incapable of handling heavy equipment and ammunition and that they should not be sacrificed on the altar of political correctness.

In his later years the Duke visited Iraq (he was highly critical of the 2003 invasion) and made a pilgrimage to the 6th Duke's grave near Salerno. He was proud when a grandson served in Afghanistan with the Blues and Royals.

Among his many appointments he was the last colonel-in-chief of the Duke of Wellington's Regiment; president of Game Conservancy; a director of Massey Ferguson; a trustee of the Royal Armouries; and a governor of Wellington College.

He was appointed LVO in 1952, OBE in 1957 and KG in 1990. He was also an officer of the Legion of Honour in France, a Knight Grand Cross of the Order of St Michael of the Wing in Portugal, and of the Order of Isabel the Catholic in Spain.

The Duke's wife died in 2010. He was succeeded in the peerages by the eldest of his four sons, Charles, Marquess of Douro, a former MEP, who was born in 1945 and married Princess Antonia von Preussen, a great-granddaughter of the last German Emperor.

MAJOR GENERAL MICHAEL GRIGG

Major General Michael Grigg (who died on January 30 2015, aged 97) won an MC in Sicily in 1943 and was subsequently the first major general of the Zambian Army.

In July 1943 Grigg was in command of a company of 6th Battalion, Seaforth Highlanders (6 SH) and took part in the invasion of Sicily. There was a battery of guns on the high ground behind the village of Cassibile, near Syracuse, which dominated the beach.

A parachute drop to capture these guns was considered vital but the operation was a disaster. The pilots dropped their load too soon and turned for home. Grigg saw men struggling in the water but his assault craft was running three minutes late and he was ordered not to delay under any circumstances. The little cove was not defended but beyond the beach the terrain was heavily mined. Grigg's best friend lost both legs but he could not stop to help him. For a long time afterwards he had nightmares in which he heard the cries of the men who had been left to die.

On the night of July 12/13, he led his company in a battalion advance on Augusta. On the outskirts of the town they came under heavy machine-gun fire. Despite being under fire himself, Grigg went forward and directed the fire of his force on to the enemy positions.

It was a dark night but he succeeded in identifying the location of the machine-gun posts and, one by one, they were knocked out. In recognition of his outstanding courage and leadership, he was awarded an MC.

Casimir Michael Grigg was born in London on February 25 1917 and spent his childhood at Bembridge, Isle of Wight, before going to Eton. After attending Sandhurst, he was commissioned into the Seaforth Highlanders.

In 1938, he served with 1 SH in Hong Kong and Shanghai. After accompanying the battalion to Malaya and then India, he also took part in the invasion of Madagascar. He saw action in the final phase of the North Africa campaign in early 1943 and moved to Syria the following year.

Grigg was in Germany during the last months of the war in north-west Europe. Reflecting on his wartime experiences, he said that decorations for gallantry could be very unfair. One night, he recalled, he led a reconnaissance patrol which had only limited success because the guide was useless.

On the way back, they had to cross a minebelt, but the guide could not remember which side of a hedge was sown with enemy mines. Grigg said to his men, "I'll walk down one side and if I'm blown up, you walk down the other." To do that, he said, took far more guts than anything he had done on the day he won his MC.

He returned to Malaya with 1 SH in October 1948 and served with 2 King's African Rifles between 1950 and 1953. Two years later he resigned his commission and joined the Federation of Rhodesia and Nyasaland Army.

In January 1964, he took command of the Northern Rhodesia Army. The country became the Republic of Zambia in October that year and President Kenneth Kaunda appointed Grigg major general. Grigg derived great satisfaction, as he said afterwards, "from running a happy and efficient multi-racial concern in emergent Africa". He was appointed CBE in 1965 and retired in 1967.

He was a director of the Migraine Trust from 1968 to 1970 and of the Cinema & Television Benevolent Fund from 1970 to 1983. His hearing was impaired by being close to two explosions during his active service but he used to joke that the worst bang that he ever received was when the doorman of a Cairo nightclub hit him on the head with a fire extinguisher. Michael Grigg married, in 1950, Audrey Vera Moore. She predeceased him and he was survived by their two daughters.

CORPORAL BERNIE DAVIS

Corporal Bernie Davis (who died on February 15 2015, aged 82) was awarded the British Empire Medal for bravery aged just 16 – the youngest ever recipient – for rescuing at great risk to himself a three-year-old girl in danger on a window ledge.

An irrepressible Cockney, Davis was also a self-styled 'street raker', used to climbing around bomb-damaged buildings. This was not without its dangers and shortly after receiving the BEM his younger brother John, aged 12, was killed when a wall fell on him as he was playing on a bombed site.

Davis was strolling from Southwark Bridge Road to Borough High Street, when he came across a group of people looking upwards, shouting and screaming, "Go back!" to a child no more than three years old and who was alone, as she teetered on a window ledge some 80ft above them.

This clearly called for immediate action but when Davis asked if anyone had gone up, he was put out to learn that nobody had. "Bloody useless," he exclaimed, before racing up the ninety-nine steps of the common staircase to the flat on the sixth floor.

When he knocked there was no reply, only a dog which barked and scratched inside. So, although only 5ft 3in tall and slightly built, he threw himself against the door.

It refused to budge, so Davis ran up a further two flights of stairs to the flat roof. This allowed him out to the rear of the bomb-damaged building and across the top of a 4ft parapet of two bricks' width, crumbling and sloping at a 45 degree angle. He successfully lowered himself enough to drop on to an unprotected ledge 8ft below. Then, having crawled until he was directly above the flat, he dropped 10ft on to the back balcony. Had he missed the ledge or slipped off it, he would have plunged down to the concrete yard below.

As Davis opened the rear door of the flat, he had to shut it when the dog attacked. Realising the need for quick action, he made a second attempt to enter, leaping on to a chair and then a table, from where he managed to lift the catch of the bedroom door with a table knife. He then burst into the bedroom and grabbed the child, who was kneeling on the window ledge inside with her hands on the outside ledge.

Davis's exploit made headlines and he was awarded the British Empire Medal for bravery on May 30 1949; it was presented to him by the Bishop of

Southwark. In addition he was given the Carnegie Hero Fund Trust's Bronze Medal. He also received a letter from No 10 but this, together with the press cuttings and both medals, went into a drawer to be all but forgotten.

The Army, Davis would later discover, did not believe in forgetting such things and it was while he was doing National Service with the Royal Ulster Rifles in Hong Kong that a record of his award came from the War Office. Brought before his commanding officer for being improperly dressed, he was told: "You should be wearing your medal ribbon" and admonished.

Promotion to corporal followed, and he was sent with another soldier to the New Territories to report on Chinese activities. Asked by his brother what he would have done if the Chinese in their millions had come across the frontier, he replied: "Ring the duty officer." "And then?" "I suppose," Davis joked, "Ron and me would have had to hold them off until the battalion arrived."

Bernard Jeffrey Davis was born in south-east London on January 6 1933 and educated at the Charles Dickens School. He went on to become a bookbinder for the Charles Letts diary makers, with whom he remained all his working life.

He married his wife Pat when he was twenty and she eighteen in 1953. His reticence was such that not even his relations or friends knew of his award, only his immediate family. Bernie Davis was survived by his wife, son and daughter.

COLONEL BILL ETCHES

Colonel Bill Etches (who died on April 12 2015, aged 93) took part in the raid on St Nazaire, one of the most audacious operations of the Second World War.

Code-named Operation Chariot, the plan was to disguise the obsolete Royal Navy destroyer *Campbeltown* as a German ship, pack her with explosives and drive her into the lock gates at the port of St Nazaire in German-occupied northern France. Success would render the port unusable as a place of provisioning, refitting or sanctuary for the battleship *Tirpitz*, which posed a constant threat to Britain's merchant vessels and naval forces.

In the early hours of March 28 1942, Etches, a platoon commander serving with 3 Commando, was severely wounded in the legs when the ship came under fire during the run-in along the Loire estuary. Despite being in great pain, he disembarked with the assault and demolition teams and supervised the destruction of a number of vital shore installations.

When the force tried to break out of the dock area, he took part in fierce street fighting in the town. Although weak from loss of blood and barely able to drag himself along, he kept up with his comrades, scaling walls and breaking into houses until all the ammunition was exhausted and he was finally captured.

After *Campbeltown* exploded, the lock gates were destroyed and much of the port was not used again during the war. The citation for Etches's MC paid tribute to his indomitable courage and stated that his bravery inspired others to go on fighting despite their wounds.

William Whitson Etches was born at Bisley Camp, Brookwood, Surrey, on May 15 1921 and was educated at Rugby, Sandhurst and later at Cambridge where he did a course in Russian interpreting. In 1940, he was commissioned into the Royal Warwickshire Regiment (RWR) which his father had commanded.

Keen to see active service, he joined 3 Commando and, in 1941, took part in raids on the Lofoten Islands, Vaagso and Maaloy, Norway. He was wounded and received a mention in despatches.

After the St Nazaire raid, Etches spent the remainder of the war in a series of German POW camps. His severe wounds made it impossible for him to try to escape, a source of great frustration.

Repatriated in 1945, he was posted to 2nd Battalion Royal Warwickshires in Palestine. Regimental and staff appointments took him to Austria, Korea, the Canal Zone, Northern Ireland, Aden and Hong Kong.

In 1961, he commanded 3rd Battalion Queen's Own Nigeria Regiment and, after Belgium withdrew from the Congo, his battalion formed part of the United Nations peacekeeping force. They performed with distinction and he was appointed OBE at the end of a most exacting tour.

In 1962, his former regiment became the Royal Warwickshire Fusiliers and, after several staff appointments, in 1968 he became the brigade colonel of the newly formed Fusilier Brigade of which his old regiment was a part. Following further

Army reorganisation, the brigade became the Royal Regiment of Fusiliers.

Etches retired from the Army in 1971 and for the next fourteen years he was the regimental secretary, known as the Godfather of the Regiment, and insisted on the highest professional standards.

Always known as Colonel Bill, he was responsible for recruiting several generations of young officers into the regiment. They soon learned that this rather formidable war hero had a heart of gold and an exceptional gift for getting on with the young. In retirement in Surrey, he enjoyed golf, gardening and writing. Bill Etches married, in 1946, Dora Finch. She predeceased him, and he was survived by their two sons and a daughter.

INDEX OF PERSONALITIES
(Italics denotes main entry)